"Cheap Travel in Michigan" is a revision and redesign of the well-known guidebook, "What's Cheap and Free in Michigan" which was published in 1993 by Glovebox Guidebooks of America. As always, please call each destination for the latest details before traveling. Have fun!

Cover design and illustration by Dan Jacalone

Copyright by Glovebox Guidebooks of America 2006

All rights reserved - revised and updated, second printing

No parts of this book may be reproduced in any form without the written permission of the publisher.

Published by **Glovebox Guidebooks of America**
3523 N. Gleaner Road
Freeland, MI 48623-8829
1-800-289-4843

Library of Congress

Bailey, William L., 1952-
DuFresne, Jim, 1956-

Cheap Travel in Michigan
(A Glovebox Guidebook of America)
ISBN 1-881139-28-X

Printed in the United States of America

***Don't miss thes other
Glovebox Guidebooks:***

Around the Shores of Lake Erie
Awake to Wildlife
Beach Freaks' Guide to Mi. Best Beaches
Cycling Eastern Michigan
Cycling Western Michigan
Fifty Hikes in Lower Michigan
Fish Ohio
Illinois State Parks Guidebook
Indiana State Parks Guidebook
Kentucky State Parks Guidebook
Lower Mich. 75 Best Campgrounds
Making Healthy Tomorrows
Michigan Antique Guidebook
Michigan State Parks
Michigan Zoos & Animal Parks
New York State Parks Guidbook
Ohio State Parks Guidebook
Pennsylvania State Parks Guidebook
Porcupine Mts. Guidebook
Spin Tactics - A Guide to Media Relations
State Parks on the Great Lakes
Thrill Sports In the Great Lakes
Virginia State Parks Guidebook
Wisconsin State Parks Guidebook

**Glovebox Guidebooks of America
3523 N. Gleaner Road
Freeland, MI 48623-8829**

Available at your local bookstore or to order call:
1-800-289-4843

Contents

Alcona County	6
Alger County	10
Allegan County	17
Alpena County	22
Antrim County	25
Arenac County	30
Baraga County	33
Barry County	39
Bay County	42
Benzie County	45
Berrien County	51
Branch County	62
Calhoun County	64
Cass County	71
Charlevoix County	75
Cheboygan County	81
Chippewa County *Sault Ste. Marie*	85
Clare County	91
Clinton County *Indian River*	94
Crawford County *Grayling*	97
Delta County	103
Dickinson County	110
Eaton County	114
Emmet County	119
Genesee County	124
Gladwin County	132
Gogebic County	134
Grand Traverse County	139
Gratiot County	148
Hillsdale County	151
Houghton County	155
Huron County *Pt. Austin*	161
Ingham County	166
Ionia County	175
Iosco County	179
Iron County	183
Isabella County	187
Jackson County	190

Kalamazoo County	196
Kalkaska County	203
Kent County	205
Keweenaw County	213
Lake County	218
Lapeer County *Imlay City*	220
Leelanau County	222
Livingston County	230
Luce County	233
Mackinac County *St. Ignace*	237
Macomb County	241
Manistee County	245
Marquette County	250
Mason County	257
Mecosta County	261
Menominee County	265
Midland County	269
Monroe County *Monroe*	272
Muskegon County	277
Newaygo County	283
Oakland County *holly Troy*	288
Oceana County	295
Ontonagon County	298
Osceola County	301
Oscoda County	303
Otsego County *Gaylord*	306
Ottawa County	309
Presque Isle County	313
Roscommon County *Houghton Higgins Lake*	316
Saginaw County *Frankenmuth BirchRun*	319
Sanilac County	328
Schoolcraft County	332
Shiawassee County	336
St. Clair County *Pt. Huron*	340
St. Joseph County	345
Tuscola County	349
Van Buren County	351
Washtenaw County *Ann Arbor*	355
Wayne County *Money Museum*	362
Wexford County	372

ALCONA COUNTY

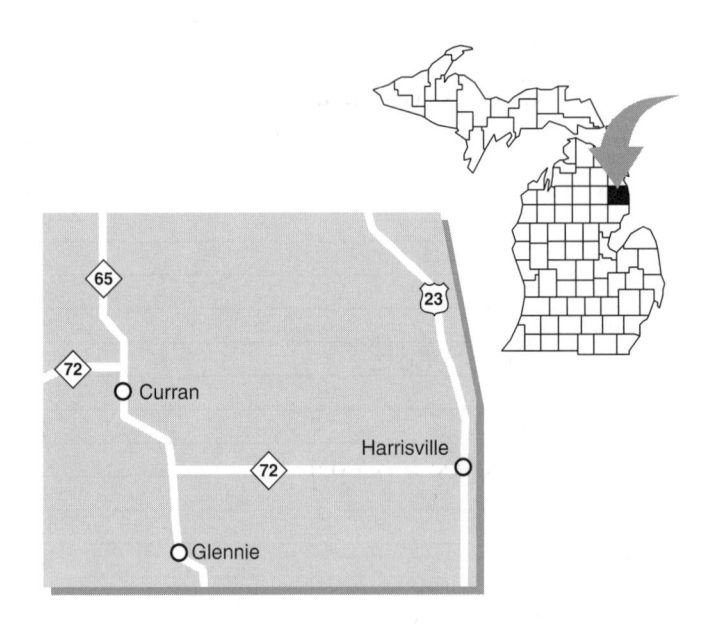

VISITOR INFORMATION

Huron Shores
Chamber of Commerce
P. O. Box 151
Harrisville, MI 48740
989-724-5107 or 800-432-2823
email: info@huronshoreschamber.com

Alcona County

JEWELL LAKE
Harrisville Ranger District
(989) 724-5431

FREE

What a pleasant little lake with a wonderful beach ideal for your children. Kids will also like the gentle one-mile long nature trails that skirt the lake in one part and passes over a beaver dam in another. The trailhead is located in the Huron National Forest's Jewell Lake Campground, which also features 32 rustic campsites. Day use is free but there is a night charge for camping. The campground is 14.5 miles west of Harrisville, reached by departing M-72 north on Sanborn Road and then west on Trask Lake Road.

CEDARBROOK TROUT HATCHERY
(989) 724-5241

Admit it. You're too cheap to buy a fishing license. In fact, didn't I see you sneaking around near the river with a cane pole and tin-can full of worms?

Fortunately, there are two ways to catch Michigan-raised rainbow trout. You can loosen up and buy a fishing license, waders, a really cool hat, rod and reel and stalk the fish in a scenic wild trout stream like the famed "Holy Waters" of the AuSable.

Or, you can schlep-off to a trout farm...like Cedarbrook Trout Hatchery north of Harrisville. At the farm you don't need to arrive with any equipment or even purchase a Michigan fishing license. But you're still guaranteed to catch a fish.

In 1950, Cedarbrook became the first private trout farm to be licensed by the state and its location in the pine forests and sandy hills just off US-23 near the Lake Huron shoreline was no coincidence.

Bubbling out of the hills behind the farm are natural springs providing a constant flow of crystal clear water that is always the same temperature - 47 degrees - and saturated with oxygen. Just what a trout farmer needs the most. "The water is even gravity-fed," says longtime owner Jerry Kahn. "I don't need any pumps here."

Worm-haters will appreciate the hooks baited with moist

Cedarbrook Trout Hatchery

vegetable-based pellets. Intrepid anglers merely stand along the banks of the pond and watch the trout boil the water. You'll see hundreds of fish here but the trick is to get your bait in front of their noses as they dart and snap at particles in the water. Eventually even fishermen with skills as good as mine will fill their pail, or spend your quota, whatever comes first. Fish are cleaned free and priced depending on the weight.

Particulars: The farm is at US-23 and Lakeshore Drive and open daily, 9 a.m. - 6 p.m., Memorial Day through Labor Day and on the weekends in October.

STURGEON POINT LIGHTHOUSE
(989) 724-6267 or 595-3632
www.lighthousefestival.org

The historic light was built in 1869 after Perley Silverthone gave the federal government the land at the end of the point. In return, Silverthone was named the first lighthouse keeper, where in the spring he opened up the navigation season by climbing the same 85 steps and lighting a kerosene lamp, which contains a huge lens that is 70-feet above Lake Huron. The light was important as it guided mariners safely around Lake Huron at the eastern-most point along its northern shoreline, a rocky reef that juts out 1.5 miles into the lake.

The lifesaving station was added in 1876 with Silverthone

captain of the crew before the light was electricified and automated in 1936. A few years later the station was closed. Since then the Coast Guard has overseen the light, but the life saving station was badly vandalized until the Alcona County Historical Society purchased the structure and renovated it.

Clean and well maintained, visitors can view the lighthouse keepers living area much the same way it appeared in the late 1800s. The six rooms of the first floor included a kitchen, work area, and furnishing. Upstairs there are four small rooms that have displays interpreting commercial fishing, ice harvesting industry, scuba diving, and past lightkeepers.

You can also see the modern light. Unlike the kerosene lamps of a previous era, today the tiny lightbulb is golfball-size. But don't let the small size fool you, it can project a guiding light more than 13 miles into Lake Huron.

Particulars: The museum is reached by continuing north past Cedarbrook Trout Farm on Lakeshore Drive and following signs.

It is staffed by volunteers who try to keep it open year-round Monday through Thursday from 10 a.m. to 4 p.m. and Saturday and Sunday noon to 4 p.m. Admission is a donation.

For information about The Lighthouse Festival: 989-595-3632 or www.lighthousefestival.com

ALGER COUNTY

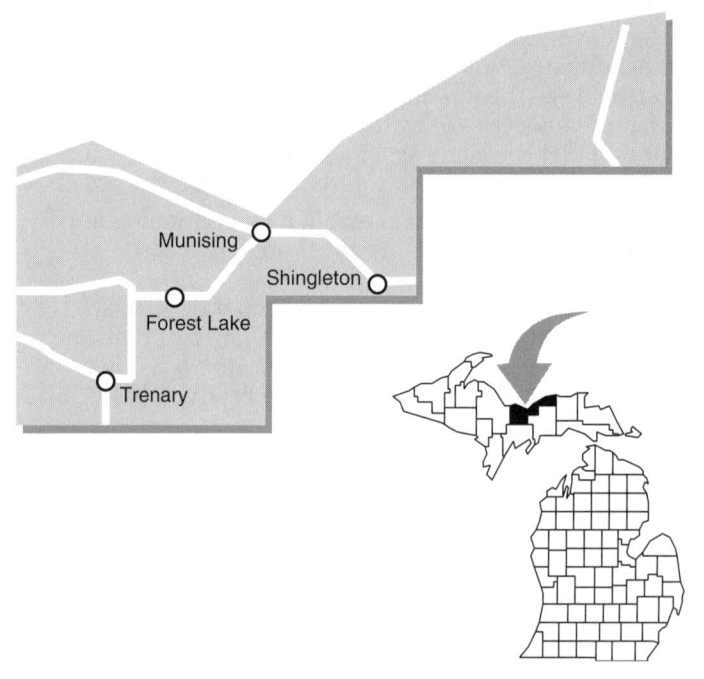

VISITOR INFORMATION

Munising Visitors Bureau, Inc.
P. O. Box 421
Munising, MI 49862
906-387-2138

www.munising.org

Alger County

▼ Grand Marais

GRAND MARAIS MARITIME MUSEUM   *FREE*
(906) 494-2669 or (906) 387-2607

Located on Coast Guard Point in picturesque Grand Marais, is this maritime museum that also doubles up as a national park service ranger station for the Pictured Rocks National Lake Shore. Inside the old Coast Guard station are exhibits detailing the ships, shipwrecks and the U.S. Lifesaving Station at nearby Au Sable Point along with the 1900 Fresnel lens from the light house. There are also displays on the once booming commercial fishery in this now sleepy hamlet of 400.

Particulars: From M-77, follow the shoreline of the Grand Marais harbor to Coast Guard Point. The museum is open daily from 10 a.m. to 5:30 p.m. from late June through early September. Free.

GRAND SABLE BANKS AND DUNES   *FREE*
(906) 494-2669

Just east of Grand Marais, are Grand Sable Dunes, a four square-mile tract of dunes that rivals those of Sleeping Bear Dunes in the Lower Peninsula. There is a small National Park Service visitor center along H-58 and nearby a picnic area, beach and boat launch on Grand Sable Lake.

Between the inland lake and Lake Superior, lie the dunes. You can trudge more than a mile across them to end up at Grand Sable Banks that rise almost 300 feet straight out of the Great Lake. For those not up for the hike, continue along H-58, which turns into a winding dirt road, to the Log Slide, the site of a 500-foot long wooden slide in the 1800s that loggers used to send timber flying into Lake Superior on its way to the mills. The walk to the banks is less than 100 yards and the view, including Au Sable Light Station to the west, is spectacular.

Warning! Many visitors make the mistake of gleefully running down the Grand Sable Banks to Lake Superior only to discover at the bottom that it's one heck of a climb back up.

Particulars: The visitor center and dunes are four miles west of Grand Marais, the Log Slide eight miles. Free.

LAKE SUPERIOR SHIPWRECKS
(906) 494-2669

FREE

Continue west along H-58 for another four miles to reach Hurricane River Campground, where you'll find a series of shipwrecks. No need to drag along the scuba gear the shipwrecks can be seen from shore.

At the east end of the campground, at the trailhead of the Lakeshore Trail, is a "Shipwreck" sign that directs you to the beach. These ruins, wooden ribs of a ship, are actually in the water, 20 yards from shore. Hike a mile down the trail and a second "Shipwreck" sign appears. These maritime ruins are on the beach where protruding from the sand are the scattered remains of two hulls. Continue another half mile along the trail and you'll arrive at the Au Sable Light Station, where the National Park Service has restored the light, keeper's residence, boat house and even a red brick privy. Interpretive displays explain how lightkeepers and U.S. Lifesaving crews worked to save ships from 1874 to 2958. But, obviously, could not save all of them.

Particulars: Hurricane River Campground is 12 miles east of Grand Marais off H-58. Free but there is a nightly fee to camp here.

▼ Shingletown

IVERSON SNOWSHOE COMPANY
(906) 452-6370

FREE

This little company is world renown for its snowshoes. Iversons are on the boots of trappers, park rangers, timber cruisers and winter enthusiasts from Maine to Alaska. Informal tours, basically they show you the single large room where the shoes are cut and laced, are offered and during the winter snowshoe rentals are available.

Particulars: Located 10 miles east of Munising in Shingleton where a sign on M-28 directs you to the factory on a side street. Snowshoe rentals, factory sales and tours are available weekdays 8 a.m. to 3 p.m. Tours are free. Day and week rentals are available.

Munising

MUNISING FALLS
Pictured Rocks National Lakeshore
(906) 387-2607

FREE

These were the famous "walk-behind-the water" falls until

part of the sandstone cliffs caved in. Rocks the size of a large pick-up truck landed on the path and the thought of a law suit made the National Park Service say no more treks behind the tumbling cascade. Still, this is a scenic, and cheap, attraction not to be missed.

There is an unmanned visitor center that explains the history of the falls and then a paved path that leads 800 feet into the small gorge to the falls themselves. Set is a stone amphitheater, Munising Falls drops 50 feet straight down then resumes as a small stream on its way to Lake Superior. In the winter when it freezes, it's a stunning sight.

Particulars: From M-28, head east on H-58 and then veer off on Sand Point Road and follow the signs. The interpretive center is open late June through early September from 10 a.m. to 4 p.m. daily. Free.

MINERS CASTLE
Pictured Rocks National Lakeshore
(906) 387-2607

FREE

The most famous attraction in this town are the Pictured Rocks, towering sandstone cliffs that change colors with the setting sun. The best way to see the Pictured Rocks is from the water. Plan to take the three-hour cruise on a tour boat from the Munising Harbor. There is a fee for the tour.

Cheapskates can still see a small portion of the shoreline from land with a drive out to Miners Castle. The castle is a monolith as tall as a nine-story building and from the day-use area you get several different views of it, including a platform that's right on the tip. Legend has it that Father Marquette once stood on the rock and gave mass to Indians bobbing below in the canoes on Lake Superior. But I don't know. Sounds like something a tour boat captain would make up.

Pack a lunch and have a picnic on Miners Beach or hike down to Miners Falls, a walk of 1.2 miles, to round out the afternoon.

Particulars: Head east on M-58 and just follow the signs. In the summer there will be a string of tour buses and fudgies heading for the monolith, reached by turning north in four miles on Miners Castle Road and driving to the end. Free.

GRAND ISLAND OVERLOOK

FREE

Another cheap way to see Pictured Rocks is to head west of town to the Grand Island Overlook. It's a winding drive up to this rest area but from the parking lot a short path leads to the edge of the hill where you can see the rocks off in the distance along with Grand Island and mils of Lake Superior. An Interpretive display points out what is what.

Particulars: Head west of Munising on M-28 two miles to the scenic area posted along the road. Free.

▼ Au Train

PAULSON HOUSE
(906) 892-8292

FREE

The Hiawatha Folk Craft and Art Museum is a unique spot in the Upper Peninsula that features on-site demonstrations by potters, carvers and weavers while selling the work of hundreds more from throughout the country.

But the most skilled artisan and contributor to the center, Charles Paulson, is no longer living and his only master piece, his homesteading cabin, is definitely not for sale. The century-old cabin is today a small but interesting museum and monument to Paulson who arrived in 1884 and built one of the first farm houses is the area. The squared-off logs were 34 feet long and 22 inches wide that had to be hoisted into place by hand. Paulson then carefully dove-tailed each log to form the joint corners, making a home that was tight and warm even during the coldest U.P. winters.

The adjacent art center was open in 1986 and is now a collection of three more buildings on whose porches might be a potter throwing clay, a Jamaican wood carver or an Arkansas craftsman demonstrating the art of broom making. Inside are even more artistic efforts, from corn shuck dolls, pewter and hand blown glass to handmade oak furniture and marquetry, pictures where veneer is used instead of paint. All of which is for sale.

Particulars: From Munising head west on M-28 for 12 miles and then south at the blinker light in Au Train Corner. The museum and art center are 2.5 miles south along H-03 overlooking Au Train Lake. The museum is open mid-May through mid-October from 9 a.m. - 7 p.m. daily. A small donation is requested for the museum, the art center is free.

▼ Sundell

LAUGHING WHITEFISH FALLS SCENIC SITE
DNR Regional Office
(906) 228-6561

FREE

Another spectacular falls in Alger County, as if this place

doesn't already have enough. The scenic site is actually a state park unit that consists of a small parking area, a couple of picnic tables, hand pump for water and a pair of pit toilets.

There is also a trail that departs into the woods. It's a half-mile hike to the falls where you'll find an impressive stairway with 160 steps and three observation platforms to view the falls. Laughing Whitefish is actually a 30-foot drop and then the stream slides down a rock bowl in a thin veil to the bottom of the gorge where the stairway ends.

Particulars: The park is posted in Sundell at the corner of M-94 and Dorsey Road and is reached heading north on Dorsey for 2.5 miles. A daily vehicle permit or annual state park pass is required but since there is no staff here to sell one I guess it's free.

▼ Trenary

Trenary Home Bakery
(906) 446-3330

There's no sales counter, glass display cases, or pimply-faced teenagers cracking gum behind the cash register. There's no stag table with coffee drinkers solving world problems, and there's no fancy furniture, but there is Trenary Toast. Famous throughout the U.P. and beyond, Trenary Toast is to Alger County what cars are to Detroit and cherry pits to Traverse City.

From Monday through Friday, the bustling bakery produces more than 600 bags of toast a day or between 3,000 and 4,000 bags weekly. Most of it is destined for grocery shelves across the U.P. or shipped to cinnamon toast lovers around the county. It's so popular, it's rare to find a bag unsold by late afternoon anywhere in this region of the state, even at the bakery.

To me it's Zwieback with cinnamon sugar on it but Yoopers love it and it is perfect size for dunking into a cup of hot coffee.

Particulars: Trenary is in the southwest corner of Alger County. From US-41, 19 miles north of Rapid City, head east on M-67 into town and then on Marquette Street. The bakery is at 208 Marquette and open weekdays 5 a.m. to 5 p.m. A bag of toast is around $2.50.

ALLEGAN COUNTY

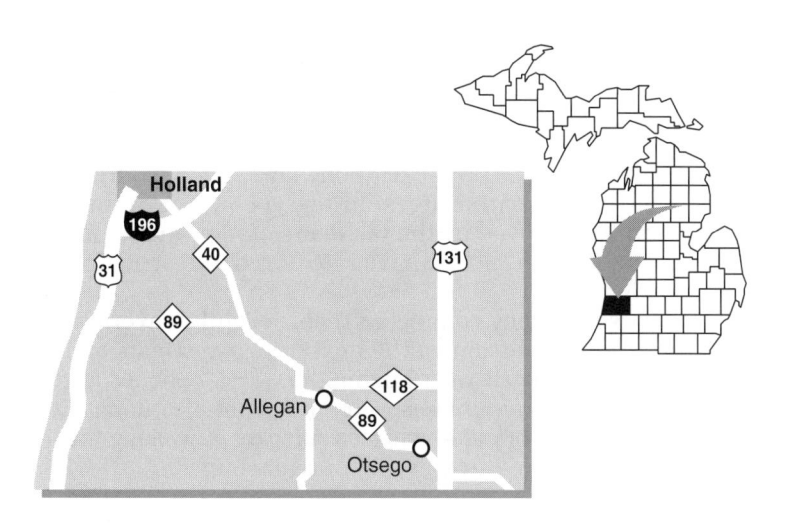

VISITOR INFORMATION

Allegan Area Chamber of Commerce
882 Marshall Street - Suite B
Allegan, MI 49010
269-673-2479
email: chamber@allegan.net

Allegan County

▼ **Allegan**

WHIPPLE TRUSS BRIDGE AND RIVERFRONT PARK
Allegan County Tourism Council
(269) 673-2479

FREE

With Kalamazoo River snaking around it, Allegan is known as the city of bridges and the most interesting bridge by far is the Whipple Truss Bridge. Built in 1886 by Kings Iron Bridge Company of Cleveland at a cost of only $7,500, the structure is an ornamental style bridge with one lane. Look before you drive over. It's one of the largest bridges of its kind in the country and so beloved by the residents of Allegan that in 1983 they raised $552,000 to have it restored to rescue it from the wrecking ball.

Two years later they completed their delightful Riverfront Park that stretches to almost the next bridge upstream and consists of a boardwalk overlooking the water, benches a pavilion and floating fountains. Continue your afternoon with a walk through historical downtown Allegan. A walking tour brochure is available through the tourism council or the Old Jail Museum.

Particulars: From US-131, depart at exit 49 and head west on M-89. The Whipple Truss Bridge is reached in 12 miles just as you enter town. Riverfront Park is on the north side of the Kalamazoo River here. Free.

ALLEGAN ANTIQUE SHOWS
Allegan County Tourism Council
(269) 673-2479

Three hundred antique dealers convene monthly for western Michigan's largest regular antique festival. Indoor and outdoors, dealers offer everything from pillbox hats to spittoons.

Particulars: The antique show is held at Allegan County Fairgrounds off Delano Street. From M-89/40 head north on Davis Street to reach Delano. Admission fee.

ALLEGAN COUNTY HISTORICAL SOCIETY
& OLD JAIL MUSEUM
(269) 673-4853 www.alleganmuseum.com

Allegan County's first jail is an imposing red brick building that was built in 1906 and features Greek Revival architecture with a peaked roof and columns along the porch. There's bars on the windows, a hexagonal turret in the corner and a three-story grandeur that's lacking in its replacement across the street.

But most unusual is the small red sign on Walnut street that says "Allegan County Historical Museum." Go to jail and get a lesson in history! Known to most as the "old Jail Museum," the historical building was spared by the wrecking ball in the mid- 1960s because the museum society lobbied for its use as a museum to house their collection of artifacts.

Inside are numerous exhibits, including a county store loaded with 19th century merchandise, a display devoted to Allegan's General Benjamin Pritchard, whose men captured Confederate President Jefferson Davis during the Civil war, and a historical laundry room.

But it's a fascination with the jail itself that attracts most visitors. To this extent the staff maintains a roll of six by eight-foot cells in their original condition complete with graffiti that dishearten convicts scratched on the walls in the 1930s. On the third floor you can walk through the maximum security cells, now filled with a historical toy collection, view the old padded cell and examine the holding pen for "ladies."

Particulars: From US-131, depart at either M-222 (exit 55) or M-89 (exit 49) and head west into Allegan. The Old Jail Museum is at 113 Walnut Street, between Hubbard and Trowbridge, a block north of the Kalamazoo River and is open from 2-5 p.m. on Friday from June through Labor Day or by appointment, Saturday's 10 -2 p.m. Admission is by donation.

▼ Holland

Holland Museum
(616) 392-9084

Explore Holland's Dutch heritage in the collections from the Netherlands and early settlers to the area. The museum includes room settings, Delftware, exhibits from the 1939 World's Fair, the lamp from the Holland Lighthouse and a dollhouse furnished with miniatures.

Particulars: The museum is located in the heart of downtown Holland on the corner of 10th Street and River Avenue. Open 10 a.m. to 5 p.m. Monday through Saturday, closed on Tuesday, 2 to 5 p.m. on Sunday and 10 a.m. to 8 p.m. on Thursday. May to Labor Day. Admission fee.

BAKER FURNITURE MUSEUM
(616) 392-9084

Grand Rapids isn't the only city with a furniture collection. This Holland museum features pieces from as early as the 16th century to the 20th century with the antique furnishing from around the world, including England, France, Italy as well as the Orient.

Particulars: Located in downtown Holland at 100 E. 8th Street. Open year-round from 10 a.m. to 5 p.m. Monday through Saturday. Admission fee.

DEKLOMP WOODEN SHOE AND DELFT
(616) 399-1803

FREE

Still not over-dosed on the Dutch? Head northeast of town to DeKlomp Wooden Shoe factory. Watch workers carve the wooden shoes on traditional Dutch machinery or observe the famous blue and white delftware as it is poured, fired and handpainted. It's the only delftware pottery factory in the U.S. Behind the factory are the Veldheer Tulip Gardens, where during the summer you can stroll through 2 million tulips.

Particulars: From US-31 head north of Holland for 2 miles and exit west on Quincy Street. The factory tours are offered year-round and are free.

▼ Fennville

FENN VALLEY VINEYARDS
(269) 561-2396

FREE

The vineyard offers self-guided tours with a viewing balcony and a wine video along with a small tasting room where you can try some award winning wines.

Particulars: From I-196 depart at exit 34 and head east on M-89 for three miles to 62nd Street, then south one mile to 122nd Avenue. The winery is a quarter mile east on 122nd Avenue. The vineyard is open year-round from 10 a.m. to 5 p.m. Monday through Saturday and 1-5 p.m. Sunday. Free.

▼ Saugatuck

SAUGATUCK CHAIN FERRY
(269) 857-2107

FREE

Near this city's impressive marina where scores of $200,000 polished cabin cruisers and sailboats bob in their slips, is the state's only handcranked, chain-powered ferry. An operator literally winds a winch for over 380 feet to fetch you on one side of the Kalamazoo River and drops you off on the other.

The original ferry, a chain-pulled wooden barge, was a much heralded event when it was put into service in 1838. Before the ferry, friends and farmers spent a half-day traveling 10 miles inland to a bridge in New Richmond just to reach Douglas which was only 100 yards across the river.

Residents fell in love with their chain ferry and even after the Saugatuck-Douglas bridge was built in the 1920s the chain-pulling tradition survived. Today, the ferry is a small barge with white gingerbread siding and the trip lasts a mere 15 minutes, delivering pedestrians and bicyclists further up the river, nowhere near Douglas.

Particulars: Saugatuck is south of Holland and reached by exiting onto Blue Star Highway (A-2) from I-96. The Chain ferry is located downtown at the foot of St. Mary St. just off of Water Street. It's operated daily form mi-June through Labor Day. Small fee.

MOUNT BALDHEAD
Saugatuck Visitors Bureau
(269) 857-5801

FREE

What to do once you cross the Kalamazoo River on the Chain Ferry? Nearby is Mt. Baldhead Park where the adventurous can climb 282 steps up the side of forested dune that rises 260 feet above the lake. At the top you'll find observation platforms which feature a spectacular view of the harbor below, Saugatuck and Douglas. There are also three trails that lead down the north side of the dune and end up at Oval Beach.

Particulars: The park is located on the west side of the Kalamazoo River along Park Street. Free.

OVAL BEACH
Saugatuck Visitors Bureau
(269) 857-5801

Dangle your toes in the sapphire waters of Lake Michigan or stretch out on the sand of one of the most beautiful beaches in Michigan. It's also one of the most famous.

Why? MTV once filmed a segment of its show here, complete with imported beach bunnies and muscle-bound lifeguards.

Particulars: From Blue Star Highway in Douglas, turn west at the blinking light onto Center Street then north on Ferry Street to the beach. There is daily vehicle entry fee.

ALPENA COUNTY

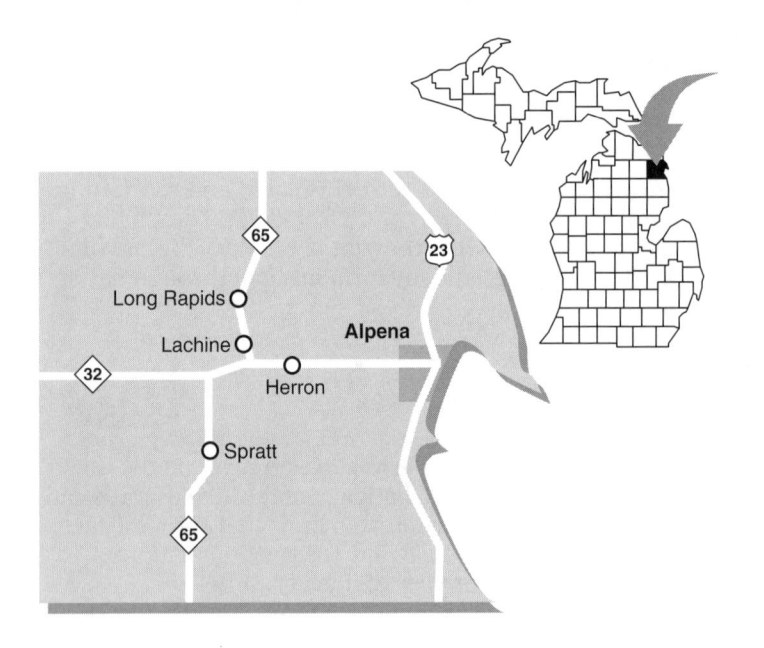

VISITOR INFORMATION

Alpena Area Convention & Visitors Bureau
235 W. Chisholm Street
Alpena, MI 49707
989 354-4181 or 800-4-ALPENA
email: alpenacvnorthland.lib.mi.us

Alpena County

ALPENA MUNICIPAL HARBOR
Downtown Alpena

FREE

A harbor of refuge that features transient slips and full service for traveling boaters. Many fancy sailboats spend time each summer at this popular downtown-area marina. There is shopping, play grounds, tennis courts and food service nearby. Maritime enthusiasts will enjoy the boating action and should consider a dive on the shipwrecks of Thunder Bay. The underwater preserve was established in 1981 offering 288 square miles of preserve. For more information on the shipwrecks/underwater preserves contact: Thunder Bay Underwater Preserve Committee, Box 65, Alpena, MI 49707. Free.

THE COUNTRY CUPBOARD
102 North St.
(989) 356-6020

There's lots of run-of-the-mill gift and antique shops scattered in every corner of the state, but few occupy a virtually unchanged landmark drug store. The Country Cupboard, which now occupies the former Sepull Drug Store that dates back to 1920, still has many remnants of the drug store.

Above you is the original decorative tin ceiling, below a polished floor. There's a wrap-around balcony on the second floor now stocked with baskets and antiques and traveling ladders to reach those high shelves.

The atmosphere is great. Some of the aged remains of the drug store are terrific. There's a nickel Coke Cola machine, a big roll of brown wrapping paper at the end of a sales counter, and overhead a display of Dr. Grabow's pipes proclaiming them as "Our fastest selling pipes because they're pre-smoked!"

But the best part of the quaint shop is all of those shelves and wooden pharmacy drawers packed with Sepull's old merchandise. Looking for some Mount Clemens bath salts, Dr. Heess powdered Louse Killer or a box of cerevim Pre-Cooked Cereal Product? How about some 1920 vintage Icelandic moss, which was once used in folk medicine?

Particulars: Downtown Alpena, block east of US-23. Open daily. Free!

JESSE BESSER MUSEUM
491 Johnson St.
Alpena, MI 49707
(989) 356-2202

One of 19 museums accredited in Michigan, the Besser facility offers three galleries devoted to changing art exhibits, the gallery of Man, lumber and agricultural exhibits, and a Sky Theater Planetarium. Lectures, workshops, and classes are also offered.

Historical Village at Jesse Besser Museum

Particulars: Just north of Alpena, one block east of US-23 North, at 49 Johnson Street. Open year round, small admission fee.

▼ Ossineke

DINOSAUR GARDEN PREHISTORIC ZOO
11160 US-23 South
Ossineke, MI 49766
(989) 471-5477

Twenty-seven life-size dinosaurs, made from concrete, wire, paint, and deer hair, were created in the 1930's. The handmade replicas are painted and have signs describing dinosaur lifestyles for the visitors. The big critters are located along a twisting, turning gravel foot trails that pass through rolling woodlands and over a small hill. Plan about 45 minutes for the tour. Open seasonally, small fee.

Sportsman's Island & the Alpena Wildfowl Sanctuary, corner of US-23 and Long Rapids Road. The island is accessible by a footbridge. Small children will love the chance to feed the waterfowl, hike a short trail, and fish from a specially constructed platform. A handicapped accessible dock is also open. Free.

ANTRIM COUNTY

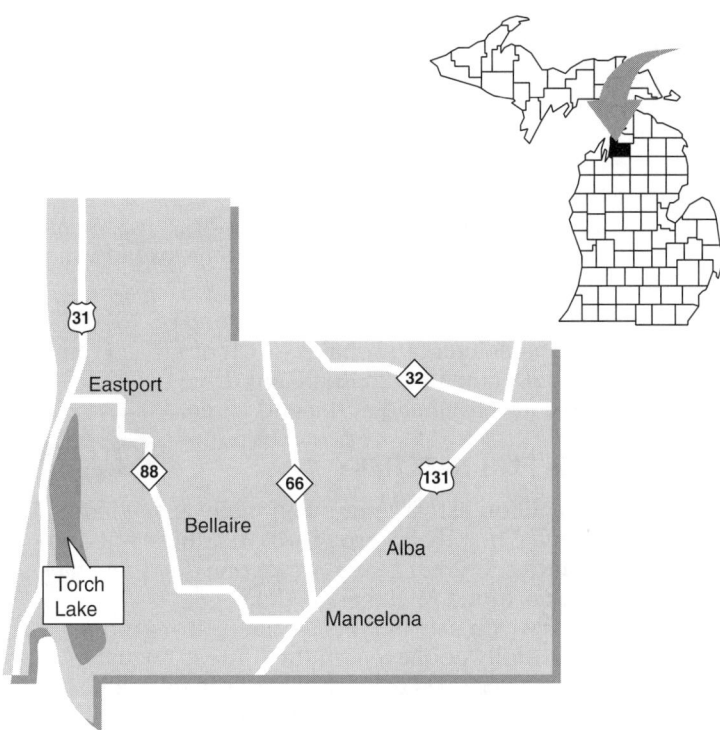

VISITOR INFORMATION

Bellaire Area Chamber of Commerce
211½ N. Bridge Street
P. O. Box 205
Bellaire, MI 49615
231-533-6023
www.bellairemichigan.com
email: info@bellairemichigan.com

Antrim County

▼ Alba

DEADMAN'S HILL
Gaylord DNR office
(231) 732-3541

FREE

Deadman's Hill is one of the best scenic overlooks northwest Michigan, a steal-your-breath panorama of the Jordan Valley that draws tourists from all over the state, especially during fall colors in October. It's also the spot where logger "Big Sam" Graczyk was run over by an overloaded "Big Wheel" on the day he was to be married in 1910, thus the name of the hill.

The scenic area has little more than a parking area, a pair of pit toilets and the trailhead to the 18-mile long Jordan Valley Pathway.

Particulars: Deadman's Hill is posted along US-131 11.5 miles north of Mancelona or six miles north of Alba. From US-131 turn west on Deadmans Hill Road and drive two miles to the parking area and trailhead at the end. Free.

JORDAN RIVER FISH HATCHERY

FREE

More than 5 million fish are reared annually at the federally funded hatchery. The tiny fry are grown to adolescent and then released into the Great Lakes where one day they may become great sport for a Michigan angler.

At the hatchery, you can step inside the visitors room where it is delightfully cool even on the hottest August afternoon due to the 23,000 gallons of water inside that's always kept at a constant 46 degree temperature. Outside you can look at trout in raceways bigger than the ones most people catch all summer.

Particulars: The hatchery is four miles north Alba. From US-131, turn west on Turner Road. The visitor's room is open 8 a.m. to 4 p.m. Monday through Saturday. Free.

▼ Elk Rapids

ISLAND HOUSE LIBRARY
(231) 264-9979

FREE

When Edwin Noble arrived in this historic iron milling town, he built sawmills, a grist mill, lumber yard and one most impressive house. He constructed the large rambling

Glovebox Guidebooks of America **27**

Deadman's Hill, Jordan River Valley

Victorian home on a five-acre island near the mouth of the Elk River. It not only featured the usual living quarters for a millionaire but also servants' rooms, two conservatories and a 50-foot porch.

In 1979 it was placed on the State Register of Historic Sites and today it's the Elk Rapids Public Library. Here you can cuddle up with a good book in any easy chair on the enclosed porch overlooking Grand Traverse Bay or in one of half dozen rooms. The library is reached by a foot bridge in the downtown area that also provides access to the Elk Rapids Harbor that bustles in the summer with pleasure boats, a kid's only fishing pond and a walkway along the Elk River to Lake Michigan.

Particulars: From US-31, turn west into Elk Rapids on River Road where bridge is located. Hours are 10 a.m. to 4 p.m. Tuesday to Friday and 10 a.m. to 1 p.m. Saturday. Free.

ELK RAPIDS HISTORICAL MUSEUM
(231) 264-8000 or 264-5147

FREE

Located in the lower level of the old Elk Township Hall, the small museum has numerous artifacts and pictures from the days when this port was a major iron milling center in Michigan. Blast furnaces once produced 55 tons of pig iron annually and in 1855 400 tons were shipped to England from here, the first "pigs" to be sent overseas from the U.S. The hall itself is an impressive building that was built in 1883 and today is on both State and National Registers of Historical Sites.

Particulars: The township hall is located on the corner of River and Spruce Street, across from the Elk Rapids tennis courts. Hours are 1-4 p.m. on Saturday and Sunday. Free.

▼ Kewadin

CAIRN MONUMENT
Elk Rapids Area Chamber of Commerce
(231) 264-8202

FREE

Michigan is a haven for hundreds of monuments. From General George Custer in Monroe and the Joe Louis "Fist" in Detroit to the Hugh Gray Cairn monument in Antrim County.

Hugh Gray, you ask? Gray was a conductor on the Grand Trunk Railroad when he decided that more people should enjoy Michigan's wonderful natural resources and began to promote tourism. He was so adamant in that belief that in 1917 he was named secretary of the newly created Michigan Tourism Association...an unpaid position.

By the 1930s, a movement began to honor Gray with a monument. The idea was to build a giant cairn on the 45th parallel using a stone from each of the state's 83 counties. A location was selected along US-31 north of Kewadin due to its hilltop location which gave way to a beautiful view of the surrounding countryside and Lake Michigan in the distance.

Then stones arrived from around the state, rocks of all sizes and shapes, weighing anywhere from 80 pounds to the 800-pound boulder from Midland County. Huron County contributed a round grindstone from Grindstone City, Houghton and Keweenaw produced reddish boulders from their copper mines and Washtenaw shipped a stone that was carried from Canada by the last glacier. Traverse County offered a boulder that featured a naturally raised face in the shape of Indian Chief Pontiac. Wexford didn't send a rock at all. At the time Cadillac was a major rubber manufacture so the county sent a two-foot-square block of black rubber with its name attached to it on a steel plate.

Gray was there for the dedication ceremony on June 28, 1938 and was deeply touched by the effort. But the major attraction everybody envisioned never materialized. As fate would have it, US-31 was rerouted more directly north from Elk Rapids in 1955, by passing the monument entirely. Despite renaming the road, Cairn highway, the tribute to Gray became a forgotten roadside treasure. And so did Gray.

Particulars: Cairn Highway departs from US-31, six miles north of Elk Rapids and heads south into Kewadin. Free.

▼ Central Lake

**BROWNWOOD ACRES
(231) 544-3910**

FREE

Established in 1945, Brownwood is a collection of historical buildings that include a fully stocked Country Store, the Country Kitchen where they make and sell Brownwood's Cherry Butter and Kream Mustard, the Honey House and the renovated Grass Lake one-room schoolhouse.

There's also Mary Lou's Tea Room in this charming group of stores that are very much off the beaten path.

Particulars: Brownwood Acres is located on East Torch Lake Drive, reached south from Eastport on US-31, and is open daily during the summer. No fee for browsing.

ARENAC COUNTY

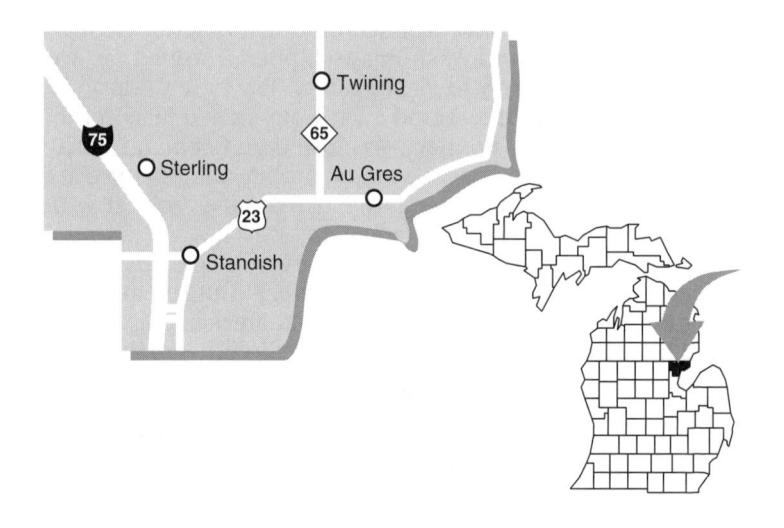

VISITOR INFORMATION

Standish Chamber of Commerce
P. O. Box 458
Standish, MI 48658
989-846-7867

www.sunriseside-mi.com

email: demunson@chartermi.net

Arenac County

▼ Omer

The smallest city in the state is the Sucker Capital of the World. It no longer sponsors an annual sucker festival but anglers still come anyhow, taking the bottom-feeding fish with corn on a hook or in dip nets. Suckers run early to mid-April.

▼ AuGres

**SINGING BRIDGE
Singing Bridge Restaurant
(989) 362-2828**

FREE

One of the best places to dip smelt is Singing Bridge, where US-23 crosses the East Branch of AuGres River. So popular is this spot among dippers that the DNR maintains public access parks on both sides of the bridge.

Never dipped smelt? The small silver fish spawns late at night during the month of April. Arrive at the bridge at midnight, or better yet 2 a.m., on a night when they're running and you'll be stunned at how many people cram into the

Nearby Saginaw Bay is a "world class" walleye fishery and hunting area.

small river with their long-handled nets. Dippers will be staggering away with buckets full of fish.

If you get caught up in the frenzy, Singing Bridge Restaurant and Grocery across US-23 sells everything you need to dip; buckets, waders, nets and Michigan fishing licenses. They also serve a delicious smelt dinner for those who just as soon not stay up until sunrise cleaning 2,000 smelt.

Particulars: From I-75, depart at exit 188 and head north on US-23 through Standish. Singing Bridge is eleven miles north of AuGres.

REST AREA I-75 *FREE*

We said this was your bargain guidebook—and there's nothing cheaper than a stop at a rest area.

But this one on the south-bound lane of the interstate has a terrific little natural area not far from the parking lot. Many of the rest areas around the state have neat little natural areas, some, and we won't tell you which ones, even have bogs nearby, complete with pitcher plants and other interesting flora.

BARAGA COUNTY

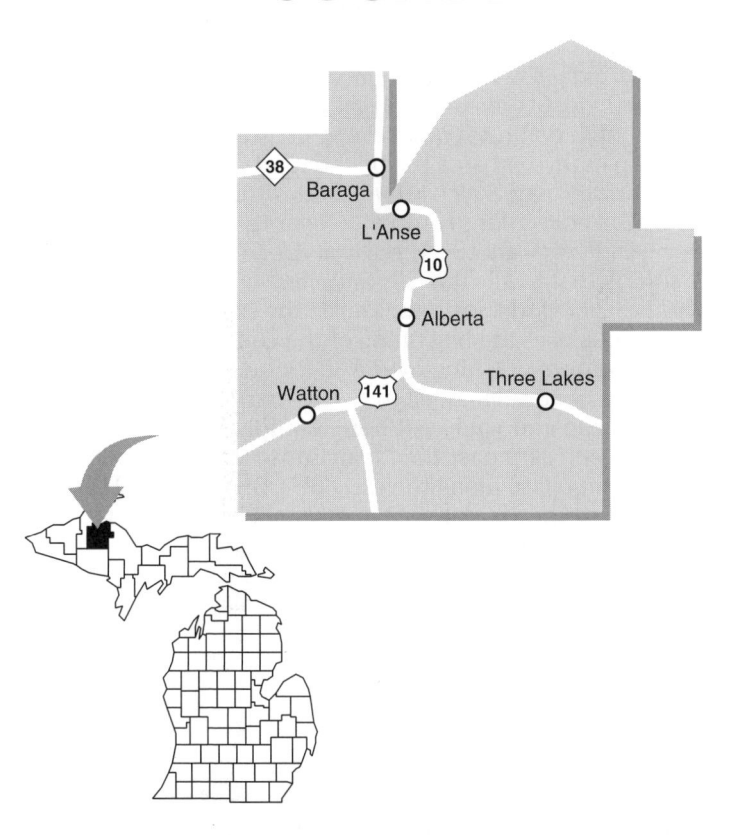

VISITOR INFORMATION

Bargara County Tourist & Recreation Association
755 E. Brodd Street
L'Anse, MI 49946
906-524-7444 or 800-743-4908

www.destinationmichigan.com

Baraga County

▼ L'Anse

CANYON FALLS AND GORGE
Baraga County Tourist Association
(906) 524-7444

FREE

There are 21 falls in Baraga County but Canyon Falls is the prettiest and most convenient offering a rest area and short walk to the observations platform and boardwalk. From a large display map in the rest area the path departs into the woods, crosses a bridge over Bacco Stream and within a third of a mile swings by the cola-colored Sturgeon River to arrive at the first falls, a cascade with about a three-foot drop. Sometimes visitors think that this is the falls and head back to the car. But just another 200 yards down the trail is the real thing.

Canyon Falls is at the beginning of the canyon with thundering waters crashing over a 30-foot ledge. Visitors can lean over the handrail and listen to the roar of the rushing waters. You can end your visit here, but for a better view of the canyon itself skip past the "Trail Ends Here" and follow and old winding path along the rim. BUT BE CAREFUL! Do not get too close to the steep edges and keep a hand on your children if you venture beyond the end of the falls.

Particulars: Canyon Falls Roadside Park is on the west side of US-41 eight miles south of L'Anse or 60 miles west of Marquette. Free.

HILLTOP RESTAURANT
(906) 524-7858

Morning road food. "Start your day with a good breakfast, Billy," Mom would always say. You bet, Mom...So over the ears I've always sought-out Egg McMuffins and a hot cup of coffee with a human hair.

But when there's no Mickey Ds in the area, which is usually a good sign, I always look for places that have a simple 'EAT" sign out front and enough room for 18-wheelers to maneuver. Give me plastic curtains, chipped china, and dried egg on my fork anytime.

So you can imagine my apprehension when I stopped at the Hilltop restaurant outside of L'Anse in the U.P. There's no "EAT" sign and no greasy lunch counter. I almost turn around and left. But the Hilltop's reputation is so unbelievable, I stayed.

A clean place, the waitress took my order of "one roll and a cup of Joe." Less than five minutes later she delivers the biggest cinnamon roll I ever seen. Setting on a dinner plate, it measures six inches across, three inches high and is covered with an avalanche of rich, creamy glaze. How big are the rolls? Go to a grocery store and hold up a one pound loaf of bread...you'll get the picture. Today, the giant cinnamon rolls are so well known by travelers, that on a good day Hilltop sells more than 200 dozen and every Monday the restaurant ships out frozen ones around the country via UPS. Do you think the UPS driver ever sneaks a roll?

Particulars: The restaurant is located on top of a hill (no Kidding) on US-41 just south of L'Anse. It's open from 6 a.m. to 8 p.m. daily. The cinnamon rolls are sooooo wonderful.

INDIAN CEMETERY
Baraga County Tourist Association
(906) 524-7444

FREE

Indian Cemetery Road indeed ends at an Indian cemetery that is situated at the top of a pine-covered hill overlooking a pair of lakes. Chippewa Indians began burying their dead here in 1840 and today there are still several dozen spirit houses scattered throughout the burial grounds. The natural beauty of this reflective spot is even more pronounced during the fall colors.

Particulars: The cemetery is five miles northeast of L'Anse and reached by heading north on Skanee Road and east on Indian Cemetery Road.

SHRINE OF THE SNOWSHOE PRIEST
Baraga County Tourist Association
(906) 524-7444

FREE

Father Frederick Baraga may be buried in Marquette, but his teachings and influence were felt throughout the U.P., especially in the county named after him. Baraga was a young, frail priest more than 150 years ago when he traveled from eastern Europe to Lake Superior to convert the Indians. He was affectionately called the "Snowshoe Priest" because of his long excursions through the U.P. wilderness on snowshoes. In 31 years, he established five major missions and eventually became the first bishop of Upper Michigan.

Today, Baraga is especially remembered near L'Anse with an impressive shrine on the Red Rocks Bluff above the Keweenaw Bay. Made of Lake Linden copper, the shrine was erected in 1972 and stands six stories high. Five laminated wood beams and concrete tepees represent his five missions while at the top if a 35-foot statue of the priest standing on a cloud of brass.

From the shrine there is a stunning view of the Keweenaw Bay while nearby you can walk the Lac Vieux Desert Trail, the same footpath the priest had journeyed along at one time.

Particulars: Located just off US-41 between L'Anse and Baraga. Free.

▼ Arnheim

HANKA HOMESTEAD
(906) 353-7116

Drive inland from Arnheim, a tiny community along Keweenaw Bay, and the smooth asphalt roadway turns to roughed gravel, then to dirt. The open fields quickly turn to forests, and pretty soon you're winding along a woodland two-track convinced you're lost, or worse yet, entering the Twilight Zone.

You're not. Welcome to the 1920s and the Hanka Homestead! The small hilltop with scattered log building is a "living museum" that is supposed to convey what life was like for the early Finnish formers who immigrated to what was then a remote and isolated region of the state.

The farm dates back to 1896 when the Hanka family applied for a homestead on two 40-acre parcels along the military road to Fort Wilkins at the tip of the Keweenaw Peninsula. The first thing Herman Hanka built was a 18 by 24-foot log house. Because he was a good Finn, the second thing he built was a "sava." A smoke sauna. It doubled as a smoke house to cure meat and as a sauna bath. When they doused the fire the steam would clear out the smoke.

Pretty ingenious. So is the self-cooling milk house Hanka constructed. It simply straddles a small spring so the farmer could slide open a trap door in the floor and drop his cans of cream into the ice-cold waters below. Eventually the family added cow barns, a stable, granary and work shop. Maybe the most amazing thing about the farm is that the farm has never been wired for electricity even though the youngest son, Jalmer Hanka lived there until the middle 1960s.

You'll see 10 buildings, including a fully equipped blacksmiths shop, root cellar, and many old tools. Handmade snowshoes and wide skis are hanging up everywhere. There's even a gentle-eyed cow and a noisy roosters that further sets the scene. The place is kind of like a mini-Greenfield Village, without the hype.

Particulars: From US-41 in L'Anse, head north towards Houghton, in 12 miles turn west on Arnheim Road. Follow the small museum signs to the museum. If you pass Otter Lake, you've gone too far. Hanka Homestead is open Saturday and Sundays, noon to 5 p.m. from May to mid-October. Admission fee.

▼ Pelkie

PELKIE GRADE SCHOOL
Baraga County Tourist Association
(906) 524-7444

FREE

Another of the one-room school houses that have been preserved throughout Michigan. What makes this one fascinating is the horse-drawn school bus that was built for the students in 1933 on display outside. It is completely enclosed with benches inside for 20 to 25 students and even has a small wood stove at one end to heat it during the winter. Imagine going to school in that?

Particulars: The grade school is a mile north of Pelkie on the corner of Pelkie Road and Mantila. Open June through September. Free.

▼ Covington

LOOKOUT TOWER

FREE

With Kantola peak in the distance, the 1700-foot hilly region is rich with visual excitement. Tibbets Falls, actually a series of small cascades, is only three miles north of M-28 off of Plains Roads.

Particulars: Just west of the M-28 and US-141, turn north onto Cemetery Road then east on Besonen Road. Free.

Indian Burial Grounds, Baraga County

BARRY COUNTY

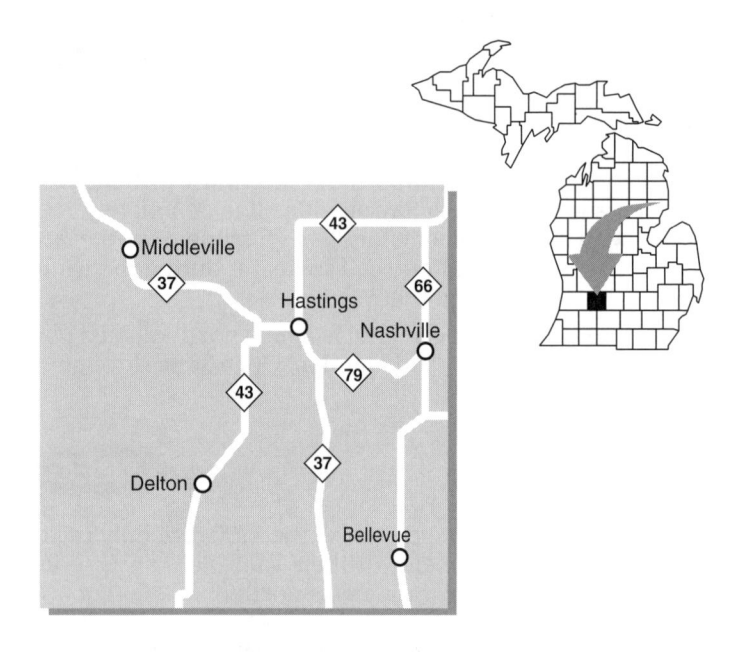

VISITOR INFORMATION

Barry County Area Chamber of Commerce
221 W. State Street
Hastings, MI 49058
269-945-2454 or 800-510-2922
www.barrychamber.com
email: bcacc@voyager.net

Barry County

▼ Hastings

CHARLTON PARK VILLAGE MUSEUM & RECREATION AREA
2545 S. Charlton Park Road
(269) 945-3775

Life in the Midwest during the last part of the 1800's is featured in the 16 historic structures that form a colorful village learning setting. A more formal museum exhibit is also open offering a number learning opportunities.

Particulars: The village is located six miles east of Hastings on M-430 and is open from 8 a.m. to 5 p.m. daily from Memorial Day through Labor Day. For Barry County residents admission is free but for the rest of us there is a small fee.

GRAVES HILL
Yankee Springs Recreation Area
(269) 795-9081

An old moraine makes a fine place for your families first "mountain climb" in southwest Michigan's Barry County. Graves Hill, the result of glacial activity, is located in the heart of the Yankee Spring Recreation Area, one of the most popular units in state park system.

The trail, winding and well marked, is not strenuous, but just steep enough to make children believe they're climbing a peak. The reward of the climb is a good view of the area, and the walk can be extended another mile to include Devils Soup Bowl, a 108-foot depression that measures 900 feet across.

Particulars: From US-131, depart at exit 61 and following county road A-42 east for seven miles to its junction with Gun Lake Road. Turn south on Gun Lake Road to enter the park and stay on it to the posted trailhead at the corner of Gun Lake and Norris Road. There is a daily fee or annual pass required for entry.

▼ Hickory Corners

W.K. KELLOGG FARM/DAIRY CENTER   *FREE*
(269) 671-2508

Mooo, Mooo. You can detect a slight trace of cow fumes in the air, too. Started by Michigan State University in 1984, the experimental dairy farm hosts over 6000 school children annually, offers tours, and has a squeaky clean milking parlor that is open year-round.

The tour takes about an hour and visitors are more than welcome to poke-around, take your time, and visit all of the area, including barns, interpretive center, and computerized milking parlor.

The center takes a holistic approach to dairy farming, teaching little negative impact techniques to professional

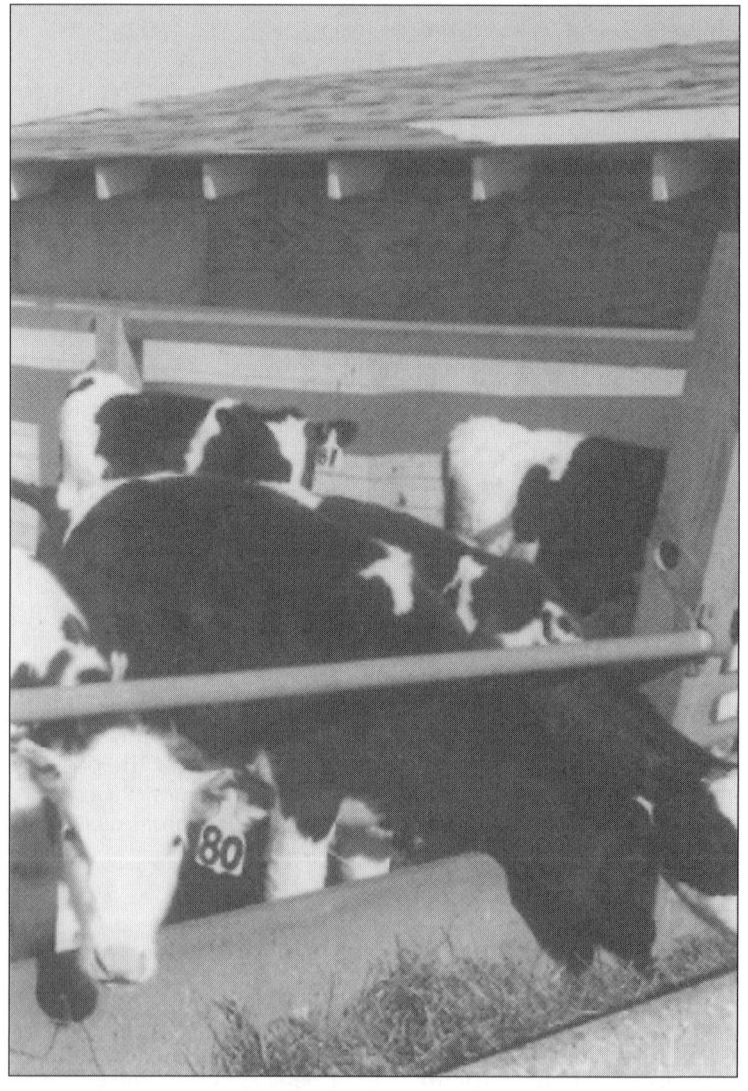

W.K. Kellogg Farm/Dairy Center

dairymen and MSU students.

From computers to labor-saving devices, the shiny white research farm is inviting and educational. You will learn how one person can handle milking sixty cows in an hour, when it used to take one farmer an hour to milk only six.

In the milking parlor, which offers a video and viewing area, you'll be impressed with tubes and piping that rival the chemical industry. Complex and clean, there is a ton of information about cow diets. Did you know an average dairy cow eats 90 pounds of food daily? They also wash down those pellets and hay with 40 gallons of water each day. The end result—manure— is captured and recycled into fertilizer which is returned to the soil to grow more forage. On and on the cycle goes, the sun and rains and cows are pretty good partners for mankind.

Kids are encouraged to pet the big wet nosed calf that has heart-breaking sad-looking eyes. This is a great educational and fun Cheap and Free side-trip.

Particulars: From I-94, depart at exit 85 and head north on 35th street for seven miles and then turn east on M-89. In three miles turn north on 40th Street where first you'll pass the entrance to the Kellogg Bird Sanctuary and then arrive at the dairy center. Hours are 8 a.m. to 8 p.m. daily with public milkings scheduled at 12:30 p.m. and 7:30 p.m. Free.

BAY COUNTY

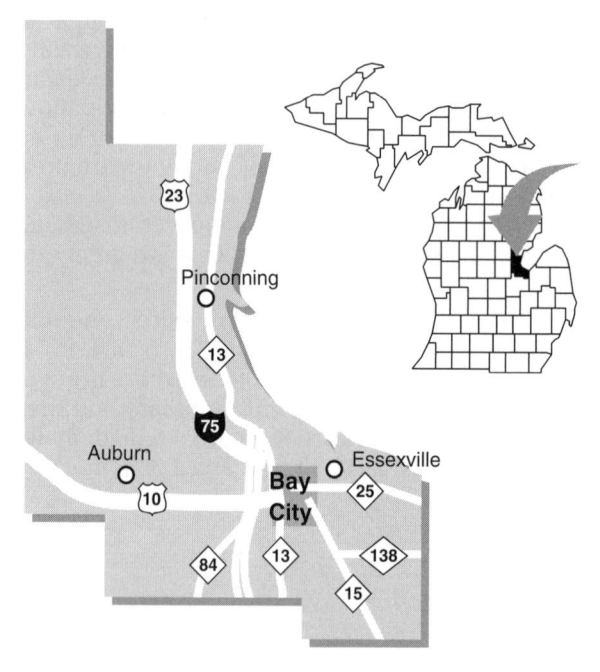

VISITOR INFORMATION

Bay Area Convention & Visitors Bureau
901 Saginaw Street
Bay City, MI 48708
989-893-1222 or 888-BAY-TOWN
www.tourbaycitymi.org
email: info@tourbaycitymi.org

Bay County

▼ Bay City

CITY HALL AND CHMIELEWSKA TAPESTRY
City of Bay City
(989) 894-8147

FREE

The southern shoreline of Saginaw Bay was the final destination for much of the lumber that was cut in the 1800s from the valley as thirty-two saw mills were clustered on the waterfront of Bay City. More impressive than the mansions of the lumber barons, however, is the Bay City City Hall.

Clock Tower, Bay City Hall, Bay City

Built in 1894, the Romanesque-style stone building dominates the city skyline with its 125-foot clock tower at the southeast corner. It was listed in the National Register of Historic Places, and in 1976 the building underwent considerable renovation to preserve the woodwork and distinct metal pillars in the huge lobby. Visitors are welcome to stroll the hallways of the massive building and view the Chmielewska tapestry that hangs in the council chambers.

Woven with hand-dyed yarn of 500 colors by a polish artist, the tapestry depicts the historic buildings of the harbor community. After seeing the colorful wall-mounted tapestry, climb the sixty-eight steps up the clock tower that brings an impressive view of downtown Bay City, the Saginaw River, boats, and the surrounding countryside.

Particulars: The City Hall is located in downtown Bay City at 301 Washington Ave. and is open 8 a.m. to 5 p.m. Monday through Friday. Inquire in the Personnel Office in Room 308 for a trip up to the clock tower. Free.

Bay County Historical Museum
(989) 893-5733

Near rows of stately homes, the museum interprets the lumbering era, ship building, and Indian cultures through displays, period rooms and seasonal exhibits.

Particulars: Located in downtown Bay City, four miles east of I-75, at 321 Washington Ave. Hours are 10 a.m. to 5 p.m. Monday through Friday and 1-5 p.m. on Sunday. Free

JENNISON NATURE CENTER AND TOBICO MARSH
Bay City State Park
(989) 667-0717

The interpretive center, which houses various natural history displays, is located within Bay City State Park and adjacent to the Tobico Marsh, one of the best birding areas in the Saginaw Bay Area. It's an ideal combination. First learn about birds, especially waterfowl, at the center then take a short hike in Tobico Marsh to see them in the wilds.

The 1,109-acre marsh offers both a mile-long loop, ideal for children, and a four-mile trail that passes a pair of observation towers and boardwalk onto the marsh itself. Trail map, bird check-off list and a key to the gate is available at the nature center.

Particulars: The state park is reached by departing I-75 at exit 168 and heading east on Beaver Road for five miles. Jennison Nature Center is open Wednesday through Thursday 10 a.m. to 4 p.m. and Saturdays and Sunday noon to 5 p.m. To reach Tobico Marsh backtrack to M-247 and head north for a mile to Killarney Road and then west to the posted entrance. A daily vehicle permit or an annual pass is required to enter the state park.

ST. LAURENT BROTHERS
(989) 893-7522

Located across the street from Michigan's finest antique mall, the Bay City Antique Center, the St. Laurent Brothers candy and nut shop is one of the most famous sweets destination in eastern Michigan. They are known for adding about three pounds of body weight per visit.

Each year the delightful shop goes through about 50,000 pounds of chocolate which arrives in huge ten pound blocks, and roasts about 800 pounds of nuts per hour, underscoring their long-time motto, "Nuts since 1904." The custom quality candy averages about $7.50 per pound, the aroma is free, and the chocolate covered pretzels are a perfect snack to munch on while roaming the huge Bay City antique mall nearby.

Particulars: The shop is located in Bay City at 1101 N. Water St. Hours are 9 a.m. to 9 p.m. Monday through Saturday and noon to 5 p.m. Sunday.

BENZIE COUNTY

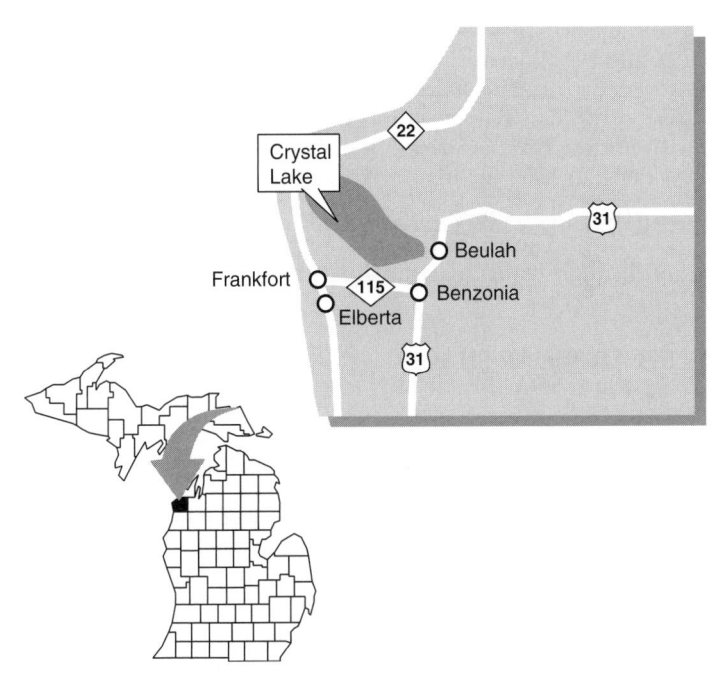

VISITOR INFORMATION

Benzie County Chamber of Commerce
P. O. Box 204
Benzonia, MI 49616
231-882-5801 or 800-882-5801

www.benzie.org
email: chamber@benzie.org

Benzie County

▼ Benzonia

BENZIE AREA HISTORICAL MUSEUM
(231) 882-5539

Housed in a century-old church building (no one steals from the donation box here) the museum features the usual artifacts and displays and tools from the early farmers, lumbermen, sailors and fishermen of Benzie County along with period rooms. The most interesting displays, however, deal with author Bruce Catton, Benzonia native who won the Pulitzer Prize in 1954 for his books on the Civil War.

Particulars: The museum is at 6941 Traverse Ave. just west of US-31 and south to River Road. Hours are 1-4 p.m. Tuesday through Saturday from June through September. A small admission fee.

HOMESTEAD SUGAR SHACK
(231) 882-7712

Diet is a four-lettered word. But not at the Homestead Sugar Shack where out front is a big sign that says, "Hang the Diet." I did.

Inside the aroma is overwhelming; sweet and heavy, the air touches off a saliva flow that will wet the front of your shirt. Hand-dipped maple sugar dollies, goobers of maple and roasted peanuts, and long-stemmed chocolate cherries are everywhere - so are samples, so don't be shy. Although goobers are a specialty, the four-inch wide Benzie Bar, a peanut crunch in white chocolate are just two of the 51 different products the owners make in the slightly weather-beaten building.

The front part of the shop is filled with display cases and shelves stocked with everything from real maple syrup and chocolate lollipops to San Francisco truffles and rum cordial cherries. In the back half of the small candy factory is the kitchen where you can watch through a window as the kettles cooks and the creations come to life.

Among the loyal customers is Linda Ronstadt, a maple creams addict. In fact, the tiny shops ships candy throughout the country. Maybe the best time to get your maple creams is during the brilliant fall color season as the shop is located along a winding rural road that blazes in autumn hues during October.

Particulars: From US-31, turn onto Homestead Road in downtown Benzonia and head east for 4.5 miles to the farm. The shop is open from May through November from 9:30 a.m. to 5 p.m. daily. Samples are free, but you won't get out that easy, even the cheapest traveler can't resist at least a small box of goobers. You'll have them eaten before you boogie back to Beulah.

GWEN FROST PRINTS
(231) 882-5505

FREE

Gwen Frost is Michigan's first Lady of art and poetry...a grand lady who seeks to share her vision of nature with heartfelt words and intriguing drawings. Frost prints are first carved in wood and then printed on-site using 15 clanking Heidelberg presses that can be viewed from a balcony from above.

The studio's interior is a blend of boulders, plants, rough-cut beams and wood paneling so natural the bark is still on. Sunlight floods the rooms through large windows and skylights while two stone fountains provide the background music of a trickling stream. Visitors are surrounded by copies of her 16 volumes of poetry and bird carvings by some of the country's leading wildlife carvers. Most of all there are her woodblock prints displayed and on sale as postcards, notepaper, placemats and napkins while one room is a gallery of framed prints.

Particulars: Gwen Frost Prints is at 5140 River Road, two miles west of US-31 in Benzonia and six miles east of M-22 in Frankfort. The gallery is open daily May to October from 9 a.m. until 5:30 p.m. and until 4:30 p.m. Monday through Saturday the rest of the year. No admission to browse or to enjoy the waterfowl that gather on her pond behind the shop.

▼ Frankfort

MIDWEST SOARING MUSEUM
(231) 352-7251

FREE

The storefront window of the Frankfort Economic Development Office is plastered with signs and the largest one shouts "Area Information" in big, bold letters. Most people stop in looking for a brochure on a bed and breakfast or for the name of a local charter captain to take them fishing.

The most obscured sign is a 8-by-10 inch yellow piece of paper, taped to the door that simply states "Midwest Soaring Museum." Imagine the surprise then of tourists who wander in looking for a good beach on Lake Michigan and leave wide-eyed

with a brochure entitled "How You can Become A Glider Pilot."
Why all these flying fantasies in Frankfort?

The Soaring Society of America has declared the town a National Landmark of Soaring and erected a bronze plaque two doors down from the Midwest Soaring Museum, the same place where you can pick the name of a good restaurant. Did I mention it's also the home of the National Soaring Hall of Fame, all due to the colorful period in the1930s when Frankfort battled Wilmira, N.Y. as the soaring capital of the country.

The high-flying sport arrived from Germany in the late 1920s and Elimira held the first national soaring championship in 1930. Soon pilots were scouring the countryside for different types of air current to test their fragile winds on. In 1935, they discovered the dunes just north of Frankfort and three years later the town hosted the first of two American Open Soaring Meets. The winds were so consistent off Lake Michigan pilots combined for a record 36 hours in the air at one meet and left proclaiming the region "excellent gliding territory, the best in the United States."

The folks in New York weren't amused and rivalry resulted. For many years Frankfort boasted one of only three sail plane factories in the country, was home of a number of nationally recognized glider pilots and in a four-month period was highlighted with major articles in reader's Digest, National Geographic and Life magazines.

The museum is not fancy, but if you take your time you'll discover hundreds of historical photos, memorabilia, and topics that will entertain and excite budding pilots. If you really get excited, you can head out to the Frankfort Airport where May through October the Northwest Soaring Club (616-352-9160) offers introductory rides to would-be pilots.

Particulars: The museum is located in downtown Frankfort in the Economic Development Office on Main Street and is open 8 a.m. to 9 p.m. Monday through Friday, Saturday 8 a.m. to 4 p.m. and Sunday 1-4 p.m. Admission into the museum is free. Introductory rides through the Northwest Soaring Club are $30 per person.

POINT BETSIE LIGHTHOUSE
**Frankfort Information Center
(231) 352-7251**

FREE

Best place to watch and photograph a sunset in Benzie is at this historical lighthouse that overlooks Lake Michigan and is surrounded by a beautiful beach.

Particulars: From Frankfort head north on M-22 to Point Betsie Road. Free.

▼ Beulah

PLATTE RIVER POINT PARK
Benzie County Chamber of Commerce
(231) 882-5801

FREE

Sleeping Bear National Lakeshore begins in Benzie County and includes one of the most scenic beaches on Lake Michigan. The Platte River Point is a long, sandy spit divided from the mainland by the crystal-clear Platte River. This narrow strip is pure sand with endless Lake Michigan on one side, the gently flowing river on the other, and panoramas of towering dunes off in the distance. The pleasant breezes and smell of Lake Michigan is delightful.

The favorite activity here is tubing. Bring an old inner tube, hike a few hundred yards up the spit and let the river give you a free ride out to Lake Michigan. The kids will love it!

Particulars: From M-22, at the corner of the Platte River Campground turn west on Lake Michigan Road and follow it to its end. Don't have an inner tube? You can rent one from Riverside Canoes (616-325-5622) at the corner of M-22 and Lake Michigan Road. The park is free but there is an hourly rental rate for a tube from Riverside.

▼ Honor

DRAKE SCHOOL
(231) 882-5539

A one-room schoolhouse that was built in 1892 and restored by the Benzie Area Historical Museum.

Particulars: The school is reached by heading north on Valley Road in Honor several miles at the corner of Fowler Road and is open Memorial Day to Labor Day from 10 a.m. - 4 p.m. Admission is by donation.

PLATTE RIVER STATE FISH HATCHERY

FREE

Honor is the "Coho Capital" of Michigan, complete with its own Coho Festival and a crowning of a Miss Coho. All due to the salmon that was first planted in the Platte River in the mid-1950s. No visit to this small hamlet would be complete without stopping at this state fish hatchery.

This is one of the state's largest and most modern hatcheries, completed in 1974 at the tune of $6 million. It produces Chinook salmon, steelhead trout and, of course, coho. The best time to come is October and November when you can watch staff member recover eggs from the spawning salmon, many 20 pounds or larger. But stop in any time to visit a small interpretive area and take a self-guided tour of the facility. What the heck, as a taxpayer you paid for it.

Particulars: The hatchery is on the north side of US-31, halfway between Interlochen and Honor. The interpretive center, next to the administrative building, is open 8 a.m. to 4:30 p.m. daily. Free.

BERRIEN COUNTY

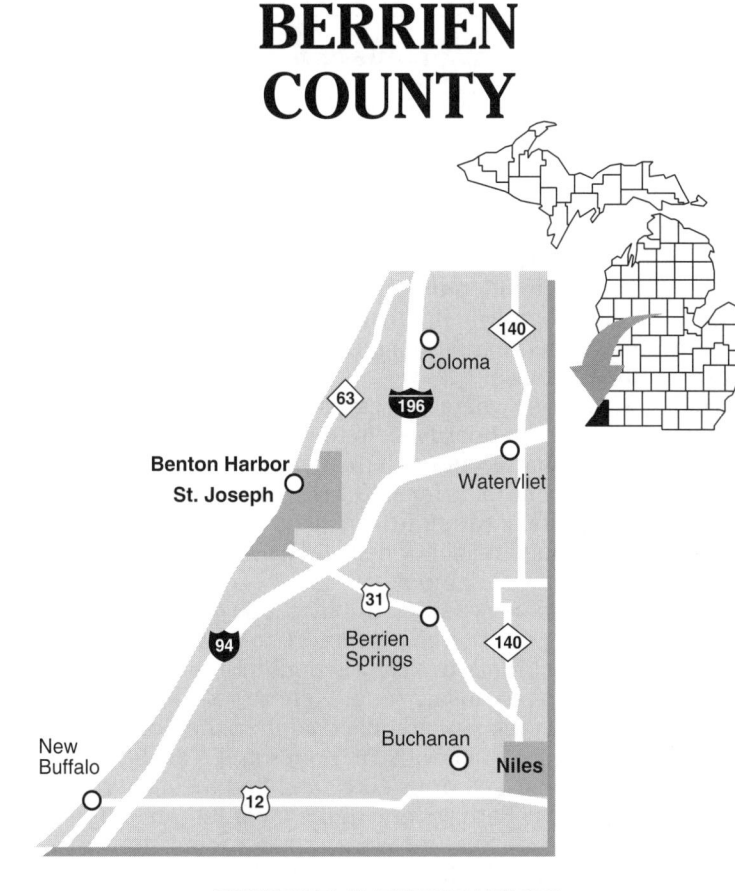

VISITOR INFORMATION

Southwestern Michigan Tourist Council
2300 Pipestone (I-94 at Exit 29)
Benton Harbor, MI 49022
269-925-6301

Four Flags Area Council of Tourism
P. O. Box 1300
(321 E. Main Street)
Niles, MI 49120
269-684-7444

MDOT Welcome Center
33 N. Thompson
New Buffalo, MI 49117
269-469-0011

Berrien County

▼ Benton Harbor/St. Joseph

CURIOUS KIDS MUSEUM
415 Lake Blvd.
(269) 983-2543

A relatively new hands-on museum, Curious Kids is a fine stop for budget-minded travelers that also want to infuse some education into the family outing. The museum is a path that winds through different rooms and areas, each with a posted theme. You begin in Kidspace where children can paint their face, serve their parents pizza and tacos in a diner, stage a puppet show.

There's Kids Port, where you can dress up as captain, sailor or pirate then climb aboard a ship to chart your course, hoist a sail, steer the boat, even swab the deck with mops that are provided. The TV studios for WKID NEWS allows children to give sports reports, weather forecasts or late breaking new stories from behind an anchor desk while watching themselves on television monitors.

There's the Discovery Room for close look at nature, an area devoted to space travel, computers to play on… and you're still on the first floor. The second floor is equally packed with thinds to do and touch. There's a hot air balloon to raise, a bubble table and bubble chamber, the Body Works area where you can dance with Mr. Bones and a display that urges children to be a "tooth sleuth" and find the cavity in a giant set of molars. Perhaps one of the most interesting exhibits is the Frozen Shadow Wall, a small room with light-sensitive walls that actually freezes your shadow momentarily.

Particulars: From I-94, depart on Business I-94, either exit 23 or exit 33 and follow it into downtown St. Joseph. From Main Street turn toward Lake Michigan on Elm Street and in two blocks turn left on Lake Boulevard. The museum is at 415 Lake Blvd. Hours are 10 a.m. to 5 p.m. Wednesday through Saturday and noon to 5 p.m. Sunday. From June through August. Curious is open Tuesday 10 a.m. to 5 p.m. Admission fee.

JOSEPHINE MORTON MEMORIAL HOME
(269) 925-7011

Built in 1849, the Josephine Morton Home is now a museum that preserves the lifestyle of the area's early pioneers with period rooms and historical displays. During the summer, guides in period customs give tours and explain the early history of St. Joseph and Benton Harbor.

Particulars: From I-94 depart at exit 33 and follow the signs to Territorial Road. The museum is at 501 Territorial in Benton Harbor and open from April through October form 1-4 p.m. on Thursday and 2-4 p.m. on Sunday. Admission is by donation.

**KRASL ART CENTER
(269) 983-0271**

FREE

One of the finest small educational art centers in the state. The ever changing exhibits that occupy the three main galleries represent the works of many types of artists, from children to exhibition quality presentations. Major shows often pull visitors from throughout the region, while one-man shows are promoted and just as important, according to the staff. You'll also find the gift shop offers some good values and unique gift ideas for the budget-wise shopper.

Particulars: The art center is downtown St. Joseph at 707 Lake Blvd. Hours are Monday through Thursday from 10 a.m. to 4 p.m., Friday from 10 a.m. to 1 p.m. Sat. from 10 a.m. to 4 p.m. and Sunday 1-4 p.m. Free.

▼ Berrien Springs

**SIEGFRIED HORN ARCHAEOLOGICAL MUSEUM
Andrews University
(269) 471-3273**

FREE

What begins as a gift of 27 pieces of ancient Megiddo pottery from the University of Chicago to the Seventh-day Adventists Theological Seminary in Washington D.C. eventually grew to become the Horn Archaeological Museum when the collection of was transferred to the James White Library of Andrews University in 1970. The museum moved to its present location in 1982 and today it has one of the 10 largest collections of cuneiform tablets in the U.S. as well as ancient coins, Egyptian figures, weapons and an eight-inch bronze statuette from Syria dating back to 15th century B.C.

Andrews University also has a Natural History Museum that is pen by appointment only and features the only complete skeletal mastodon discovered within Michigan. This museum is open by appointment only. Call (616) 471-3243.

Particulars: The Horn Museum is located across from the seminary building on campus off of US-31, two miles northwest of Berrien Springs. Hours are 8 a.m. to noon and 1-

5 p.m. Tuesday through Thursday and weekends 2-5 p.m. Free.

1839 COURTHOUSE MUSEUM
(269) 471-1202

FREE

At various times in history the Courthouse was used for militia drills, college, and even a church. The Greek Revival-style is Michigan's oldest county government facility, which features a gift shop and local historical artifacts. The courthouse, the centerpiece of the five-building County Courthouse Square, provides visitors and interesting insight into the early machinery of old fashion country and state government.

Also open is the Murdock Log House which was built in the 1830s by Francis Murdock, the first lawyer in Berrien County, and is now restored and furnished to reflect the simple lifestyles of early Michigan settlers.

The Sheriff's residence is also restored which was originally built in 1869. The two-story brick building was considered one of the finest jails in Michigan had cell space for 16 men on the lower floor and "eight women or boys on the upper floor." Other buildings include a replica of a blacksmith's shop and wagonmaker's shop.

Particulars: The historic complex is located in Berrien Springs on the corner of US-31 and Union Street. Berrien Springs is 11 miles southeast of I-94 from exit 27. The courthouse complex if open Memorial day through Labor Day from 9 a.m. to 4 p.m.. Tuesday through Friday and 1-5 p.m. Saturday and Sunday. Free.

▼ Bridgman

COOK NUCLEAR POWER PLANT
9587 Red Arrow Hwy.
(269) 465-5901

FREE

Pumping out over two million kilowatt of electricity, the nuclear plant on the lakeside has safely operated for many years. The facility offers complete tours that include three theater show, energy video games. The tours are presented by professional guides and includes "Vistascope" a wide-screen film presentation that gives unique view of Cook Plant.

When in the area call first, often there are special events, tours and programs offered on summer an autumn weekends. Picnics are permitted on the grounds where you can enjoy lunch with a panoramic view of Lake Michigan or the Cook

Plant.

Particulars: From I-96, depart at exit 15 and head north on Red Arrow Highway for 3.5 miles. The plant is open mid-January through mid-December from 10 a.m. to 5 p.m. Tuesday through Sunday. Free

▼ Sawyer

WARREN DUNES STATE PARK
(269) 426-4013

The 1507-acre park, just 12 miles north of the Indiana border, is the beginning of Lake Michigan's string of parks that preserve the greatest collection of freshwater sand dunes in the country. The park draws 1.3 million visitors annually and the attraction is its 2.5 miles of Great Lake beach and huge dunes that border it. Each season thousands climb the wind-blown dunes, some reaching 200 feet above the lake.

Warren Dunes is the only state park that permits hang gliding and is considered by most gliders as the best place in Midwest for soaring. The smooth winds and soft, forgiving sand below attract hang gliders mostly in the fall. During the heyday of the sport in the mid-1970s, you could see up to 20 gliders in the air at one time during a windy weekend. The broken legs and arms of rookie flyers were so common back then that the park finally had to institute a permit system and stricter regulations. The attraction of the sport has since died down (Hey! Let's go break our legs at Warren Dunes!) but you can still occasionally see a handful flying on a nice September weekend.

Particulars: Depart I-94 at exit 16 and follow the park signs south along Red Arrow Highway. There is a vehicle entrance fee or a state park pass required for entry. Warren Dunes is the Michigan state park that sticks it to non-Michigan residents for higher entry fees.

▼ Buchanan

BEAR CAVE
(269) 695-3050

Located in the Bear Cave Campground, a condo-style resort, only three miles north of Buchanan. The campground is private, but Michigan's only large natural cave, which once played a role in the Underground Railroad is open for tours. Narrow paths takes visitors through the cave, where limestone formations can be seen.

Particulars: Located on the Red Bud Trail, three miles south of Buchanan. It's open from May through October and there is an admission fee.

**PEARL MILL
(269) 695-9758**

Buchanan was founded in 1833 because of the 60-foot gradual drop in McCoy Creek that provided a constant source of power. Of the 13 known water-powered mills along the creek only one remains today - Pears Mill, a gristmill constructed in 1853. You can still enjoy the sight and sound of splashing water at the mill as the waterwheel powers belt-driven gears which turn grinding stones to produce flour and meal.

There are also demonstrations at this fully restored mill in weaving, blacksmithing and basket making. A mill gift counter allows you to take home some stone-ground flour (does it really make better pancakes?) and thus a bit of Buchanan's history.

Particulars: The mill is located on Front Street between Days Avenue and Oak Street, in downtown Buchanan. It is open from late May through September from noon to 4 p.m. on Saturday and Sunday. Admission is by donation.

▼ Eau Claire

**TREEMENDUS ORCHARDS
9351 E. Eureka Road
(269) 782-7101**

When Grandpa was farmer many of us had an opportunity to have a "country" experience, a chance to roam the field, learn about man's role in nature, and understand the farming lifestyle. Today, thanks to a bit of commercialism, places like Tree-Mendus offers orchard tours, cider mills, old-time apples, famous cherry spitting contest, cherries in July and pumpkins in October. The highpoint of the 400-acre farm is the Cherry Pit Spitting Championship Contest held every July.

Particulars: The farm is just six miles north of Berrien Springs and east of Eau Claire on Eureka Road. It's open daily from late June through September from 10 a.m. to 6 p.m. It's free to wander around but there is a fee for everything else from wagon rides to orchard tours.

▼ New Buffalo

**THE ROUNDHOUSE
(269) 469-3166**

Located in an actual roundhouse, where Pere Marquette locomotives were once overhauled, your family will discover railway history in the New Buffalo Railroad Museum. You'll also discover shopping as the Roundhouse is a unique shopping experience with upscale shops and a 25-dealer antique mall.

The museum includes local history and railroad memorabilia from the Pere Marquette, Michigan Central, C & P, Chessie and Amtrak Lines. There is also a delightful exhibit of model trains that will charm any child's heart.

Particulars: I-94 Exit 1, one mile north to 530 S. Whittaker. The Railroad Museum is open Thursday through Saturday from 10 a.m. to 6 p.m. and Sundays from noon to 6 p.m. There's a small admission fee.

▼ Harbert

SWEDISH BAKERY
13698 Red Arrow Hwy.
(269) 469-1777

Carl Sandberg was one of Harbert's most famous visitors. In fact, much of his Pulitzer Prize winning account of Abraham Lincoln was accomplished in Harbert. When this Glovebox Guidebook wins a Pulitzer, we will disclose that the authors have pigged-out repeatedly at the Swedish Bakery.

Lace curtains and knotty pine covered, the friendly bakery has picnic tables outside, where the authors sometimes burp and sleep-off a dozen pastries. This place is great, a dozen kind of crunchy cookies, breads, and an aroma that wafts in the lakeshore breezes. Do not, we repeat, do not blame us if you gain seven pounds in one visit!

Particulars: The bakery is located in Harbert at 13746 Red Arrow Hwy. Open mid-March-the day before Thanksgiving, during the summer from July 4-Labor Day they are open Wednesday-Saturday, 7:30 a.m. - 6 p.m., Sunday 7:30 a.m. - 4:30 p.m. Early spring and autumn they are open Friday - Sunday.

▼ Niles

Fernwood Botanic Garden and Nature Center
(269) 695-6591

The 105-acre preserve is located northwest of Niles and features six acres of gardens, a 45-acre arboretum, a reconstructed tall grass prairie, woods and four miles of trail, much of it skirting the banks of the St. Joseph.

But it is the variety of ferns seen at Fernwood that is

astounding. They range from tree ferns that thrive in the tropic, reaching heights of 60 to 100 feet, to the smallest American fern that is usually mistaken for moss because colonies of it found on the limestone cliffs of Alabama are no larger than a quarter.

If it's spring or summer, you can hike the trails, especially the half-mile long Guide Yourself Nature Trail, and see and read about ferns. If it's winter, visit the Fern House. Inside the 1,000-square foot conservatory, there is a huge limestone peninsula, 72 tons of rocks and boulders, that are surrounded by a waterfall, stream and pond and covered with ferns. There are more than 100 different species of ferns inside, each with enough Latin in its name to tie up your tongue for a week.

Particulars: From the US-12 west of Niles, head north on the US-31 Bypass and then southwest on Walton Road just after crossing the St. Joseph River. Turn north on Range Line Road and the entrance of the nature center will be reached in a mile. The visitor's center and Fern House is open Monday through Saturday 9 a.m. to 5 p.m. and Sunday noon to 5 p.m. Admission fee.

FORT ST. JOSEPH MUSEUM
508 E. Main Street
(269) 683-4702

FREE

Unlike many town museums - often tiny halls of dusty local lore, the Niles museum is very impressive, especially for a community of less than 13,000 residents. Niles, the city of four flags, has a colorful past and this museum does a wonderful job of preserving it.

In 1842, a private museum opened its doors here, making it one of the earliest museums in the U.S. Eventually the local government took over the responsibility of preserving the past and today city hall and city heritage sit side-by-side in downtown Niles.

The Chapin Mansion, a beautiful Queen Anne-style home built in 1884, is where you'll find the mayor, clerk, and dog catcher. Right behind it is Henry Chapin's carriage house, no the Fort St. Joseph museum, where more than 10,000 historic items have been preserved on tow floors. Much of the museums collection related to its namesake fort that the French built the stockade in 1691, the British took over in 1761 and the Spanish raided 20 years later. In 1783, the Americans arrived and raised the fourth flag over Fort St. Joseph.

The museum's most noted exhibits are devoted to the Sioux

Indians of the Great Plains, however, not the citizens of Niles. The collection ranges from head dresses, buffalo robes and rawhide saddles to dolls, weapons and tobacco pouches that belonged to Sitting Bull.

Most of the complex artifacts were obtained by Capt. Horace Baxter Quimby, whose daughter was a resident of Niles. Captain Quimby was based in the Dakota Territory in the 1881-1882 when he became friends with Sitting Bull. Among the gifts Quimby received were 13 autobiographical photographs of the chief's greatest battles. The set of pictures is one of only three known collections by the famous warrior.

Particulars: Located behind the Niles City Hall at 508 E. Main Street. Niles can be reached from US-12, 23 miles east of I-94 or 33 miles west of US- 131. Museum hours are 10 a.m. to 4 p.m. Tuesday through Saturday and 1-4 p.m. on Sundays. Free!

▼ Three Oaks

DRIER'S BUTCHER SHOP
(269) 756-3101

FREE

You'll find lots of bologna at Drier's Butcher Shop, some in the display cases, and some from Ed Drier, a sausage maker with a spicy sense of humor. The shop has changes little since opening shortly after the Civil War and still has good service, fine cuts of meat, especially the double-smoked hams, and signs chiding vegetarians. Built in 1875 and listed as on the National Register of Historical Sites, the butcher shop features the original meat hooks, a potbelly stove in the corner and wooden floors covered with sawdust. A cheap and free favorite, especially the liverwurst, which Drier compares to fine liver pate.

Particulars: Located on 14 S. Elm Street in Three Oaks.

THREE OAKS SPOKES BICYCLE CLUB
(269) 756-3361

FREE

In downtown Three Oaks, in the southwest corner of Berrien County, is the year-round bike museum where dozens of the wheeled vehicles hang from the walls, and crowd the building. From Boneshaker (no rims or tires) to side-by-side, two seater called the Companion two-seaters, bikes of all types are displayed. Zany? Yea, you bet and I love it. The museum also offers bunches of information and even organizes one of the largest road events in the state (Apple Cider Century).

Drier's Butcher Shop

Promoting recreational cycling in Michigan was the aim of the Three Oaks Spokes Bicycle Club when it was formed in 1974. Along with museum, the busy club has also set up the Backroads Bikeway, a selection of 10 tours throughout the region that have been posted with color coded bike route signs.

The bike museum also rents bikes for those who want to follow a portion of the Backroads Bikeway. They aren't exactly top-of-the-line touring bikes, but they definitely have something a little newer and a little more comfortable than the vintage Boneshaker.

Particulars: The Bicycle Museum is located in the east of Three Oaks on 110 North Elm Street. Three Oaks in 16 miles west of Niles on US-12 or 71 miles southwest of Kalamazoo. Hours are 9 a.m. to 5 p.m. daily. Free.

Wineries of Berrien County
LEMON CREEK FARM WINERY
(269) 471-1321

FREE

One of the smallest, family owned wineries in the state, visitors will enjoy an opportunity to buy fresh fruit, take a tour, and taste some elegant medium-priced wines.

Particulars: Lemon Creek is 5 miles east of Bridgman. From I-94, depart at exit 16, head north on Red Arrow

Highway through Bridgman to Lemon Creek Road. The winery is at 533 East Lemon Creek Rd. Free.

MADRON LAKE HILLS
(269) 695-5660

FREE

A small, far-from-fancy owner operated winery, Madron Hills offers limited tours during the summer and autumn, and offer middle market prices for spirits.

Particulars: Take I-94 to exit 28 (US-31 South) and head eight miles south. Continue south on Red Bud Trail another eight miles to Miller Road and head west 2.8 miles to Madron Road. The winery is south at 14387 Madron Lake Rd. Free.

TABOR HILL WINERY
(800) 283-3363 or (269) 422-1161

FREE

This is a big-money winery with all the bells and whistles. But also a lovely restaurant with sophisticated design and graphically appealing. From the restaurant terrace you have a panoramic view of the rows of grapes, orchards and in the distant Lake Michigan dunes.

Tabor Hill produces wines from every market, there are bottles of sangria to expensive award winning Chardonnay. Tabor Hill has a comprehensive tour where visitors, which, depending on the season, can witness the entire process of winemaking.

Particulars: Take I-94 to exit 16 and go one mile north on Red Arrow Highway to Bridgman. Turn east on Lake Street and then follow the lively colored directional signs to the winery at 185 Mount Tabor Hill Rd. Tour hours are 11 a.m. to 5 p.m. Monday through Saturday and noon to 5 p.m. Sunday. Dinner is served from 5-9 p.m. daily. Tours are free.

BRANCH COUNTY

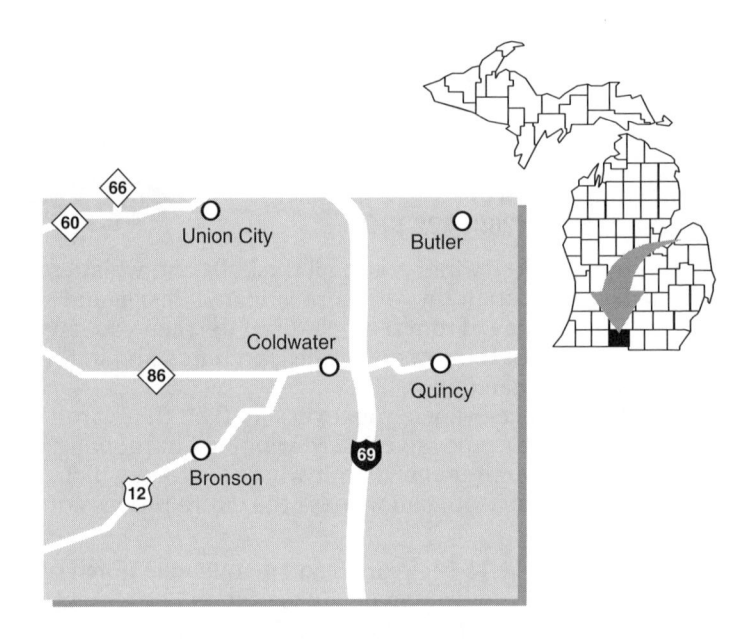

VISITOR INFORMATION

Coldwater/Branch County Chamber of Commerce
20 Division Street
Coldwater, MI 49036
517-278-5985

MDOT Welcome Center
I-69 Northbound at 6 mile marker
Coldwater, MI 49036
517-238-2670

Branch County

▼ Coldwater

WING HOUSE MUSEUM
(517) 278-2871

The Second Empire style mansion was built in 1875 and then sold to Lucius Wing in 1882, where it remained in the Wing family until the Branch County Historical Society purchased both the home and much of its furnishing in 1974. It's an excellent and , better yet, cheap way to see how people lived a century ago.

Particulars: Located in Coldwater at 27 S. Jefferson and open from 1-5 p.m. Wednesday through Sunday. Admission by donation.

TIBBITS OPERA HOUSE
(517) 278-6029

Completed in 1882, this Victorian-style opera house is the professional summer stock and special vocal arts events. The historic house offers free tours and art exhibits, but summer performance require an admission fee.

Particulars: Located in downtown Coldwater at 14 S. Hanchette St.

MDOT WELCOME CENTER
(517) 278-2670

FREE

On I-69 just north of Coldwater Lake is a Michigan Department of Transportation Welcome Center, known to most travelers as simply a rest area.

But hey, it's chucked-full of brochures for businesses and attractions for every budget. I know, that's where I did half the research for this book (the other half was done at the MDOT Welcome Center north of Clare).

Particulars: The bathrooms are open 24 hours, the visitor's center 8 a.m. to 5 p.m. daily. Free.

CALHOUN COUNTY

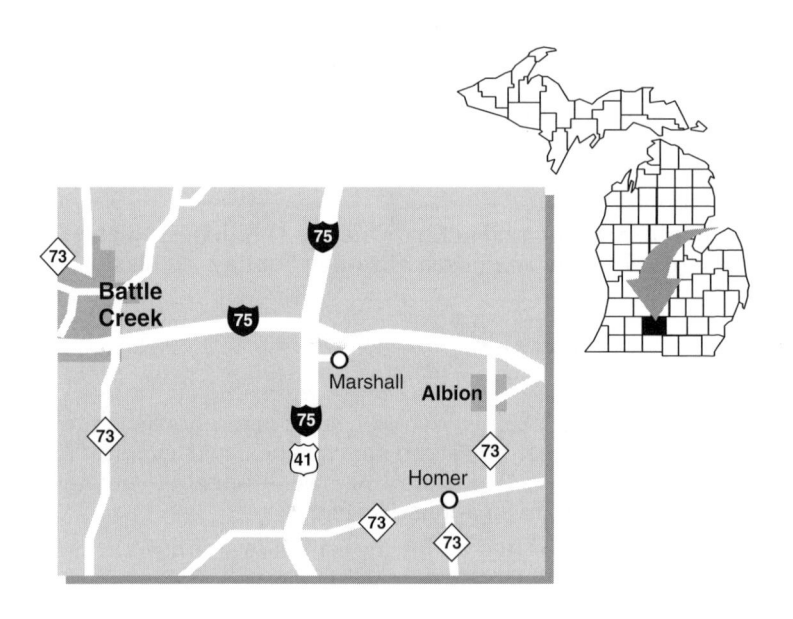

VISITOR INFORMATION

Greater Battle Creek/Calhoun County Visitor & Convention Bureau
77 E. Michigan, Suite 100
Battle Creek, MI 49017
800-397-2240
www.freeinfo@battlecreekvisitors.org

Calhoun County

▼ Albion

STARR COMMONWEALTH SCHOOLS *(FREE)*
(517) 629-5591

The historic school helps troubled children and also operates the Brueckner Museum featuring fine arts, Gladsome Cottage Museum displaying examples of Victorian furniture, and Chapel-in-the-Woods, an English cruciform church with 17 lancet stained-glass windows.

Particulars: From I-94 depart at exit 119 and head south on 26 Mile Road to the Starr Commonwealth School. Hours are by appointment. Free.

GARDNER HOUSE MUSEUM
(517) 629-2443

This 1869 Second Empire-style Victorian mansion is now the home of the Albion Historical Society. Listed on the National Register of Historic Places, the Gardner House features five rooms restored as a typical dwelling of the 1869-1900 period. The rest of the building has local historical displays and rotating exhibits.

Particulars: The museum is at 509 S. Superior Street in Albion and open May through October from 1-4 p.m. Saturday and Sunday or by appointment. Donation requested.

ALBION'S HISTORIC WALKWAY
Albion Chamber of Commerce *(FREE)*
(517) 629-5533

Walk around the historic heart of the city using a self-guided tour map which interprets sites and landmarks. Maps are available for a small fee at Gardner House Museum.

▼ Battle Creek

BATTLE CREEK ART CENTER *(FREE)*
(269) 962-9511

The center houses galleries, featuring changing art exhibitions and an extensive collection of Michigan Art.

Particulars: From I-94 head north on I-194/M-66 at exit 98 and then head west on Emmett Street. The art center is at 265 E. Emmett and is open 10 a.m. to 5 pm. Mondays through Fridays and 1-4 p.m. on Saturday. Free.

BINDER PARK ZOO
(269) 979-1351

More than many traditional zoos, Binder Park is a regional cultural center providing outdoor recreation, wildlife conservation and natural history education for its quarter-million annual visitors. At Binder more than 20 days per year are scheduled for significant special events.

Cobblestone paving, elevated boardwalks, colorful interpretive signs, smiling uniformed staff, and a terrific collection of interesting wildlife are on display. Over 290 specimens and 70 species are exhibited at the 170 acres zoo.

The Miller's Children Zoo, dedicated in 1989, is a two-acre delight for all ages. Although the traditional fair of petting animals occupy the contact yards, the design of the exhibits are clean and attractive. Sure-footed pygmy goats, complete with tiny romping babies; the "servant of man," camels, which can sometimes drink 35 gallons of water at one time, also gawk and gently plod around the small area. Kids will love the mini-playground, pot-bellied pigs, and Buelah's restaurant.

Particulars: From I-94, depart at exit 100 and head south on Beadle Lake Road to follow signs to the entrance. The zoo is open from mid-April to mid-October from 9 a.m. to 5 p.m. Monday through Friday and 9 a.m. to 6 p.m. Saturday and Sunday. There is an admission fee.

KIMBALL HOUSE HISTORICAL MUSEUM
(269) 965-2613

Restored 1886 Victorian home, features a furnished first floor, four rooms on the second floor and the basement that is open to the public. Basement includes a old country store and a pioneer kitchen filled with kitchen gadgets of long ago and by-gone items.

Perhaps the most noted display in the museum is dedicated to Solourner Truth (1797-1883), the famous black, anti-slavery reformer who was Battle Creek's first nationally known figure. Several mementoes, including her attempt to write her name and her address are on exhibit on the second floor. The museum staff can also give you directions to Sojourner Truths grave, at 222 South Haven in Oak Hill Cemetery, shady and calm.

Glovebox Guidebooks of America **67**

Binder Park Zoo, Calhoun County

Particulars: From I-94 depart at exit 98 and head north on I-94/M-66. The museum is right off M-66, labeled as 196 N.E. Capital Avenue in downtown Battle Creek. Hours are 12:30 - 4:30 p.m. Tuesday through Friday. Admission is by donation.

KINGMAN MUSEUM OF NATURAL HISTORY
175 Limit Street
(269) 965-5117

Overlooking the beautiful Leila Arboretum, near M-37, the Kingman Museum specializes in comprehensive natural history exhibits and programming. Part of the Battle Creek public School System, the hands-on museum features exhibits that includes The Ice Age, The Wonder of Life, Astronomy and Space Science, In the Footsteps of Dinosaurs, and many other adventures in learning. Planetarium shows are offered on the weekends.

Particulars: From I-194 head west on Van Buren through downtown Battle Creek which merges into West Michigan Avenue. The museum is at West Michigan and 20th Street and open from 9 a.m. to 5 p.m. Tuesday through Saturday and 1-5 p.m. Sunday. Admission fee. Planetarium show is an additional fee.

LEILA ARBORETUM
928 Michigan Avenue W.
(269) 969-0270

FREE

With grand ideas in mind, Leila Post Montgomery donated 70 acres of rolling hills and picturesque land, the original site of the Battle Creek Country Club, for development as an arboretum. Brilliant landscaping has reshaped the lands as the originally planted 250,000 trees are reaching maturity offering both beauty and recreational opportunity. Sledding hills, Kingman Natural History Museum, pioneer homestead, picnic area, botanical collection, scenic overlooks and aquatic display areas are open to the public.

Particulars: The grounds are at West Michigan Avenue and 20th Street (see Kingman Museum of Natural History above). Open dawn to dusk. Free.

▼ Marshall

TURKEYVILLE USA
(800) 888-7933 or (269) 781-4293

FREE

A mix of zany events and facilities unlike anywhere else in

the state. Giant flea markets monthly during the summer, antique shows, art and craft fairs, famous jumbo turkey sandwiches, dinner theater, petting farm, ice cream parlor and more.

Particulars: From I-94, head north on I-69 to exit 42 and then west on N. Drive North (also known as Turkeyville Road). Turkeyville USA is half mile west of I-59 and the season runs from mid-February to late December. Hours are 11 a.m. to 8 p.m. Monday through Saturday. Free Admission.

EDUCATION OAK
Marshall Chamber of Commerce
(269) 781-5163

FREE

A stately oak was the location chosen by the Rev. John Pierce and Issac Crary for their discussion of the founding of an educational system for the new territory that was to become Michigan. A statue of the founders of public education was carved from the original oak tree.

Particulars: The tree is located at 310 N. Kalamazoo Avenue in Marshall. Free.

HISTORIC TOURS
Marshall Chamber of Commerce
(269) 781-5163

FREE

Take a two hour van or foot tour of the historical community that once battled Lansing to be named the new state capital.

Particulars: Walking tour maps are available throughout the community of the Marshall Chamber of Commerce at 109 E. Michigan. Free.

HONOLULU HOUSE MUSEUM
(269) 781-8544

A classic example of rare Victorian architecture, the Honolulu House was built in 1860 by a former U.S. Consul to the Hawaiian Islands. The Honolulu House, which have been completely restored, is listed in both the Historic American Building Survey and the National Register of Historic Places. Outside there are rose and herb gardens.

Particulars: From I-94 depart at the Marshall exit to the Fountain Circle in the heart of downtown. The museum is at 107 N. Kalamazoo Avenue and open May through October from noon to 5 p.m. daily. Admission fee.

CAPITOL HILL SCHOOL
(269) 781-8544

FREE

Owned and operated by the Marshall Historical Society this Victorian school museum features a typical classroom of the 1860s and second room housing a historical toy collection and a marionette theater.

Particulars: Located at Washington and Maple Street near the Calhoun County Fairground. There are no regular hours. Call for information regarding tours. Free.

CASS COUNTY

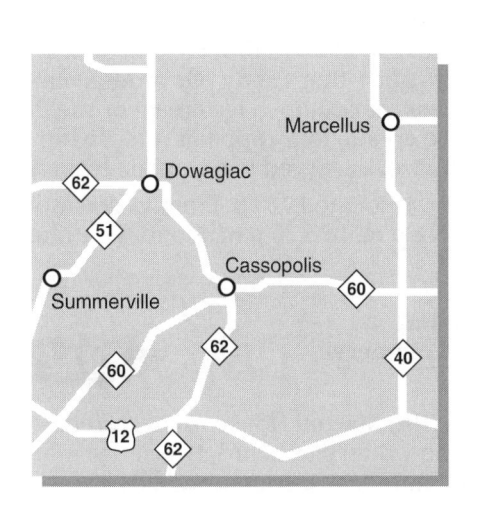

VISITOR INFORMATION

Greater Dowagiac Chamber of Commerce
200 Depot Drive
Dowagiac, MI 49047
269-782-8212
www.dowagiacchamber.com

Cass County

▼ Dowagiac

CARUSO CANDY KITCHEN
(269) 782-6001

It's as if time stood still since the 1920s in this charming Dowagic candy shop. Pull up a tall pedestal stool to the Italian marble soda fountain, make faces in the wavy mirror behind it, plop down in a high wooden booth that's been there since Model A's were arriving at the shop.

The shop, which has been in the same family for more than 70 years, has display cases full of hand-dipped chocolates, caramels, peanut clusters and other candy. Or order a malt, still served in a metal glass, hand0diped ice cream or the Pig Dinner: four flavors of ice cream, four toppings, nuts, whip cream, split bananas, the works served in a wooden trough.

Particulars: The shop is located 130 S. Front in downtown Dowagiac and open from 8 a.m. to 5:30 p.m. Monday through Saturday.

NEWTON HOUSE MUSEUM
Dowagiac Chamber of Commerce
(269) 782-8212

FREE

Built in the mid-1800s, the Newton House is a restored Quaker family home. The white, clapboard, two-story structure is set off by an impressive cupola and has a landscaped herb garden.

Particulars: The house is located five miles east of Dowagiac on Marcellus Highway and Decatur Road near Russ Forest County Park. It's usually open 1-4:30 p.m. Sundays. Free.

FRED RUSS FOREST PARK
Cass County Road Commission
(269) 445-8611

Located on a rural road between Dowagiac and Marcellus, Cass County's Fred Russ Forest Park is a delightful 10-acre park surrounded by Michigan State University's 580-acre Russ Forest Research Station. The area is laced by more than 4 miles of foot trails while gently flowing through the middle of

Cass County Park

it is Dowagiac Creek, a class A trout stream.

At one time the site of a farm, a huge red barn still stands near the parking area while nearby is a display containing a third of what was once the largest tulip tree in Michigan. Known simply as the "Big Tree" it was 200 feet tall with a girth of 23.6 feet when a violent storm blew it down in 1984. To see the rest of the trunk and its massive stump you have to hike 1.6 miles along Big Tree Loop.

It may be lying on the ground in several pieces but it's still an impressive piece of lumber. And it's not hard to imagine what it looked like stretched out to the sky at the end of its 300-year life. Nearby is another towering tulip tree that somehow survived the storm and still forces you to look up.

It may be lying on the ground in several pieces but it's still an impressive piece of lumber. And it's not hard to imagine what it looked like stretched out to the sky at the end of its 300-year life. Nearby is another towering tulip tree that somehow survived the storm and still forces you to look up.

Particulars: From M-60, two miles east of Cassopolis, turn north on Decatur Road and then in six miles east on Marcellus Highway. The park entrance is posted just to the east. The park is open daily. Free.

▼ Cassopolis

Pioneer Log Cabin
Southwestern Michigan Tourist Council
(269) 925-6301

FREE

The museum is made of logs donated by area farmers 50 years ago to celebrate Cassopolis' centennial. Inside there are displays of old tools and farm equipment, quilts and a dollhouse. South of Cassopolis, along M-60 on the way to Edwardsburg, there is the Red Brick Schoolhouse that is being restored and has roadside picnic tables.

Particulars: Pioneer Log Cabin is near downtown Cassopolis on the edge of Stone Lake. It's usually open during the summer. Free.

CHARLEVOIX COUNTY

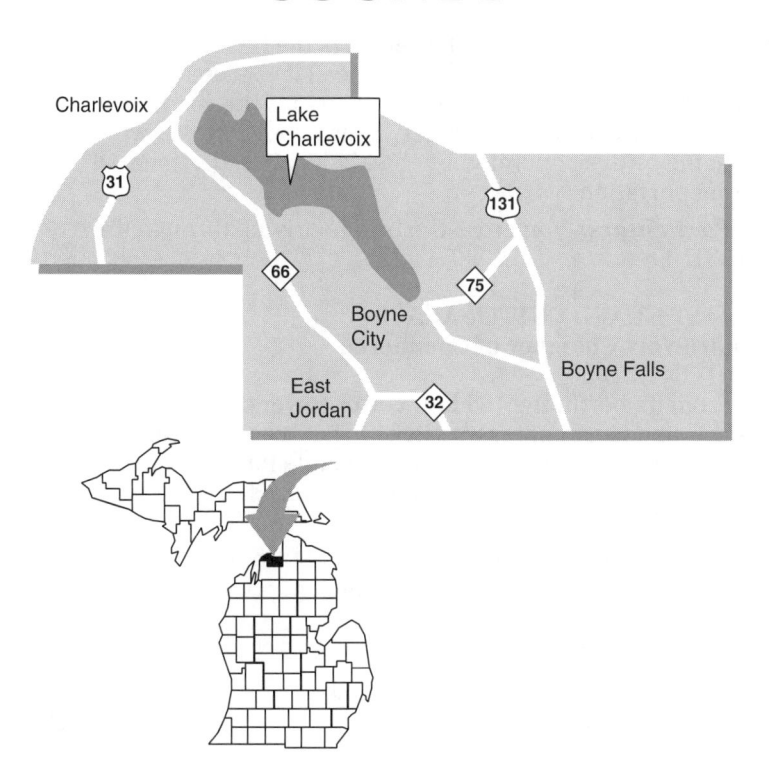

VISITOR INFORMATION

Charlevoix Area Convention & Visitors Bureau
408 Bridge Street
Charlevoix, MI 49720
231-547-2101
www.info@charlevoix.org

Charlevoix County

▼ Charlevoix

CHARLEVOIX MEMORIAL BRIDGE
Charlevoix Chamber of Commerce
(231) 547-2101

FREE

A visual focal point in Charlevoix is the Bascule-type bridge, (not a draw bridge as most people call it) because it has a huge counter-weighed system that swings the roadways vertically by turning on hinges. This is only one of two bascule bridges operated by the Michigan Department of Transportation.

Particulars: You cross the bridge driving through town on US-31. Free.

COAST GUARD CUTTER ACACIA
Charlevoix Chamber of Commerce
(231) 547-2102

FREE

From its berth, the 180 foot cutter towers over the nearby shops and is an impressive sight. The Acacia is primarily a buoy tender and ice breaker responsible for the shipping lanes of northern Lake Michigan, northern Lake Huron, and occasionally eastern lake Superior.

Particulars: The cutter is moored at Bridge Park in the Bridge Street Shopping Area. When in port the cutter often has tours. Free.

EARL YOUNG HOMES
Charlevoix Chamber of Commerce
(231) 547-2101

FREE

Earl Young "liked" rocks. With no formal architectural training, Earl A. Young, during the 1920s mostly, built a number of fanciful houses with stone and dramatically curved roof lines. Young built 30 homes over a 40 year career, including the "Mushroom" homes along Park Avenue. Often referred to as "stone cottages," the symmetrical structures seem to squat on their lots, blending into neighborhoods and the texture of the Charlevoix region.

Particulars: The homes are located at the west end of town. A detailed map is available from the Chamber of Commerce office just off US-31. Free.

FISHERMAN'S ISLAND STATE PARK
(231) 547-6641

Search for "Hexagonaria" on the sandy beaches of northwest Michigan. Thousands of people do it. You'll see half-stooped people scratching in the sand, filling tin buckets, and hoarding their finds. What are they doing? If you haven't guess... they're collecting Petoskey stones. Although many Michigan beaches yield the official state stone, Fisherman's Island State Park is one of the best areas to hunt for them.

Even is you can resist pocketing a few Petoskey stones, the five miles of undeveloped beach is fascinating. Low rolling dunes second growth maples, birch and black spruce offset the azure water of Lake Michigan. There are also 90 rustic campsites, a picnic area and five miles of trails.

A reminder; once collected, display your stones in a glass jar filled with water and compare them with Petoskey stones from the east side. There's a big difference. Can you tell what it is? The answer will be in the second edition of "What's Cheap and Free."

Particulars: Fisherman's island State Park is five miles south of Charlevoix. From US-31, turn west on Bell Bay Road where the park is posted and follow signs. You need either a daily vehicle permit to enter the park or a state park pass.

SALMON WEIR
Charlevoix Chamber of Commerce
(231) 547-2101

FREE

In the autumn when Lake Michigan salmon begin their spawning run, they unfortunately (for them) find themselves caught in a weir where they are harvested by the tons. Visitors can watch as the fish make heroic aerial leaps trying to swim up stream.

Particulars: The weir is located at the end of Lake Shore Drive. Free.

▼ Horton Bay

HORTON BAY GENERAL STORE
5115 Boyne City Road
(231) 582-7827

FREE

This is the main stop on any Ernest Hemingway pilgrimage to the northwest Michigan. Built in 1876 with a high false front, the general store most prominent feature is its large front porch where the author himself idled away many

Horton Bay General Store

youthful summers. Eventually the store appeared in the lead of his story "Up in Michigan."

Little has changed since then. Horton Bay General Store is a classic where you enter through a flimsy screen door that closes with a BANG! Inside you'll find well worn wooden floors, the morning coffee drinkers at the counter and on the walls an assortment of photos, guns mounted deer and other bits of Hemingway history.

Particulars: From US-31 north of Charlevoix, turn couth on Boyne City Road to reach Horton Bay. The general store is open 8 a.m. to 9 p.m. Monday through Saturday and until 5 p.m. Sunday. Free.

▼ Boyne City

AVALANCHE OVERLOOK
Boyne City Chamber of Commerce
(231) 582-6222

The best high point in the Lower Peninsula is this sledding hill on the edge of Boyne City. How steep is Avalanche Overlook? It was downhill ski run in the 1950s and today it's a climb to 473 steps and 11 rest benches to the top.

Once on the peak, you'll find a viewing platform and more benches from which you can see all of Boyne City and Lake Charlevoix, from one end to the other, as well as the hills that surround it to the north.

Particulars: To reach the park from US-131, take M-75 into town and then head west on Division Street. Just before Division Street turns into Lake Shore Road, turn left on Lake Street and then left on Ann Street. The park is a quarter mile at the end of Ann Street. Free.

▼ Ironton

IRONTON FERRY
The Landing Restaurant
10231 Ferry Road
(231) 547-9036

Thousands of people annually hop aboard the tiny Ironton Ferry, a cable-driven barge that is a 15 mile shortcut around the South Arm of Lake Charlevoix.

Most years the busy ferry operates 25 to 30 weeks, basically from ice break-up to freeze up, and transports 73,000 cars along with 6500 walkers. On a single summer week the ferry has carried up to 4000 vehicles.

Regular ferry service on the South Arm dates back to 1876 when the first barge was pulled back and forth by heavy horses. It was a money maker right from the start as the 1884 rates are still listed on the side of the ferry office.

Double teams (of horses) were 30 cents, beast a dime, sheep a dime up to six and then a nickel a piece and "footman without beast" a nickel. If you wanted to haul your threshing machine across the arm, that was a buck.

The present barge was installed in 1926 and it guided by cables 35 feet down on the lake bottom, making it, say officials, one of two cable-operated automobile ferries in the country. That's only one of the Ironton Ferry's little oddities, the reason it was once featured in "Ripley's Believe It or Not," column. Consider its size (so small it holds only four cars) the length of its trip (a mere 575 feet of water), or the fact that it doesn't have a rudder.

Perhaps most bizarre is the Ironton Ferry doesn't make regularly scheduled crossings. The South Arm is so narrow they can see you waiting on the other side so it's operated on demand. "We come when you come," the operators will say.

To those who live and work in the county, the small ferry is critical cog in their efforts to get to work. But to increasing numbers of tourists, it's a summer tradition; taking the ferry to Boyne City. Try dinner at the Landing while you watch the ferry go back and forth, back and forth, back and forth...

Particulars: Landing Restaurant and the ferry are just off M-66, seven miles south of US-31. There are ferry charges for cars and for walkers.

CHEBOYGAN COUNTY

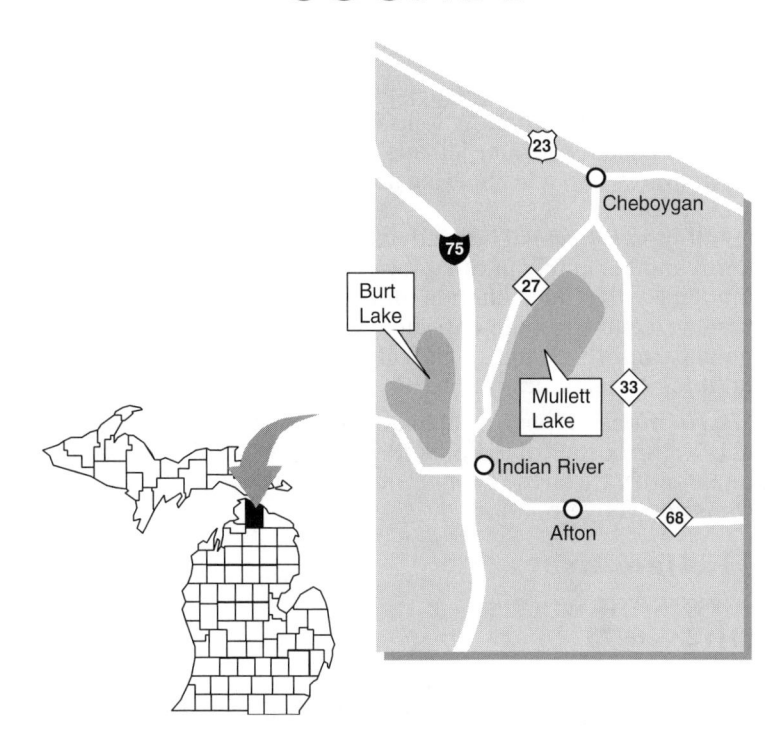

VISITOR INFORMATION

Cheboygan Area Chamber of Commerce
124 N. Main Street
P. O. Box 69
Cheboygan, MI 49721
231-627-7183 or 800-968-3302
www.cheboygan.com

Cheboygan County

▼ Cheboygan

CHEBOYGAN HISTORICAL MUSEUM
404 S. Huron Street
(231) 627-9597

When you visit Cheboygan, go to jail and do not collect $200. Actually, the friendly folks in Cheboygan, a town of 5,000, has taken a former jail and carefully converted the cells and hallways into a fascinating museum that chronicles the local history.

Built in 1870, the jail housed not only criminals but also the sheriff and his family in the attached house. The house, complete with a huge kitchen for preparing inmate meals, is preserved and the main entrance where over 1000 visitors annually tour the facility that features exhibits in each cell and thick metal doors that remind you where you are.

Particulars: From US-23, head south on Huron Street. The jail is at the corner of Huron and Court Street and open 1-3 p.m. Monday through Friday from June through Labor Day. Admission is by donation.

▼ Indian River

CROSS IN THE WOODS
(231) 238-8973

FREE

Towering skyward, straining for the heavens in the crisp northern Michigan air, the world's largest Crucifix is carved from a 55-foot California redwood. The bronze sculpture of Jesus casts a long shadow over beautifully landscaped grounds, which includes an outdoor church, shrines and a famous religious doll museum.

Particulars: From I-75 depart at exit 310 to Indian River. The cross is on M-68 south of town. Open from April through November. Free.

▼ Mackinaw City

MACKINAC BRIDGE
(231) 643-7600

Mackinac Bridge a tourist attraction??? Are you kidding! It's

Museum of Cheboygan County

one of the cheapest (the more people you pack in the car the cheaper it gets) and one of the most scenic. Building a bridge across the straits was first proposed in 1884, but Mighty Mac (the bridge not the hamburger) didn't become a reality until 1957. Today it's the world's longest total suspension bridge at 8,344 feet from cable anchorage to cable anchorage.

The total length of bridge is five miles and the height of the main towers is 552 feet above the water (fact: the authors briefly considered parachuting off the bridge in a bold attempt to promote this book-fortunately we are only cheap, not stupid). The best part is the view. On a clear day you can see two Great Lakes, the shoreline of the Upper and Lower Peninsula, two forts and a dozen islands, including Mackinac, Drummond and Bois Blanc.

There's even a special radio station that will pass along other interesting tidbits about bridge while you drive across it.

Particulars: The Mackinac Bridge is part of I-75 and is open 24 hours a day, 365 days a year. There are fare fees to cross.

TYSENS INDIAN MUSEUM
(231) 436-7011

The walk-through museum on the second floor on Tysen's restaurant features 35 glass-enclosed exhibits on the Indian history of the area. Just what you need after your morning coffee.

Particulars: Like the rest of this town, the restaurant is open seasonally. It's located at 416 N. Huron across from Arnold Mackinac Island Ferry docks, and there is an admission fee. The restaurant serves meals throughout the day.

MACKINAC BRIDGE MUSEUM
Mama Mia's Pizzeria
(231) 436-5534

Lots of information about the bridge, statistics and all of that, but more interesting are the many personalized hardhats, photos and insights into the iron workers trials and frustrations as the span was erected.

Particulars: The seasonal pizza restaurant is the heart of Mackinaw City's business district at 231 Central Ave. and open 8 a.m. to midnight daily. Free.

MCDONALD'S RESTAURANT
(231) 436-7371

Come to Mackinaw City in January or February and see the only McDonald's Restaurant that is closed in the winter. Almost 13,000 restaurants in 63 countries worldwide and this is the only one that turns off its Golden Arches. Come during the summer and a box of Chicken McNuggets is like no other.

Particulars: Located in the main business strip at 401 E. Central.

CHIPPEWA COUNTY

VISITOR INFORMATION

Sault Ste. Marie Convention & Visitors Bureau
536 Ashman Street
Sault Ste. Marie, MI 49783
906-632-3366 or 800-MI-SAULT

www.saultstemarie.com

MDOT Welcome Center
1001 Eureka Street
Sault Ste. Marie, MI 49783
906-632-8242

www.saultstemarie.com

Chippewa County

▼ Rudyard

JILBERT RUDYARD CHEESE PLANT
(906) 473-4731

FREE

Using 100 percent U.P. milk, the small plant produces cheeses, ice
Cream, and other dairy products and occasionally offers tours.

Particulars: From I-75 depart at exit 373 and head west on M-48 two miles to Rudyard. The cheese plant is on Mackinac Trail in town and is open 10 a.m. to 5 p.m. Monday through Saturday. Free.

▼ Sault Ste. Marie

SOO LOCKS
Sault Area Chamber of Commerce
(800) 647-2858

FREE

This National Historic Site, and adjacent park and viewing area is a pretty significant man-made project. Years in the making, and incredibly engineered, much like my bathroom remodeling job, the locks control water levels allowing huge ships to pass to the lower lakes. More than 12,000 vessels pass through the locks annually, some carrying up to 70,000 tons of stuff, that's more than a fully packed family of four on Labor Day weekend.

The St. Mary's River, the only waterway between Lake Superior and the rest of the Great Lakes, has drop of 21 feet, the reason for the locks. Originally the Ojibway Indians portaged their canoes around the rapids as did the furtraders and other early settlers. By 1797 the Northwest Fur Company constructed the first lock and remained in use until it was destroyed in the War of 1812. It was back to portaging furs and transporting ships around the rapids on logs until the next lock was built in 1855.

Today there are four locks on the American side with the largest, the Poe, 1,200-feet long. All of them are operated by the Corps of Engineers, those zany engineers that built dams all over the place. They also maintain a nifty visitors center that includes a working model of the locks, a small theater with a film on their history as well as charts, maps and historical artifacts on display.

Outside there is a viewing platform that provides a birds-eye view of ships being raised and lowered in the locks. During the busy shipping season, you rarely have to wait long before a freighter comes along.

Particulars: From I-75, depart at exit 392 and follow Ashmun Street across the Power Canal into downtown Sault Ste. Marie. Park anywhere along Water Street. The interpretive center is open daily from April to Mid-November. Free.

**LOCKS PARK WALKWAY
Sault Area Chamber of Commerce
(800) 647-2858**

FREE

Stretching from Soo Lock Park to the freighter, S.S. Valley Camp (now a maritime museum) is Locks Park Walkway, which provides an excellent view of Sault Ste. Marie's 350-year history as well as a little exercise. The walkway is marked by blue symbols of freighters while interpretive plaques explain the history of various areas and renovated buildings along the way.

You'll pass the 1864 home of missionary bishop Frederic Baraga, the Snowshoe Priest, and then the John Johnston House, which was constructed in 1794 for the Irish fur trader, making the oldest surviving home in Michigan.

The site of Fort Brady is also marked and it was here in 1820 that the Americans lowered and removed the last British flag to fly over U.S. soil.

Particulars: The walkway begins in Soo Locks Parks and parallels Water Street for several blocks. Open year-round. Free.

▼ Brimley

**POINT IROQUOIS LIGHT STATION
Hiawatha National Forest
(906) 635-5311**

FREE

Activated in 1858, Point Iroquois Light Station has guided freighters through the narrow and foggy waterways at the east end of Lake Superior for more than a century. Even with the aid of the light, ships occasionally foundered in the passage as going from the open water of Lake Superior to the St. Mary's River was difficult. In 1919, the steamer Myron went down and 16 crewmen lost their lives during the fierce November storm . As the bodies washed ashore, lightkeeper

Elmer Byrnes would take them to an undertaker in Brimely who paid him $10 for every "floater" he brought in.

In 1962, the light was replaced by an automatic signal beacon inside the channel across Whitefish Bay and in 1975 the scenic lighthouse and lightkeeper's quarters were added to the National Register of Historical Places. The handful of small rooms on the first floor reveal the always interesting tales of the lightkeepers and their efforts to save the ships. Then from the museum climb the 72 steps to the top of the tower for a picturesque view of Lake Superior. Often during the summer you can watch freighters pass by.

Particulars: The lighthouse is 20 miles west of Sault Ste. Marie. From I-75, depart at exit 386 and head west on M-28 for eight miles and north on M-221 three miles into Brimley to pick up Lakeshore Drive. Follow Lakeshore Drive to the museum. Hours are 10 a.m. to 5 p.m. and 7-9 p.m. daily from Memorial Day through Labor Day. Free.

▼ Paradise

WHITEFISH POINT BIRD OBSERVATORY
SE shore of Lake Superior, Paradise

FREE

To date, 287 species of birds have been sighted at Whitefish Point, a peninsula only a short distance from Canada, that is one of the finest places to witness the spring migration of songbirds and hawks. Common loons, cormorants, owls, and many other species are also seen. During the summer there is a small visitor's room where bird lists are maintained as to what has been seen in the area.

Raptor (hawk) banding has been conducted for two decades at Whitefish Point, which receives some funding from the Michigan Audubon Society. Scientists use the station to obtain information on migratory patterns, length of life, recapture data, plumage and much more.

Particulars: The observatory is at the end of Whitefish Point Road across from the impressive Great Lake Shipwreck Museum (sorry, too expensive to be in this cheapskates guidebook) which heads north from M-123 from the town of Paradise. Free.

TAHQUAMENON FALLS
(906) 492- 3415

Tahquamenon Falls State Park is best known for the Upper Falls, the second or third largest east of the Mississippi River

Tahquamenon Falls, Chippewa County

depending on whether your measuring water volume of length of drop. This Upper Peninsula jewel measures 200 feet across, descends 50 feet into a sea of mist and foam and has a thunder that can be heard from the minute you step out of the car. The spectacular sight is only a quarter-mile walk from the parking lot and if you're up for some long stairways, you can descend into the surrounding gorge to a pair of observation platforms that put you right above the brink of the falls, so close you can feel the mist.

As far as children are concerned, however, the Upper Falls are impressive but the Lower Falls are much more fun. While not nearly as stunning, this series of cascades are still beautiful and are best viewed by combining a short boat trip across the river with a short walk around an island, an outing ideal for any short-legged hiker.

You can rent rowboats from a park concessionaire. The trip across is easy while step-for-step this is one of the most beautiful foot paths in the state, only there's not a lot of steps. It's a loop of less than a mile that skirts the outside of the island, passing one display of tumbling water after another. Within minutes you'll come to the first cascade and learn the reason for the popularity of the Lower Falls. Everybody, we mean everybody; kids, moms and dads, kick their shoes off, wade out on the ledges and let the river cascade across their legs.

Particulars: Tahquamenon Falls State Park is on M-123 between Paradise and Newberry. The Lower Falls is 12 miles west of Paradise and 23 miles northeast of Newberry. A daily vehicle permit or an annual pass are needed to enter the park.

The rowboats are rented from May to mid-October.

Just north of Clare on US-27/10 is the largest "inland" visitor center in the state. Unlike other centers that are located near our borders, this visitor center, which is tucked among rolling hills, has piles of brochures, lots of economy vacation ideas, and skilled staff.

Particulars: the welcome center is just north of where US-10 merges into US-27 and can be reached by traffic heading both north and south. The center is open 8 a.m. to 5 p.m. daily. Free.

CLARE COUNTY

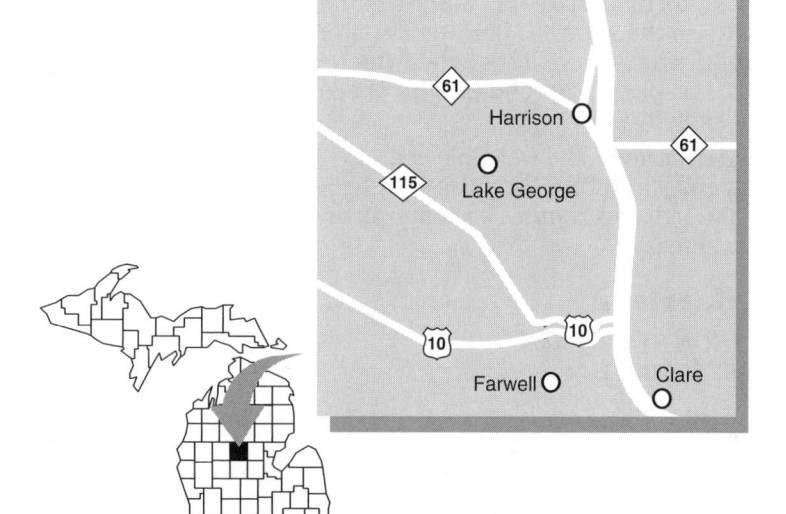

VISITOR INFORMATION

Clare Area Chamber of Commerce
429 N. McEwan Street
Clare, MI 48617
888-AT-CLARE

MDOT Welcome Center
9599 U.S. 27
Clare, MI 48617
989-386-7634

www.claremichigan.com
e-mail: chamber@claremichigan.com

Clare County

▼ Clare

CLARE WELCOME CENTER
(989) 386-7634

Just north of Clare on US-27/10 is the largest "inland" visitor center in the state. Unlike other centers that are located near our borders, this visitor center, which is tucked among rolling hills, has piles of brochures, lots of economy vacation ideas, and skilled staff.

Particulars: The welcome center is just north of where US-10 merges into US-27 and can be reached by traffic heading both north and south. The center is open 8 a.m. to 5 p.m. daily. Free

▼ Harrison

WILSON STATE PARK
(989) 539-3021

Wilson State Park is one of the smallest tracts in the system at 38 acres. It was originally a sawmill for the Wilson Brothers Lumber Company before it was deeded to the City of Harrison in 1990. The land was transferred to the state 22 years later, and in 1927 the park was dedicated.

Sorry, there are no trails, boat launches or significant natural area but there is a Rent-A-Tipi. That's right, an authentic tribal replica. The 20-foot tall, tipi-like tent sets on a wooden platform, offering lots of space and a wonderful experience for youngsters. Bring your six-shooter, partner

Kids will love the adventure. The DNR is using the tipi as a marketing tool to get families away from the TV and into the woods. The tent, which has 15 poles lashed together, has a flap door and a small totem pole nearby.

Economy-minded families should reserve the tipi well in advance.

Particulars: Wilson State Park is a mile north of Harrison on Business US-27. You need either a daily vehicle permit for entry or a state park pass.

Rent-A-Tipi during your stay. Contact park office for fees at 989-539-3021.

Wilson State Park's Rent-a-Tipi.

CLINTON COUNTY

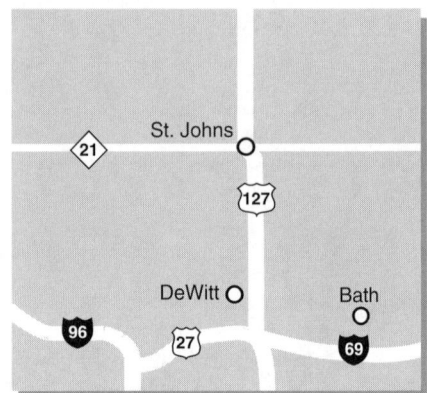

VISITOR INFORMATION

St. Johns Area Chamber of Commerce
P. O. Box 61
St. Johns, MI 48879
989-224-7248

Clinton County

▼ Bath

FREE

**ROSE LAKE RESEARCH STATION
(989) 641-4638**

Like the Houghton Lake and Shingleton research stations, Rose Lake is made possible by revenues from hunting and fishing licenses to provide a scientific place for wildlife research and management study. The 3574-acre station is only 12 miles northeast of Lansing and located in rolling farmlands, abandoned fields, oak and lowland woods and marshes divided into color designated areas for research purposes.

Canada geese at Rose Lake

The natural area offers hunting, wildlife observation, and hiking. Also, behind the research building is a small enclosure where wildlife are occasionally housed.

Particulars: Located on the Clinton-Shiawassee county line, the research facility is 12 miles northwest of Lansing. From I-69, turn north on Upton Road and then east on Stroll Road. The office is open 8 a.m. to noon and 1-5 p.m. Monday through Friday. The trails are open dawn to dusk daily. Free.

▼ St. Johns
PAINE-GILLAM-SCOTT MUSEUM
(989) 224-2894 or 224-7402

This imposing home was built in 1860 by John Paine and is the oldest brick residence in St. Johns. At the time, St. Johns was only a six-year-old village on the edge of the frontier and two years before Paine's built his new home a "wild bear" had been shot across the street.

Eventually a series of doctors and a dentist occupied the home and based their practice here until the Clinton Country Historical Society obtained it in 1978 and restored it to its 1890 period.

Upstairs the rooms have displays on local history as well as exhibits covering the turn-of-the century medical methods of the doctors who lived and worked in the home.

Particulars: The museum is on St. John's Courthouse Square at 106 Maple St. Hours are 1-5 p.m. Sunday and 2-8 p.m. Wednesday. Admission is by donations.

CRAWFORD COUNTY

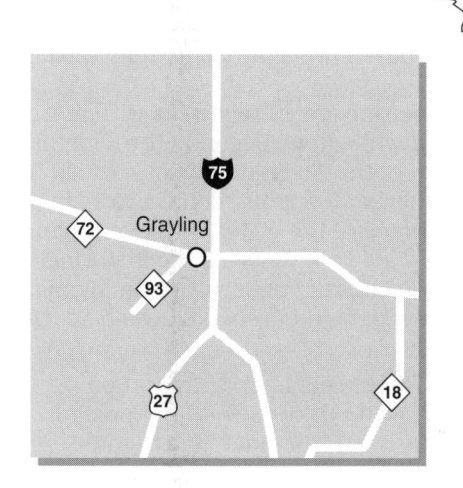

VISITOR INFORMATION

Grayling Area Visitors Council, Inc.
213 James Street
Grayling, MI 49738
989-348-2921 or 800-937-8837
www.grayling-mi.com

Crawford County

GRAYLING FISH HATCHING
Grayling Chamber of Commerce
(989) 348-2921

FREE

The facility, built in the 1920s, was one of the first state-run hatcheries in Michigan. Trout were hatched and raised here until the 1950s and then the raceways were used for research. After the DNR closed down the then out-dated ponds in 1972, the hatchery sat vacant for 10 years until a local sportsmen's club reopened it to the trout-curious public passing through the land of AuSable.

Located in a park-like setting are 12 raceways with more than half of them stocked while flowing gently through the middle is the East Branch of the Au Sable River. You can buy bags of fish pellets and then watch trout, some 1 to 14 inches long, exploded on the surface of the water with every handful you toss in. The hatchery also contains a state historical marker describing the grayling that once swarm in Michigan rivers and a display showing the difference between species of trout.

Particulars: From I-75 Business Loop turn east on Michigan Avenue and follow it out of town to the posted entrance. The hatchery is open from mid-May to mid-September from 8 a.m. to 6 p.m. daily. Admission is free, bags of fish feed are available for a small fee.

GRAYLING HISTORICAL VILLAGE
(989) 348-4461

A restored railroad depot, that was built is 1882, is the home of the county museum and the cornerstone of the Grayling Historical Village. To the north of the depot, alongside the D&M tracks, the rest of the village contains exhibits that offer visitors a nostalgic trip to the turn of the Century when Grayling was a leading lumbering center.

The village also contains the former Grayling Township Hall, that now houses military displays including uniforms and weapons, and the machine gun that was used by Maj. Edward Hartwick during World War I. Also on the property is a full-size caboose, an authentic trapper's log cabin and a turn-of-the-century fire barn that houses two equally old fire engines.

Particulars: From the I-75 Business Loop, turn west on Michigan just after crossing the Au Sable River and then north on Norway. The village is at 401 Norway. Open Wednesday through Sunday during the summer. Admission is by donation.

▼ The Monarch
HARTWICK PINES STATE PARK
(989) 348-7068

Come October, Michigan's Monarch stands in a royal setting just north of Grayling. Outlined by an autumn backdrop of orange, yellow and a bit of red is this dark brown trunk. But it's impossible to overlook the tree even if you can't see its greenery. The trunk is huge, three people couldn't join hands around it, and it makes visitors walking down the paved path in Hartwick Pines State Park stop, strain their neck to glance at the top...

And whisper things like "this sure don't make them like this anymore." They sure don't!

Make no mistake about it, this 155-foot white pine, the most beloved tree in Michigan and the only one that is a legitimate tourist attraction, is worthy of its nobility. More than 200,000 visitors arrive from around the state not so much to see a big pine but to walk through the woods as they once were.

After loggers depleted the eastern forests by the 1830s, they turned their attention to abundant white pine found out the Great Lakes and within 30 years Michigan was producing more lumber than any other state. By the turn of the century the loggers had cut more than 60 million board feet of Michigan pine that held a dollar value greater than all the gold mined during the California Gold Rush.

But one of the few tracts spared the swinging acs of lumberjacks was an 49-acre parcel now known as The Pines. It's the center piece of the largest state park in the Lower Peninsula and it's where the Monarch hold court.

The tree is 45-inches in diameter, contains more than 6,000 board feet of lumber and is estimated to be between 300 and 400 years, making it not only one of the most visited trees in the state but also one of the oldest. Foresters don't know the exact age of the Monarch but they do know one thing.

The tree is so old it's dying. Visitors, who arrive with a set of binoculars, can see that the tree's bark has aleady fallen off a seven-foot section at the top, the first segment of a aging pine to die. Most experts say it will be dead within 10 years.

The Monarch

The white pine is only one of several interesting stops along the mile-long path. Others include Big Wheels that were used to transport logs during the lumbering era, a reconstructed logging camp, the tranquil Chapel in the Pines and a new interpretive center and logging museum.

Particulars: From I-75, north of Grayling, depart at exit 259 and head north on M-93 for three miles to the park entrance. The park is open year round. The interpretive displays in the museum and in the logging camp are open from 8 a.m. to 4 p.m. daily from May through October. A daily vehicle permit or an annual state park pass is needed to enter the park.

KIRTLAND'S WARBLER TOUR
Grayling DNR Office
(989) 348-6371

FREE

With a bobbing tail and distinct yellow breast, the Kirtland's warbler has turned Grayling into something of a pilgrimage for birders around the country. Almost extinct in the late 1970s, today the number of warblers fluctuates around 300. Wintering in the Bahamas, where it is rarely

Kirkland's Warbler Tour, Crawford County

seen, the tiny birds nest each summer in Crawford, Oscoda, and Roscommon counties in jack pine forests and tours out of Grayling and Mio allow birders to spot the warbler and mark it off on their check list.

The tours begin with a movie and discussion on the unique aspect of the warbler, a bird the size of a sparrow with a distinct yellow breast and what one biologist described has a "liquid, bubbling song." The tour is followed by a one to two-mile walk into the Kirtland's Warbler Habitat Management Area, a 135,000-acre preserve of federal and state land for the opportunity to sight the species. Nothing is guaranteed but there's a pretty good chance to see it in late May and early June. The morning tours are the best because once it begins to warm up, the males stop singing around 10 a.m.

Particulars: Mio tours begin at the U.S. Forest Service Ranger Station, 401 Court, and are offered Wednesday through Friday at 7:30 p.m. and Saturday and Sunday at 7:30 a.m. and again at 11 a.m. In Grayling, they begin at the Holiday Inn on the I-75 Business Loop and are offered at 7 a.m. and 11 a.m. daily through the Fourth of July weekend. Free.

DELTA COUNTY

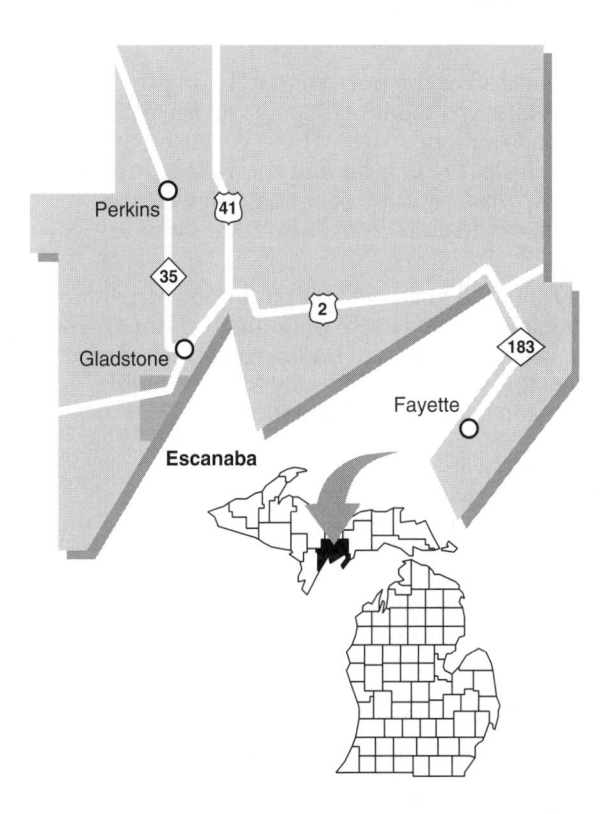

VISITOR INFORMATION

Delta Chamber of Commerce
230 Ludington Street
Escanaba, MI 49829
906-786-2192

www.deltami.org

Delta County

▼ Escanaba

DELTA COUNTY MUSEUM
(906) 786-3428

The museum is located at the north end of Ludington Park and features local history, including displays on the early logging, shipping and rail industries. There is also an old fashion parlor and drugstore exhibit and the 16-foot rudder from the Nahant shipwreck in the Escanaba. On a clear day you can see the rest of the shipwreck from Sand Point Lighthouse next door.

Particulars: From US-2 head east on Ludington Street into downtown Escanaba, past the House of Ludington Hotel. The museum is on the waterfront where Ludington Street curves into Jenkins Drive. It opens at 1 p.m. daily May through September. Admission is by a small donation.

SAND POINT LIGHTHOUSE
(906) 786-3428

Before the Delta County Historical Society put the top back on the light, you really wouldn't know the Sand Point Lighthouse was a lighthouse. Built in 1867, the one-and-a-half story structure was your routine light, featuring an attached brick tower topped off by a cast iron lantern room with a fourth order Fresnel lens. The beacon was in service from 1868 to 1939, except for a short time in 1886 when a fire swept through it, damaging the building and killing Mary Terry, one of the first women light tenders to serve on the Great Lakes.

In 1939 the harbor was dredged, leaving the steady light some distance from the hazards it was supposed to be warning of. So, in a modernization effort, the U.S. Coast Guard constructed a crisp light off shore then turned the lighthouse into a family residence for the officer-in-charge of Escanaba station.

When they converted the light to a house they removed the lantern room and stairway and thus reducing the tower by 10 feet. Eventually aluminum siding was installed and the light no longer looked like a lighthouse. But in 1985, the historical society saved the structure from the wrecking ball and,

Sand Point Lighthouse, Delta County

amazingly, found a duplicate lantern room and lens rusting away on nearby Poverty Island. Using a crane, the cast iron structure was returned to its lofty place.

Today, you'll see a restored kitchen area, period rooms, and artifacts. The best part of the tour is climbing 41 steps up to the top to inspect the huge lens or enjoy a panorama of the city's shoreline.

Particulars: From US-2, head east on Ludington Avenue to the north end of Ludington Park where the lighthouse can't be missed. The lighthouse is open from May through September the same hours at the museum next door. Admission fee.

WILLIAM BONIFAS FINE ARTS CENTER
(906) 786-3833

FREE

The center is home to a variety of visual, performing and cultural arts unique to the Upper Peninsula. The Alice Uren Powers Gallery, just one part of the center, showcases the work of regional artists and stages special exhibits and craftsmen demonstrating their trade, whether it pottery or weaving.

Particulars: From US-2, head east on Ludington Avenue into the heart of Escanaba and then south on 7th Street a block. The center is on the corner of 7th and 1st Avenue. Hours are Monday through Friday 10 a.m. to 5 p.m. and Sunday noon to 4 p.m. Free.

DOBBER'S PASTIES
(906) 786-1880

For most people, simply eating pasties in the Upper Peninsula is enough of a treat. But for those who want more than just to savor the turnover of meat, onions, and chopped potatoes and rutabaga, this pasties shop offers tours of its bakery along with a little history on how Cornish miners bought the meat pies with them from England.

Particulars: The shop is at 827 N. Lincoln, just west of US-2. The shop is open daily and offers the tours in the morning. The tours are free but not the pasties.

▼ Gladstone

HOEGH PET CASKET CO.
(906) 428-2151

FREE

You never see any big dogs along I-75 and I doubt they have found their way to custom pet caskets manufactured by the Hoegh Pet Casket Company in Gladstone, after being splattered by an 18-wheeler at exit 101. Nevertheless, many dogs, cats, even birds are tearfully buried in one of the seven sizes of caskets made at the plant. They even have blue and pink models in smaller sizes for those pastel loving canines. The plant tour is free and includes a peak at model cemetery where a brass plaque on the crematorium informs tour goers, "If Christ had a dog, he would have followed Him to the cross."

Particulars: From US-41, turn east onto Delta Avenue in Gladstone. The plant is at 317 Delta Ave. and can be visited from 8 a.m. to 4 p.m. Monday through Friday, year round. Free.

▼ Stonnington

PENINSULA POINT LIGHTHOUSE
Rapid River Ranger District
(906) 474-6442

FREE

There are two ways to reach Peninsula Point; you can drive to it or hike in. If you're thinking about driving, the U.S. Forest Service warns that the final mile to the 19th century light is a narrow, winding and very bumpy one-lane road not recommended for recreation vehicles more than 16 feet long or eight feet high.

Wouldn't that just make your trip; getting the RV stuck 25 miles from the nearest gas station.

If you decide to hike in, the walk is a pleasant and scenic stroll of only 1.5 miles to Peninsula Point Lighthouse, the guiding light at the very tip of Stonington Peninsula that was built in 1865. Congress authorized the funds the year before because wooden sailing ships, hauling lumber, iron ore and fish from Escanaba and Fayette, were no match for the treacherous shoals and reefs that separated Big Bay de Noc from little Bay de Noc.

The structure consisted of a 40-foot tower, lit by an oil lamp and reflectors, along with an adjoining home for the lightkeeper and his family. The light went out for the last time in 1936 and the house portion of the lighthouse burned to the ground in 1959. But the view from the point was so spectacular that the Forest Service made it into public picnic area in 1937.

Climb the 40 steps to the top of the square brick tower and you're greeted with a 360-degree panorama that includes the Escanaba waterfront to the west, the limestone bluffs of Fayette State Park to the east and the length of Lake Michigan in front of you.

Particulars: To reach the lighthouse from Rapid River head east on US-2 to the Stonington exit. Head south 19 miles on County Road 513 to Stonington and then take Forest Road 2204. The RV parking area and trailhead are reached before the forest road turns into a narrow, one-land road in the final mile. Free.

▼ Garden

GARDEN PENINSULA HISTORICAL MUSEUM
Delta County Chamber of Commerce
(906) 786-2192

FREE

The former one-room schoolhouse is packed with local history on logging and fishing as well as the old classroom itself.

Particulars: From US-2, head south on CR-483 for 16 miles into Garden where the museum is in the heart of town. Who knows when it's open.

I've been there twice and still had to look at the displays through the school windows like a peeping Tom.

FAYETTE STATE PARK
(906) 644-2603

In the middle part of the 1800s huge loads of iron ore was shipped from the Upper Peninsula mines to the foundries in the lower Great Lakes at a tremendous cost to the companies. Fayette Brown, innovative manager of the Jackson Iron Company, studied the problem and decided to construct a company-owned furnace near the mine, so the ore could be smelted into pig iron before it was shipped.

In 1866 Brown chose a spot on the Garden Peninsula overlooking Big Bay de Noc because of the natural harbor, limestone deposits, and hardwood forests needed to smelt the iron. The company town was built and called, Fayette.

Twenty-five years later the town died, the furnaces cooled, and the ghosts took over the 20-odd buildings that stand within the park. In 1959 the state designated the 750-acre tract a state park and historic site.

With towering limestone cliffs near, the town that overlooks Snail Shell Harbor, booms again each summer as tourists flock to the peninsular park. The interpretive area contains a modest museum and 20 buildings, nine of which are completely renovated and fully furnished with artifacts from the iron ore days of the late 1800s.

The difficult life of Fayette residents are told during a tour, which includes a visit to the Visitor Center and around the various buildings that include an Opera House, Machine Shop, Company Office.

Particulars: From US-2 head south on CR-483 for 16 miles

Kiln at Fayette State Park

to the posted entrance, 8 miles beyond the town of Garden. Although you can visit the town anytime, the museum and buildings are open from mid-May to October from 9 a.m. to 6 p.m. daily. A daily vehicle entry fee or an annual state park pass is required to enter.

▼ Fairport

One of the few remaining commercial fishing villages in the state. At the tip of the Garden Peninsula, there are many private beaches and turn-offs in the area.

A favorite is the small Sac Bay Point where you can have a shoreside lunch and a brisk walk. By the way, bring your own lunch, there are no restaurants this far south on the peninsula.

Particulars: From Garden continue south on CR-483, past Fayette State Park to its end at Fairport.

DICKINSON COUNTY

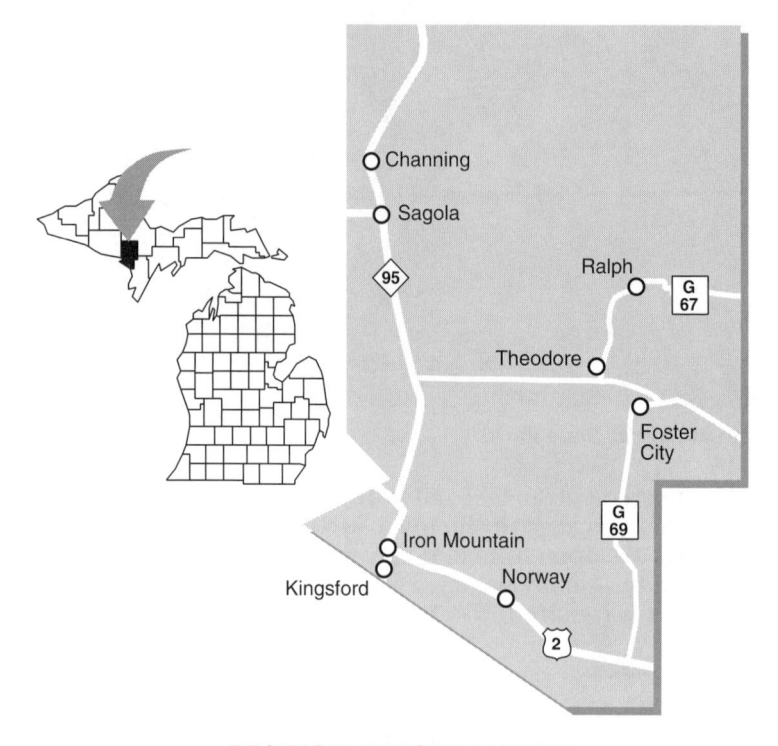

VISITOR INFORMATION
Tourism Association of Dickenson County
Iron Mountain, MI 49801
800-236-2447
www.ironmountain.org
MDOT Welcome Center
618 Stephenson Avenue
Iron Mountain, MI 49801
906-774-4201
email: tadca@up.net

Dickinson County

▼ Iron Mountain

CORNISH PUMPING ENGINE AND MINING MUSEUM
(906) 774-1086

America's biggest steam-driven pumping engine once belched steam as it pumped 4.5 million gallons of water a day from the tunnels of the Cornwall iron mines. The copper and brass pump has a huge weighed wheel and a 725-ton steeple that rises 54 feet from the engine floor. A variety of other mining equipment is also on display including mining cars, lugger, cages, and skips.

Particulars: From US-2 on the north of Iron Mountain, turn west on Kent Street and follow the signs. The museum is open daily May through mid-October from 9 a.m. to 5 p.m. Monday through Saturday and noon to 4 p.m. Sunday. Admission fee.

MENOMINEE RANGE HISTORICAL MUSEUM
Iron Mountain, MI
(906) 774-4276

Over 101 dramatic, turn-of-the-century exhibits and dioramas depict 18th century lifestyles on the Menominee Range. Thousands of artifacts are meticulously displayed in an authentic setting, the life-size exhibits offer interesting insights into a wide variety of occupations, pioneer lifestyles, a barn interior, blacksmiths shop, mine interior, one- room school, and more. All exhibits are fitted with appropriate tools, supplies, and objects of the era they interpret. The museum is located in the former Carnegie Library, built in 1901, and designated as a historic site.

Particulars: The museum is one block east of US-2 at 300 East Ludington. It's open daily May through mid-October 9 a.m. to 5 p.m. Monday through Saturday and noon to 4 p.m. Sunday. Admission fee.

PINE MOUNTAIN SKI JUMP
Pine Mountain Lodge
(906) 774-2747

FREE

Scraping the sky, nearly 12 stories high, the slightly rusty scaffold supports a steep 395 foot runway where adrenalin-crazed skiers fly off the end. From the top of the scaffold to the end of the landing field is a run of more than 1,000 feet for the skiers. The current jumping record holder is Werner Schuster when in 1991 he flew his entire body 400 feet. I am happy to report he is still alive, just slightly shorter.

The 90-meter ramp is a spectacular sight any time of the year but the best time to come is the weekend of the Pine Mountain Ski Jumping Championships. It's the biggest winter tailgate party anywhere in Michigan. Locals pack their coolers and bring their lawn chairs (who cares if it's 10 below zero) and then ring the landing field, oooing and ahhhing every time one of those jumpers come down the ramp at 60 mph. The championship is generally in mid-February.

Particulars: For the closest view of the jump depart west from US-2 on Kent Road and then continue onto Fairbanks Street past the Cornish Pump Museum and then Walker Street, where signs will direct you to the Pine Mountain Ski Resort and the ramp. Free.

BOCCE BALL COURTS
Iron Mountain Chamber of Commerce
(906) 774-2002

FREE

Many of the miners recruited at the turn-of-the-century were from Italy and today the weekend rage in Iron Mountain is playing bocce at the City Park. It's Italian lawn bowling played with eight balls that are thrown at a small one called a Pallino. You'll find a series of public courts are at this scenic park and, if it isn't league night, you can generally drop by and learn the game and lose your shirt all in a few hours.

The kids will love this park as there are swings and a war plane to play on as well as a deer yard in the middle with some impressive eight and 12-point bucks.

▼ Norway

PIERS GORGE SCENIC AREA
Kosir's Rapid Rafts
(715) 757-3431

FREE

Michigan's wildest white water is a stretch of the Menominee River that flows through Piers Gorge, the frothing waters attract kayakers from around the Midwest. At this stretch of the turbulent river the waters sliced through bedrock to form an area of holes, hydraulics, swirls, and a 10-foot drop known to kayakers as "Misicot."

A hiking path that follows along part of the shoreline offers an exciting view of rafters crashing through the waters and frantically steering around jagged rocks, holes and obstacles.

Economy-minded travelers will enjoy the 1.5-mile hike that stays in sight of the white water. Come on Saturdays from May through September and you can watch rafters flipping their boats in the wild currents. But if a mere hike along the turfed waters isn't enough adventure for you, contact Kosir's Rapid Rafts (715-757-3431) for a rafting trip.

Particulars: From US-2 in Norway, head south on US-8. Just before crossing the bridge to the Wisconsin side of the Menominee River, a sign for the scenic area pops up and directs you west. Stay to the left and in half a mile you will arrive at a dirt parking area where a wide path continues into the woods. Free.

EATON COUNTY

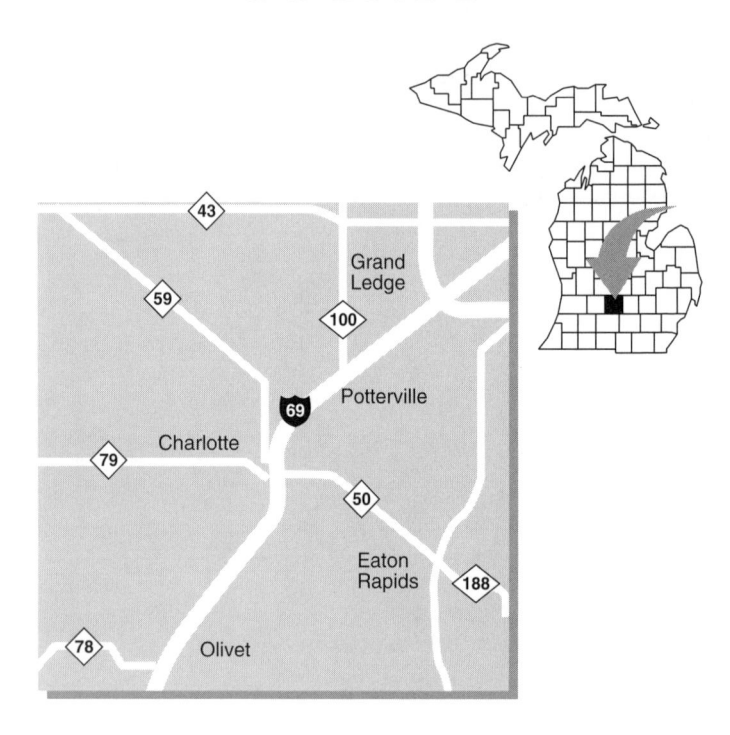

VISITOR INFORMATION

Charlotte Chamber of Commerce
100 W. Lawrence
P. O. Box 356
Charlotte, MI 48813
517-543-0400
www.charlottechamber-mi.com
email: chamber@ia4u.net

Eaton County

▼ Bellevue

BELLEVUE HISTORICAL MUSEUM
Bellevue Library
(517) 763-3369

The small museum interprets the community's journey through time, its industry, the people, and the important moments that impacted the community.

Particulars: From I-69, depart at exit 48 and head west three miles on M-78 into the hamlet of Bellevue. The museum is attached to the Bellevue Library which is at 212 N. Main St. The library is open weekdays, 1-6 p.m. Admission is by donation.

EDWARD KEEHNE ENVIRONMENTAL AREA
(517) 763-9571

FREE

Seventeen acres with fishing, picnic area, and nature study area all near the quiet hamlet of Bellevue.

Particulars: From M-78, turn south on Williams Street to reach the entrance of the park. Open from sunrise to sunset daily. Free.

DYER LIMESTONE KILN

FREE

Built in the 1870s, the limestone kiln stands as a reminder of the limestone industries impact and important role in Bellevue's development.

Particulars: From M-78 on the west side of town turn north on Old Belleuve Road, a gravel road located across from the Bellevue Middle School. The kiln is 100 yards up the road and posted with a state historical sign. Free.

▼ Charlotte

EATON COUNTY COURTHOUSE
Eaton County Historical Commission
(517) 543-6999

Listed in the National Register of Historic Places, the 1885 building has undergone considerable restoration since its last official use in 1976.

Particulars: From I-69, depart at exit 60 and follow M-50 west through downtown Charlotte. The courthouse is open weekdays and can be viewed for a small donation. Call Eaton County Historical Commission about guided tours.

▼ Grand Ledge

Grand Ledge Historical Museum
(517) 627-5170

Volunteers man the Gothic-area home which houses rotating history displays, research materials, and special programming. Small donation requested.

Particulars: From I-96, depart at exit 93 and head west on M-43 and then north on M-100 into Grand Ledge. The museum is at 118 E. Lincoln St. and is open from 2-4 p.m. on Sunday. Admission is by donation.

THE LEDGES
Fitzgerald County Park
(517) 627-7351

Grand Ledge, one of the few places to do any serious climbing in Michigan, makes a fun side-trip for budget-minded travelers. "The Ledges," towering faces of sheer rock that border the Grand River are ancient sedimentary outcroppings

Climbers at Grand Ledge, Eaton County

that were formed 270 million years ago when most of Michigan was covered by water. Serious rockclimbers can ascend the bold face on the north side of the river while hikers can head for the south side where the Ledges Trail, a 1.1 mile one-way trail, begins at the base of the cliffs, linking Fitzgerald County Park with Island Park.

Except for the initial decent to the river, the trail is an easy stroll that provides a close view of this unique geological formation and a good vantage point from which to watch daring climbing across the river. The county park also has picnic areas, other nature trails, a fish ladder and a small nature center as well as the Spotlight Theaters (517-483-1623), from which the Ledges Trail begins.

Particulars: Fitzgerald County Park is 1.5 miles west of town at 3808 Grand Ledge Highway. The park is open year round from 8 a.m. to dusk but the nature center is open only May through October from 1-5 p.m. on Wednesday, Saturday and Sunday. There is a vehicle entry fee that is collected from mid-April through October.

▼ Vermontville

Academy-Chapel Museum

Constructed in 1843, the museum displays many artifacts from Vermontville history. Hours vary.

Particulars: From I-69, exit at Potterville and head west on Vermontville Road to reach the town in 14 miles. The museum is at 109 N. Main St.

FIRST CONGREGATIONAL CHURCH
(517) 726-0258

FREE

Listed on the National Registry of Historic Building, this picturesque rectangular white-frame building has a lofty steeple reaching 120 feet toward Heavens. The interesting feature of this church is the historic and beautiful cathedral windows. Unlike plain old stained glass windows, these windows, which were installed in 1900, have color ground into them.

Particulars: From I-69, exit at Potterville and head west on Vermontville Road to reach the town in 14 miles. Church is at 110 S. Main Street. Free.

THE OPERA HOUSE
(517) 627-2383

The humble residents of Vermontville aren't exactly sure

when construction of the Opera House began, it was either 1883 or 1886. Nonetheless, the small, two-story red brick structure with cut stone foundation, is popular when featuring a production.

Particulars: From I-69, exit at Potterville and head west on Vermontville Road to reach the town in 14 miles.

The opera house is at 219 S. Main Street. Plays are scheduled at various times in the historic building, admission is reasonable.

EMMET COUNTY

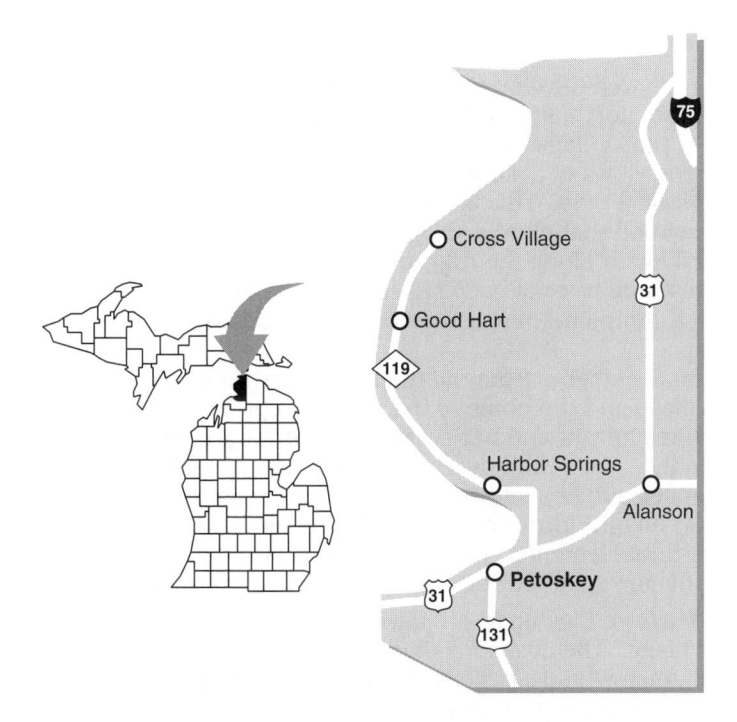

VISITOR INFORMATION

Petoskey - Harbor Springs - Boyne Country Visitors Bureau
401 E. Mitchell Street
Petoskey, MI 49770
231-348-2755 or 800-845-2828
www.boynecountry.com
email: info@boynecountry.com

Emmet County

▼ Cross Village

TUNNEL OF TREES
Legs Inn
(231) 526-2281

FREE

From the well-developed resort town of Harbor Springs, M-119 departs north and hugs the coastline for 31 miles until it ends at Cross Village. It is often cited as a scenic drive, but not for the views of Lake Michigan you might expect when tracing it on a map. This is the "Tunnel of Trees" Shore Drive, a narrow road that climbs, drops, and curves its way through the thick forest along the rugged coast. At times the branches from trees at each side of the road merge overhead to form a complete tunnel, shading travelers from the noon day sun.

You finally emerge from the thick forest Cross Village, a small village and the home of the famous Legs Inn. The Inn is a polish restaurant and bar created by Detroit-area refugee, Stan Smolak. On a bluff overlooking the lake, Smolak scoured the beaches and fields for stones and drift wood pieces that were turned into furniture, tables, fireplaces, and other architectural elements. The bizarre Inn is fascinating with its clutter of curved driftwood and aroma of hearty Polish foods.

Particulars: Pick up M-119 in Harbor Springs and take it to Cross Village. The Legs Inn is located in the heart of Cross Village (some would say Legs Inn is Cross Village) and is open May through October from 11 a.m. to until midnight, even later on Friday and Saturday an until 10 p.m. on Sunday.

The drive through the Tunnel of Trees is free. Get dinner at Legs Inn very reasonably priced.

ANDREW BLACKBIRD MUSEUM
(231) 526-7731

The local Odawa tribe operates the small museum, which has the distinction of being the state's only Indian-run museum. Inside the cultural center you can browse through quill and bead work as well as old tribal clothing, art of band members and historical exhibits.

Particulars: The museum is at 368 E. Main St. It's open

daily from Memorial Day through Labor Day and on weekends through October. Admission fee.

SHAY HOUSE
Harbor Springs Chamber of Commerce   *FREE*
(231) 347-0200

Near Ford Park, a really unusual house with protruding hexagonal eels demonstrates how inventor Ephraim Shay used creativity in all areas of his life. Although not open to the general public, visitors can step into the lobby for a quick peak.

Particulars: Located next to Blackbird Museum. Free.

▼ Petoskey

BAYFRONT PARK
Boyne Country Visitors Bureau
(800) 845-2828

The view is worth a million bucks, even if you and your humble authors aren't. Nonetheless, anyone can enjoy the view, blue waters of little Traverse Bay, sandy beach, and a walk near the mouth of the Bear River. In the summer, outdoor concerts and other special events are staged here.

Particulars: Located off of US-31 near the Little Traverse Historical Museum. Free.

▼ Bay View

BAY VIEW ASSOCIATION   *FREE*
(231) 347-6225

What began as a religious encampment, has evolved into more than 400 Victorian cottages with elaborate designs and architectural detail. The entire village is on the National Register of Historical Places while during the summer concerts and lectures are open to the public.

Particulars: Located off of US-31 just north of Petoskey. There is a charge for special events and programs.

GASLIGHT SHOPPING DISTRICT
Petoskey Chamber of Commerce   *FREE*
(231) 347-4150

Well bargain hunters, this area represents one of the first resort-area shopping spots in the Midwest. It ain't cheap but it's great fun to stroll the district and dream. The six block area has nearly 80 fancy shops, galleries, crafts, and restaurants. For those who want a horse-drawn carriage tour of the shopping area, Gaslight Carriage Tours (616- 347-7301) can offer one from mid-June through Labor Day. For a fee of course.

Particulars: From US-31, signs will direct you to the Gaslight District\Downtown area of Petoskey. No charge here for window shopping or people watching.

HEMINGWAY TOUR
Little Traverse Historical Museum
(231) 347-2620

Many famous writers, including the incredibly talented Bailey & DuFrense of Glovebox Guidebook fame, have literary ties to northwest Michigan, but none are as well-known as Ernest Hemingway. Many Hemingway fans, after reading his dazzling prose, want more, so they head to northern Michigan where they can tour and retrace many places where the master lived, fished, worked, and hung-out.

Hemingway spent all of his first 18 summers in the area, later meeting his wife and married her in Horton Bay. Some years later, after being wounded in WWI, he spent a winter in Petoskey writing The Torrent of Spring.

Thus many begin their tour at the Little Traverse Historical Museum where Hemingway memorabilia and some rare first edition books are displayed. The handsome museum, located near the marina in the old Chicago and West Michigan railroad depot, also exhibits historical remnants of the lumbering era, fascinating quill boxes, and other artifacts important to the community as well as a small display devoted to another northwest Michigan author, Bruce Catton, a 1953 Pulitzer Prize winner. From here the Hemingway tours continues on to the Horton Bay General Store and in this guidebook continues in the Charlevoix County section.

Particulars: The museum is on Dock Street on Petoskey's picturesque water front. It is open April through October from 9 a.m. until 4:30 p.m. Monday through Saturday. Admission fee.

PETOSKEY STATE PARK
(231) 347-2311

Oh, those sunsets. The blazing fireball in the sky takes a gorgeous nightly dip into Lake Michigan, and the air cools. Petoskey State Park is one of the best places along the west coast of the state to watch Old Sol end the day. But even more popular among visitors is the scattering of Petoskey stones along the parks 1.25 miles of beach. Serious collects snap-up the corals to be polished and later cut, plain old folks like us enjoy taking a pocket full home to remind us of our leisure days in Michigan's great Northwest.

Particulars: The park is located off M-119 halfway between Petoskey and Harbor Springs. It's campground is a dandy but busy. Make reservations in advance if you plan to camp there. For entry to the park a daily vehicle permit or an annual pass is required.

GENESEE COUNTY

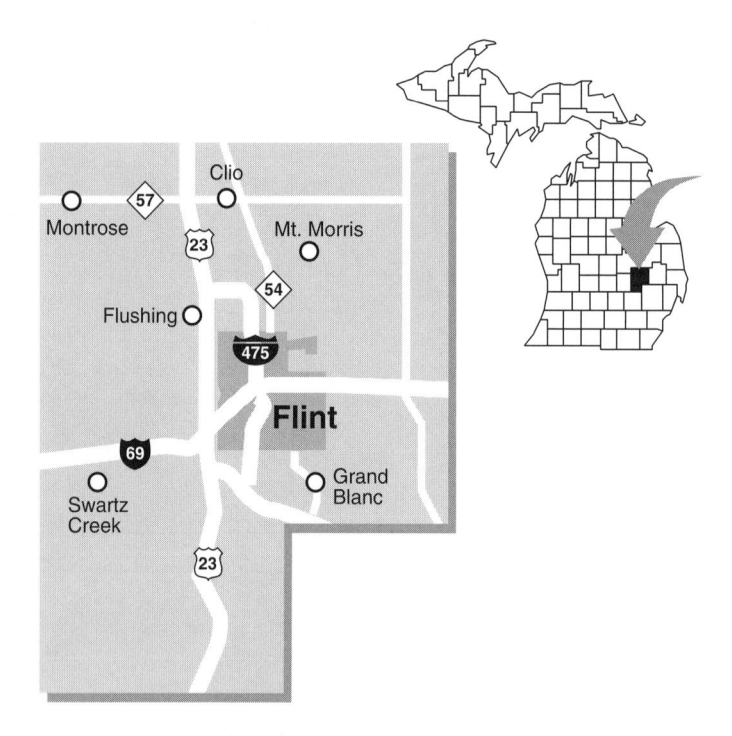

VISITOR INFORMATION

Flint Area Convention & Visitors Bureau
316 Water Street
Flint, MI 48503
800-25-FLINT OR 810-232-8900
www.visitflint.org

Genesee County

▼ Flushing
ALMAR ORCHARDS
(810) 659-6568

FREE

Over 100 acres of orchards with a cider processing operation each autumn. A small retail shop offers maple syrup, tours, and a petting zoo each fall.

Particulars: From I-75, depart exit 126 and then head west on Mt. Morris Road for seven miles to Duffield Road. The orchard is at 1431 N. Duffield Rd. Free.

▼ Flint
FLINT CHILDREN'S MUSEUM
(810) 238-6900

More than 50 hands-on experiences, youth programming, and ever-changing displays turn curiosity into learning. The strategically designed educational presentations provide lots of chances for children (and their parents) to interact with exhibits and programs.

In one room of the Children's Museum in Flint there is a small red banner hanging from the ceiling that simply says "Imagination." Underneath it there was an anchor desk without the newscasters for meteorologists, a judge's chamber with a judge, a stage and customs without the actors, and a television talk show set without the host.

The museum provides the props, kids supply the imagination and what you end up with is a "hands on" learning experience.

Unlike the Lansing and Ann Arbor facilities, Flint's museum concentrates on everyday items and how they work. Kids can jump behind the wheel of a fire engineBand even connect the fire hoseBclimb into the driver's seat of a bus and cars, even a Cris Craft boat, all ready to drive away in the child's imagination.

Particulars: From 1-75, take I-475 and depart at exit 8A head west on Robert T. Longways. Turn south on Saginaw Street and the museum is located in the basement of the Northbank Center at 2nd Avenue. The museum is open from 10 a.m. to 5 p.m. Tuesday through Saturday and noon to 5 p.m. Sunday. Admission fee.

FLINT INSTITUTE OF ARTS
Flint, MI
(810) 234-1695

FREE

Making art fun, the Institute was completely renovated in 1993 and offers tours, classes, museum area, and art gallery for all ages. Local artists are featured, while many lithographs and reprints of national artists are displayed. The Flint Art Fair is held the second weekend of June.

Particulars: From I-475, depart at exit 8A and head east on Longways Boulevard and then south on Kearsley Street. The center is at 1120 E. Kearsley St. in the College and Cultural Center and open from 10 a.m. to 5 p.m. Tuesday through Saturday and 1-5 p.m. Sunday. Free.

LABOR MUSEUM
(810) 762-0251

Billed as the only museum that explores and illustrates the history of Michigan's working men and women, at Flint's Labor Museum visitors learn about labors role in building America and its products. Displays include historical photographs of striking workers and factories during the 1936-37 sit-down strike in Flint that led to the recognition of the UAW by General Motors. Also on exhibit are billy clubs used by the police, buttons worn by strikers and other paraphernalia from labor dispute while film "The Great Sit Down Strike" is run continuously.

Particulars: From I-475, depart at exit 8A and head west on Longways Boulevard to N. Saginaw. The museum is at 711 N. Saginaw St. and open 10 a.m. to 5 p.m. Tuesday through Friday, noon to 5 p.m. on Saturday and noon to 5 p.m. the first Sunday of every month. Admission fee.

LONGWAYS PLANETARIUM
(810) 760-1181

With a seating capacity of 286, The Longways Planetarium is Michigan's largest and best equipped planetarium and one of the top twenty in the U.S. Using the latest developments in multi-media and computer technology, visitors can travel to distant worlds or be dazzled of the visualization to music by laser beams. Topical programs, regular weekend shows, and rock laser shows are always scheduled.

Particulars: From I-475, depart at exit 8A and head east on Longways Boulevard and then south on Kearsley Street. The planetarium is at 1310 E. Kearsley St. and offers family astronomy shows every Saturday and Sunday afternoon. Admission fee.

MOTT FARM
(810) 760-1795

There are some animal attractions in the state where the animals are real snoozers, they just lie around in muck filled cages, looking like they've been out drinking for a wee. But not at Mott Farms. On tiny Mott Lake, the rustic farm was established in 1961 and became part of the Genesee Recreation Area in 1969. (See Glovebox Guidebook's "Zoo and Animal Parks," $10.95, for lots more details).

A 14-point, self-guided interpretive tour brochure is available in the Orientation Building near the restroom and parking area. The property features pre-1960s farm buildings, including barns and service buildings, and older farm buildings, including barns and service buildings, and older structures like the farmhouses, help to teach rural life-styles. Mott Farm is laid-back, open and relaxing.

The farm focuses on education urban kids to rural living and farming. Maybe the most vital of the farm museums in the state, Mott Farm combines a historic and scenic setting under mature trees and a trace of cattle in the air. In the distance the steam locomotive from neighboring Crossroads Village chugs past a dozen or more times daily, spouting puffs of steam and a click-clack that helps enhance the atmosphere at the farmstead. More than many similar attractions, here you actually feel like you are "down on the farm."

Particulars: From I-475 take exit 11 (Carpenter Road) and follow the signs to Crossroads Village/Genesee Recreation Area. The farm is at G-6140 Bray Road and open My through October from 10 a.m. to 5 p.m. daily. Small admission.

PENNY WHISTLE PLACE
(800) 648-PARK

There must have been two hundred kids, from ages two through ten, all with blood sugar levels of 4000. All in a fenced in area with giant toys that quirt waters, bang drums and bouncing off the walls. Frankly, it's an adult's nightmare.

But the kids love it!

The high-energy play park is operated by Genesee Bounty parks and Recreation Commission. This is not a playground with swings and teeter-totters, this is a go-for-broke

128 *Cheap Travel in Michigan*

Penny Whistle Place, Genesee County

instructed play area where colorful imaginative play is the objective.

It was the 50th anniversary of the Flint Junior League who began the project in 1978 by securing the services of Eric McMillan, Inc., a design firm that specializes in kids play area. After a few years of fund-raising and design, the park opened in 1984.

There's Bean Bag Forest where you run through an area of swinging, suspended punching bags, taking your best shot at them. There's the Buick Bounce, a version of a moonwalk. The Cable Guide sends you flying across the park and Together Toys are the best described as giant Logos of sorts used to build forts and other things.

There's the Net Climb where kids scramble across on all fours to reach a platform high above the park and the Ball Crawl, where they swim or sink through hundreds of thousands of colorful plastic balls. Parents will be happy to know the park has never lost a kid.

Particulars: From I-75, follow I-475 and then depart at exit 13 and head north on Saginaw Street, east on Stanley Road then south to Bray Road to the park's entrance. Penny Whistle Place is open Memorial Day - through Labor Day from 10 a.m. to 7 p.m. daily. Admission fee.

SLOAN MUSEUM
(810) 760-1169

The Sloan Museum is a general museum that contains the Pierson Gallery of American History with its collection of more than 200 dolls, a health section and an area dedicated to the history of Genesee County. But it's best known for its collection of more than 50 automobiles, showcasing a variety of eras in the development of the car, especially GM vehicles.

Particulars: From I-475, depart at exit 8A and head east on Longways Boulevard and then south on Kearsley Street. The museum is at 1221 E. Kearsley St. in the College and Cultural Center and open from 10 a.m. to 5 p.m. Tuesday through Friday and noon to 5 p.m. Saturday and Sunday. Admission fee.

THE WHO
Days Inn
(810) 239-4681

Formerly the Holiday Inn, The Who's drummer Keith Moon, who died of a drug over dose a year or later, swam naked and had a cake fight at the motel as he celebrated his birthday.

You can do the same.

Particulars: From I-75 depart at exit 116A and head east on Bristol Road. The hotel is at 2207 Bristol Rd.

**WHALEY HISTORICAL HOUSE
(810) 235-6841**

The elegance and graciousness of the Victorian era as it was lived in Flint during the late 1800s is carefully preserved at Whaley Historical House. The house is a museum, and one visit through the massive carved doors will take you back in time to a lifestyle of affluence and quiet decorum.

Particulars: From I-475, depart at exit 8A and head east on Longways Boulevard and then south on Kearsley Street. The house is beyond the College and Cultural Center at 624 Kearsley St. and open the first and third Sundays of the month from 2-4 p.m. Admission fee.

▼ Swartz Creek

**SPORTS CREEK RACEWAY
(810) 635-3333**

Many of the harness horses that trainers paid $250, or roughly $25 per brain cell, run nightly during the winter season at Sports Creek Raceway. Seriously, many top race horses pace and trot their hearts out for our betting public's attention. Cheap and free fans can place a $2 bet and then go home.

Particulars: From I-69, west of Flint, depart at exit 128 and head south on Morrish Road. The track is at 4290 Morrish Rd. Admission fee.

**HISTORICAL & TELEPHONE PIONEER MUSEUM
144 E. Hickory
(810) 639-6644**

FREE

It may be located in a former bank (complete with a drive-thru window) but this is Michigan's only telephone museum. Inside you'll find hands-on working exhibits of antique telephone equipment so you can enjoy the experience of listening in on a party line. There is also a museum store, an entire collection of candlestick desk phones and local artifacts including farm implements and historical household items.

Particulars: From I-75, depart at exit 131 and head west on M-57 to Montrose. At the stoplight in town (you can't miss it, there's only one!) Turn north on Nichols Road for a block and then east on E. Hickory. The museum is at 144 E. Hickory St. and open 1-5 p.m. Saturday and Sunday. Free.

GLADWIN COUNTY

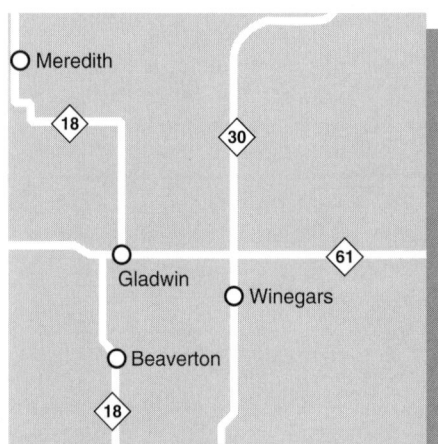

VISITOR INFORMATION

Gladwin County Chamber of Commerce
608 W. Cedar Avenue
Gladwin, MI 48624
989-426-5451
www.gladwincountychamber.com
email: chamber@ejourney.com

Gladwin County

▼ Meredith

HOISTER LAKE RECREATION AREA
Roscommon DNR Regional Office
(989) 275-5151

FREE

The lightly used recreation area of the Au Sable State Forest is at the north end of Hoister Lake and includes a picnic area, vault toilets and a small dock on the lake for shore anglers. There is also a large blue arrow that points to the Trout Lake Pathway, a 2.7 mile path that skirts both Hoister and Trout Lakes.

But the best part by far is the 1.7 mile loop around Hoister Lake as most of it follows bluffs above the shoreline for scenic views of the water. There is also a rustic state forest campground at the south end of Trout Lake where it's usually easy to get a shoreline site... even on a weekend in July.

Particulars: The easiest way to reach the area is to exit onto M-61 either from I-75 (exit 190) or from US-27 at Harrison. Follow the state highway into Gladwin where you turn north on M-18 to reach Meredith.

Once in the small town, turn east onto Meredith Grade Road for 1.5 miles then north on a dirt road that is posted "state forest campground." Follow this for 0.8 mile and you reach a posted junction saying Hoister Lake Picnic Area is a mile north and Trout lake Campground is to the south. There is camping fees, but the recreation area is free.

GOGEBIC COUNTY

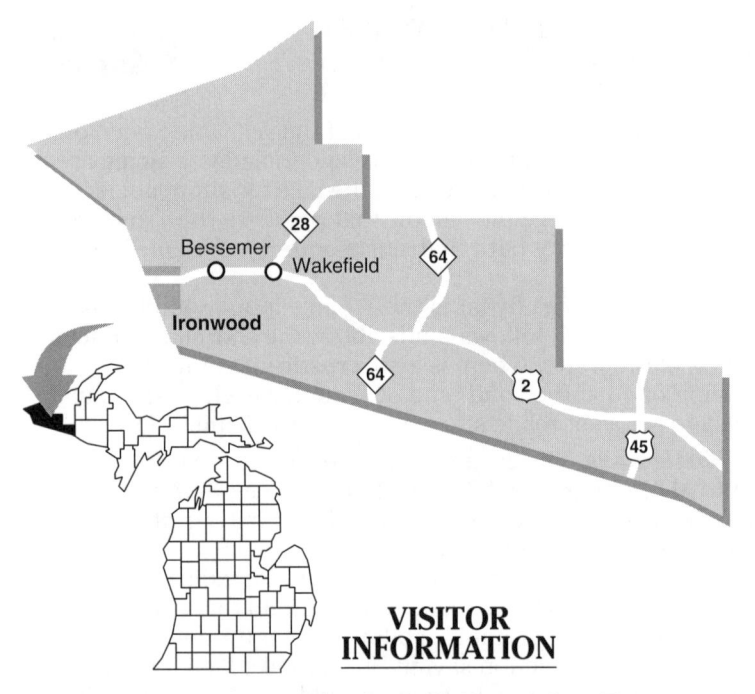

VISITOR INFORMATION

Gogebic Area Visitors & Convention Bureau
137 E. Cloverland Drive
Ironwood, MI 49938
906-932-4850

Ironwood Tourism Council
100 E. Aurora
Ironwood, MI 49938
906-932-1122

MDOT Welcome Center
801 W. Cloverland Drive
Ironwood, MI 49938
906-932-3330

Gogebic County

▼ Bessemer

BLACK RIVER HARBOR DRIVE
Bessemer Ranger District
(906) 667-0261

FREE

The 15-mile road departs from Bessemer on US-2 and enters Ottawa National Forest, ending at scenic Black River Recreation Area on Lake Superior. After passing Copper Peak Ski Flying Hill, Black River Road enters a scenic stretch and passes five posted waterfalls, each just a short trek from a parking lot.

Gorge and Potawatomi Falls are among the most spectacular and easiest to reach. The two falls are within 800 feet of each other and only a five-minute walk from the parking lot. Potawatomi is the largest with a 130-foot-wide cascade that drops 30 feet into the Black River. Gorge Falls is smaller with a 25-foot drop and is wedged in a small canyonBa red rocky natural wonder. A well used and marked trail leads you to observation decks. Other falls include Great Conglomerate, Sandstone and Rainbow Falls.

Particulars: From US-2 head north on North Bessemer Street to the Ranger District office (open 8 a.m. to 5 p.m. Monday through Friday) where you can pick up maps of the trails. Continue north and follow CR-513 which becomes Black River Drive.

COPPER PEAK SKI FLYING HILL
(906) 932-11222

Copper Peak is the largest artificial ski slide in the world and the site of 500-foot jumps during the winter (This is ski flying, not ski jumping. Don't ask me what the difference is). In the summer, it's a chair lift and elevator that takes visitors to the top for a view of three states plus Canada. You can't imagine how big these structures are until you're on the ground looking up at it. It looks like a Rube Goldberg erector set, giant metal beams sprouting off in every direction, with a ramp step atop two spindly stations.

Particulars: The sky flying ramp is off Black River Drive north of Bessemer and US-2 and open May through

One of the falls along the Black River Drive, Gogebic County

September. There is a small fee to take a trip to the top, but just to view it is free.

▼ Ironwood

HIAWATHA
Gogebic Area Visitors Bureau
(906) 932-4850

FREE

Hiawatha, the "world's tallest Indian" stands 150 feet above downtown Ironwood and make up to 55 yards of concrete, 5,000 pounds of steel, 15 yards of crushed rock and has 32-foot steel support beams that can withstand winds of up to 140 mph. The fiberglass Native American looks north to the shores of gitchee gumee, and prays those 140 mph winds never test him.

Particulars: From US-2 follow Business Route US-2 into downtown Ironwood and continue south on Burma Road to reach the Statue. Free.

OLD DEPOT MUSEUM
Gogebic Area Visitors Bureau
(906) 932-4850

As you might expect, with Ironwood's history being so intertwined with mining, there is a lot of mining artifacts and displays at the Ironwood Area Historical Society's Old Depot Museum, But you'll also find displays depicting life on the Gogebic Range as well as much railroading memorabilia.

Particulars: Take Business Loop US-2 into downtown Ironwood. The depot is located a block behind the post office on Ayers Street and is open Memorial Day through Labor Day from noon to 4 p.m. daily. Admission is by donation.

MT. ZION
Gogebic Area Visitors Bureau
(906) 932-4850

FREE

Conveniently located on the campus of Gogebic Community College north of Ironwood, Mt. Zion is one of the highest points on the Gogebic Range at 1,750 feet in elevation and 1,150 feet above Lake Superior. From the top you're rewarded with a panoramic view of the area.

Particulars: From US-2, head north Douglas Boulevard for a mile.

▼ Wakefield

PRESQUE ISLE FALLS
Porcupine Mountains Wilderness State Park
(906) 885-5275

Porcupine Mountains Wilderness State Park is so large it spans across two counties and the portion in Gogebic is stunning. The Presque Isle section of this 60,000-acre park is where the wild river descends through a series of spectacular waterfalls before emptying into Lake Superior.

From the picnic area you can descend a stairway to a suspension bridge across the rushing waters of the Presque Isle or follow board walk south along its west bank to view several more falls. For the best views follow the East and West River Trails which can be combined for a two-mile trek along the river. Also in this area of the park is a campground and trails leading into the wilderness heart of the park.

Particulars: From Wakefield head north on CR-519 which deadends at Presque Isle in 16 miles. A vehicle permit or an annual state park pass is needed to enter the area.

▼ Watersmeet

SYLVANIA VISITOR CENTER
(906) 358-4724

Sylvania Wilderness is a 21,000-acre area of pristine lakes and big fish. It's a non-motorized haven for canoeists who paddle and portage their boats from lake to lake. Even it your plans don't include any paddling, plan to stop at the visitor center, which makes for an ideal break on the long drive from Iron Mountain to Ironwood along US-2.

The center includes an exhibit hall which covers Indians and early settlers of the Sylvania lakes as well as the wildlife you'll find there today.

There is also an auditorium with programs on the area and conservation, a gift and book shop and information counter for the Ottawa National Forest. Just outside is a quarter-mile long Forest and Man Interpretive Trail through the woods.

Particulars: The center is right off US-2, west of Watersmeet. From Memorial Day to Labor Day the center is open from 9 a.m. to 5 p.m. daily. Hours are shortened to Monday and Friday 10 a.m. to 4 p.m. in the winter. Free.

GRAND TRAVERSE COUNTY

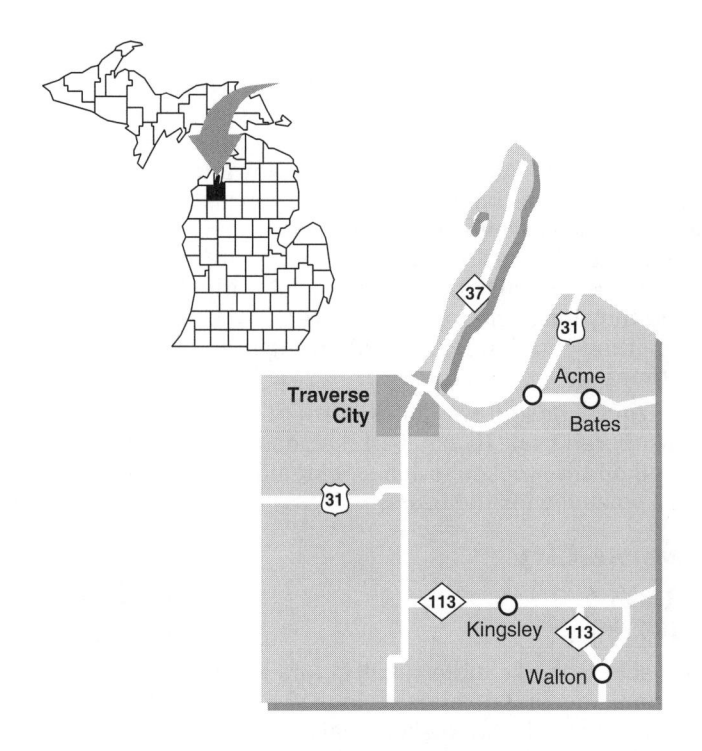

VISITOR INFORMATION

Traverse City Convention & Visitors Bureau
101 W. Grandview Parkway
Traverse City, MI 49684-2252
231-947-1120 or 800-TRAVERS

Grand Traverse County

▼ Acme

AMON ORCHARD
(231) 938-9160

Cherries are very berry, or are they a fruit, because a tomato isn't a vegetable, at least I don't think so. Well, to clear up this confusion a guided tour of a working cherry farm is certainly in order. Aside from a horse-drawn tour of the operation and a narrative about farming, you also get a FREE sample of tongue-snapping tart cherries.

The family-run farm is farmy. Also offering fresh bakery goods, produce, and all kinds of stuff made with cherries. Why don't they make cherry toothpaste? The kids will also love the petting zoo that is featured during blossom and harvest times.

Particulars: Located two miles north of Acme on US-31. Tours are offered from 10 a.m. to 4 p.m. daily in July and August and on the weekends June, September and October. There is a small fee for the tours.

▼ Traverse City

Candle Factory
(231) 946-2280

FREE

A huge selection of candles of all colors and types, plus regular candle making demonstrations. There is an area where you can watch the workers make candles and candlemaking demonstrations can often be arranged by calling in advance. If you're just dropping by, it's hit or miss whether they will be making candles that day. Saturday is by far the best day while the candle shop is open daily.

Particulars: The factory is just off the US-31 along the waterfront at 301 Grandview at Cass St. Hours are 10 a.m. to 5 p.m. Monday through Saturday and noon to 5 p.m. on Sunday. Free.

CLINCH PARK ZOO
(231) 922-4902

The entire animal collection at the Clinch Park Zoo is

comprised of native Michigan wildlife. Most of which are unreleaseable victims of gun shots, accident, and uninformed people. The small, but quality zoo is next to the Traverse City beach and downtown district. It's certainly a picturewq1ue setting in the heartland of the Midwest's finest resort area. Stroller rentals, wishing well, plenty of shady benches, and golf course-like lawn and landscaping is a hallmark of the 3.5 - acre zoo where 75 specimens reside.

Clinch Park's collection is a solid representation of Michigan's wonderful array of native species. Seven main exhibits, all of which have been improved recently, display healthy animals that are viewed by over 65,000 visitors annually.

Once inside the intimate zoo, passing through the tunnel under M-31 or crossing from the downtown street-level entrance, you'll see the covered turtle pavilion to the right, and the aroma of the four concessions in the air. Hopefully, your visit will be on a perfect summers day, a day only Michigan can display; zephyr fresh with a sky the color of infinity.

Just a few steps inside this tiny zoo is a five-section, ten-foot tall flight aviary. The older wire cage exhibit is planted with cedars, sand and gravel floors support timbers and other improvements. All of the birds of prey are unreleaseable. Barred owl, great horned owl, American bald eagle, red-tailed hawk, and hungry-looking turkey vultures fill the cages. Next door is small brown brick indoor exhibit with outdoor runs and cages on three sides. An unusual albino porcupine slept during my visit. Next are a couple of frolicking otters, cruising silently back and forth the bottom of a small concrete pond. Of all the zoos I visited (Michigan Zoos & Animal Parks, by Bill Bailey, $10.95) and of all the species viewed, otter are hard to beat for entertainment value.

The featured exhibit at the zoo is the educational center and adjoining modernized display dedicated in 1990. Using cooperative funding and significant local fund-raising, the $60,000 building offers an ecology lab, hands-on touch tables, furs, skulls, a video, and many aquarium tanks filled with small snakes, frogs, and other small animals. Surrounding the educational center are attractive updated exhibits complete with moving water, natural surroundings, and granite rock formations. Simple, but elegant design, combined with high-quality specimens, makes this the best exhibit.

A visit isn't complete unless you take a ride on the quarter-sized train, "The Spirit of Traverse City, Engine No. 400," began operation at the zoo in 1982, circling the entire zoo on a half-mile-long 24 inch wide track. Nearly 50,000 people annually ride the locomotive as it clanks and chugs around the shoreline zoo.

Particulars: The zoo is downtown Traverse City on US-31 between Union and Cass Street. Hours are 9:30 a.m. to 7:30 p.m. daily in the summer and 9:30 to 4:30 p.m. in the spring and fall. The facility is closed from November to mid-April. There is a small admission fee.

DENNOS MUSEUM
(231) 922-1055

The most amazing thing at Dennos Museum Center is called a Recollections Piece. It's like you're painting with your body. When children stand in front of the huge screen they see an outline of their image within a splash of changing colors. Then when they move their arms or jump the combination of video cameras and computer generated images makes the screen appear as if a series of outlines are moving or jumping before dissolving into more colors.

The staff at Dennos invites children of all ages to step into the Recollections exhibit and watch themselves "come alive in color." But what's even more amazing than your colorful image on the screen is the fact you're in Michigan's newest art museum..

The Hitching Cider Mill, Grand Traverse County

That's right, an art museum. But this is no stuffy gallery with ancient master pieces in gilded frames. Located on the campus of Northwestern Michigan College, the center includes the William and Helen Milliken Auditorium, the summer home for the Michigan Ensemble Theater, and three changing galleries that will feature invited artists and exhibits from other museums around the country.

But the jewel of the Dennos Museum Center is its permanent Inuit Art Gallery, a collection that began in 1960 and was housed in the college library. Today there's 550 pieces of sculptured soapstone and colorful prints depicting the harsh life and fascinating culture of these Arctic people. Cravings and prints depict hunters pulling a walrus out of the ice with a rope, caching through the open seas, bedding down in an igloo, waiting patiently at a breathing hole in the frozen Arctic Ocean for a seal to surface.

Just as popular as the Inuit collection, however, is its Discovery Gallery with 11 more hands-on exhibits as intriguing as the Recollections Piece.

Particulars: From downtown Traverse City head north on US-31 to the Northwestern Michigan College campus. The museum is posted from US-31. The center is open Monday through Saturday 10 a.m. to 5 p.m. and Sunday 1-5 p.m. Admission fee.

▼ Williamsburg

HITCHING CIDER MILL
(231) 264-8371

FREE

Mike Maten and his family don't live on the banks of a river and the orchards surrounding their place produce cherries, not apples. But none of this stopped the family from operating one of the few cider mills in northern Michigan. The way Maten see it, who needs a water well and a river when you have Norwegian Fiord horses and hay. The does and claims he has the only horse-powered apple crusher in Michigan.

Like at other mills, the process, from fruit to juice, can be seen in its entirety, beginning with an elevator taking the apples to the loft of the mill where they are chapped up aby a grander. The pulp then drops down a chute onto the press and, with a 1,400-pound horse outside supplying the power, you can actually see that sweet brown juice trickle from between the layers of rack, much to the delight of parents. That's because most kids are usually outside watching the horse work.

Particulars: The mill is six miles north of Acme, just off US-31 and east on Townline Road. The cider season is from early September to mid-November when the mill operates Saturday and Sunday 10 a.m. to 6 p.m. Viewing the operation and petting the horses is free. There is also a small country store sells apples, produce, doughnuts and cider in season.

OLD MISSION POINT   *FREE*

What do you like with your fall color drive? Antique hunting, a country store, a vineyard, fine dining or maybe a roadhouse inn? How about watery views, beautiful beaches of a lighthouse? How about all of it?

M-37 begins in Battle Creek, winds it ways through Grand Rapids and then heads north through the heart of the Manistee National Forest. But in October you can skip the first 189 miles for the final 20 that dips and climbs along the crest of Old Mission Peninsula. For that spectacular combination of autumn reds and Great Lake blues, Old Mission Peninsula rates right up there with the Brockway Mountain Drive in Keweenaw Peninsula.

UNDERWOOD ORCHARDS   *FREE*
(231) 947-8799

Within three miles of leaving the bustle of Traverse City, a sign pops up to Underwoods Orchards, a delightful country store and a place to taste the harvest fall or continue north where This Old Barn pulls a few more travelers off the road. The 1910 barn was restored by Walt and Susan Feiger and now houses, not hay and cows, but three floors packed with antiques.

Particulars: Underwoods Orchards is on Center Road and posted along M-37 three miles north of the city, This Old Barn is on Nelson Road eight miles north. Underwoods Orchards is open from 9 a.m. to 6 p.m. June through December, This Old Barn 10 a.m. to 5 p.m. daily from March through December. Free.

CHATEAU GRAND TRAVERSE WINERY   *FREE*
(231) 223-7355

At one point M-37 climbs a hill and, for the first time since you departed the city eight mils ago, you can see both bays in a colorful panorama. You can also see the rolling vineyards of the Chateau Grand Traverse Winery, a popular stop for a little wine tasting.

The winery has a delightful little tasting room and a deck off the back where you can enjoy your own lunch with a bottle of Michigan's finest. There are also guided tours of the operation.

Particulars: Chateaau Grand Traverse is right off M-37, eight miles north of Traverse City. It's open April through November from 11 a.m. to 6 p.m. Monday through Saturday and noon to 6 p.m. Sunday. Scheduled tours run daily June through August on the hours from noon to 4 p.m. Wine tasting is free and so are the tours.

LARDIE'S GENERAL STORE
(231) 223-4310

FREE

One of the more interesting places along the drive is Lardie's Grocery and it appears like nothing more than an outdated convenience store in the heart of Old Mission. At one time there were seven general stores along the peninsula because it took a farmer in a wagon here all day to go to town and back.

Lardie's can trace its roots back to when Old Mission was first settled and was first a post office. Rev. Peter Dougherty arrived from Mackinaw City and established a Presbyterian missionary here in 1839 and 12 years later a post office was set up. Postmaster Stone received no pay and it is said that he kept the mail in an empty box nailed to his kitchen wall. When the letters arrived at Elk Rapids across the bay, smoke signals were sent up and somebody would paddle a canoe over to pick it up.

When the mission moved to the west side of the bay in 1852, Stone also took over the trading activities with local Indian tribes and built the present store. It was moved once and for 82 years managed by three generations of Lardies.

What to do when you arrive at the rambling wooden porch of the general store? Pick up some provisions for a picnic, visit the replica of Old Mission Church just down street for historical insight on the store and the area and then continue north on M-37.

Particulars: The turn off to the Lardies's Grocery and the village of Old Mission is 18 miles north of Traverse City. It's open daily during the summer. There is no charge wasting away the afternoon on it wooden porch watching the traffic go by.

Mission Peninsula Winery, Grand Travers County

OLD MISSION COUNTY PARK
Traverse City Area Visitor's Bureau
(800) 872-8377

FREE

The state highway, that began at Battle Creek, finally ends at Old Mission County park, where you'll find a historical lighthouse to photograph, beautiful beaches to stroll and picnic tables to enjoy the cornucopia you gathered along the peninsula.

The 136- acre park lies at the tip of Old Mission Peninsula and contains less than four miles of trails. But few areas in the Lower Peninsula combine history, geological significance and stunning lakeshore views as well as this township park. It's crowned by the restored Old Mission Point Lighthouse, a classic light that was built in 1870 and automated in 1933 when electric lights replaced the kerosene lamp in the tower. There is a beautiful beach on the west side of the point and trails that wind through the woods to the east side (rocky shoreline here).

There are also several interpretive displays because the point ends at the 45th parallel, putting the park on the same latitude as Minneapolis and Mongolia.

You are, in effect, standing halfway to the North Pole, or if you are an optimist, halfway to the warm Equator.

Particulars: From US-31 in Traverse City, the park is located 20 miles north at the end of M-37. Open daily. Free.

OLD MISSION TAVERN
(231) 223-7280

Old Mission Tavern is a rustic inn that is a combination restaurant and art gallery. Grab the closest table to the glowing wood stove, study the original paintings around you and have one of the dozens of imported beers on display behind the polished wood bar.

Is there a better way to finish a tour of Old Mission Peninsula?

Particulars: The restaurant is only a few miles south of the park at the end and is open for lunch and dinner Monday through Sunday.

GRATIOT COUNTY

VISITOR INFORMATION

Gratiot Area Chamber of Commerce
110 W. Superior Street
P. O. Box 516
Alma, MI 48801
989-463-5525

www.gratiot.org

Gratiot County

▼ Alma

REPTILE LAND ZOO
Alma Tropical Fish, Inc.
(989) 463-2364

"Reptiles are quiet — they don't bark at the neighbors, like dogsBand they are easy and inexpensive to care for," says owner, John Nemeth. "A beginner can purchase a small boa for less than $30, and have a fine pet for many years." The Reptile Land Zoo is located in the large basement of the Alma Tropical Fish store, featuring over 200 glass-fronted exhibits, providing up-close viewing of over 200 specimens of snakes and other reptiles.

The winding basement corridors, and dim lights offers an exciting adventure into the world of reptiles. A book collection with plenty of how to information offers visitors a chance to learn about reptiles, plus learn how to even own one as a pet. The animal attraction is one of the most unique in the state and well worth a stop.

Down a narrow stairway, near the front of the store, is the entrance to the largest private reptile exhibit in the Midwest. The collection is huge, and eerie at first, but as your eyes and senses adjust to the space you're rapidly drawn along the corridor passing a 20-foot reticulated python, then hearing the startling rattles of a number of rattlesnake species.

I headed immediately for the hissing of the rattlesnakes, with senses tingling, the rush of wind from a floor fan stood the hairs on the back of my neck straight up. Surely several millimeters of adrenaline rushed my brain bucket, making the experience in the slightly musty basement even more exciting. Two healthy species of diamondback rattlers and a timber rattler shook their tails in unison sounding mad as hell, but looking pretty calm behind the safety of the thick glass.

Established in 1969, John Nemeth first began collecting reptiles in earnest in the early 1970s. "I've had many zoo professionals compliment by collection and assure me that this is the biggest private collection in the Great Lakes region," said Nemeth. Frogs, toads, and lizards are also part of the collection. "We used to market the Reptile Land Zoo intensively several years ago...billboards, brochures, and promotions," he said, "but I found word-of-mouth advertising, especially among reptile enthusiasts, is my best promotion." Today, hundreds of school children and families visit the zoo.

A 13-foot African rock python is one of the first "big" snakes you'll see, but nearby is also a large yellow anaconda, native of South America. Many species of rat snakes are also on exhibit. In this section of the basement display is the Argentina rainbow boa, a beautiful snake, but maybe the most handsome snake in the collection is the speckled king snake.

Michigan's only poisonous snake, the eastern massasauga rattler, is also on display in one of the lower cases at the back of the basement. The massasauga reaches a maximum of 30 inches in length and is considered gentle and species that will avoid confrontation. Another reason why Michigan is a great place!

Other poisonous snakes, which are locked in their sturdy plexiglass cases, are not for sale. Toward the back of the exhibit is a group of huge banded Egyptian cobras. They are the size of your arm and look pretty sleepy, but they are considered very dangerous. For Florida vacationers, a number of native species including the cottonmouth, an ornery looking serpent, is on display.

Ball python, California banded king snake, red-tailed boa, Burmese python, black-tailed rattlesnakes, Florida kingsnake, and water monitors, a native of southeast Asia which can reach a length of 108 inches. A couple of alligator-like caiman also float about in a small indoor pool, motionless, hungry looking. This is a great educational experience with visits available year-round during normal business hours.

Particulars: The zoo is in downtown Alma at 228 E. Superior St., across the street from the clock tower and the La Fiesta Restaurant. Hours are 9:30 a.m. to 5:30 p.m. Monday through Saturday and until 9 p.m. on Friday. Admission fee.

HILLSDALE COUNTY

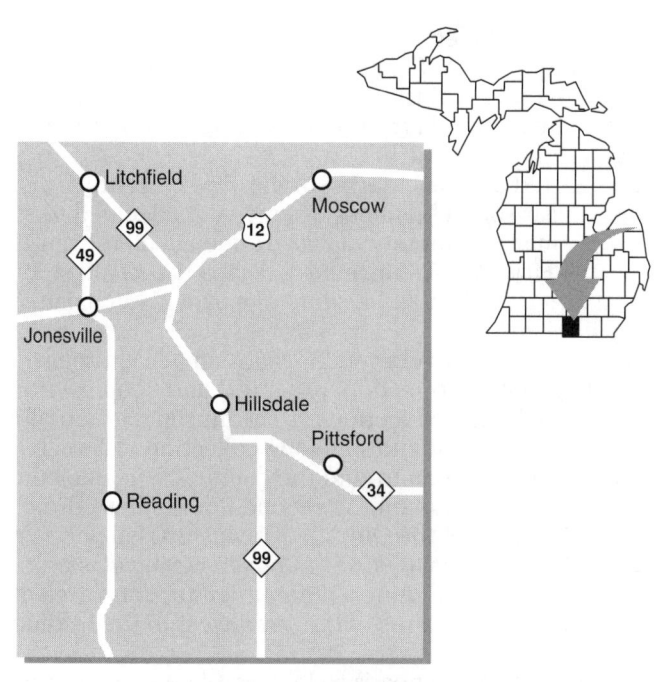

VISITOR INFORMATION

Greater Hillsdale County Chamber of Commerce
116 N. Broad Street
Hillsdale, MI 49242
517-439-4341
www.hillsdalecountychamber.com
email: info@hillsdalecountychamber.com

Hillsdale County

▼ Allen

FIRST PEOPLE MUSEUM
(517) 869-2575

Allen is for antiques
Huge antique malls (See Glovebox Guidebooks' Michigan's Only Antique & Flea Market Guidebook), housing hundreds of dealers is the featured attraction, drawing visitors from throughout the Midwest.

What started as a flea market in the 1960s, eventually became a year-round business when dealers decided to stay put in the small community of 300. Hidden in all the clutter of Allen is the First People Museum, perhaps the smallest, but finest American Indian and Eskimo museum in Michigan. Indians in Allen?

"I don't publicize it very much," said Janine Fentiman. "Mostly I open it up for school programs and people who are serious about Indian collections." The museum is actually Fentiman and her husband's lifelong collection of Native American artifacts from around the country. The museum is situated in a large room on the second floor of her Ethnic Arts Shop which is part of the Old Allen Township Hall Shops right on US-12. The room is lined with floor-to-ceiling glass cases with each case representing a different culture and area of the country, from the Navahos of the southwest to the Eskimos of Greenland.

There's lots of arrowheads to look at, of course, but there are also hundreds of other items, ranging from powder horns, rawhide mortars, head work and complete hand tooled saddles to a seal-gut rain coat, ivory carvings, and a walrus hide from north of the Arctic Circle.

Particulars: The small museum is located in Janine Fentiman ethnic Arts Shop in the Old Township Hall Shops on the corner of M-49 and US-12. Open by appointment or by accident. Admission fee.

GREEN TOP ANTIQUE MALL
(517) 869-2100

FREE

The mall is a slightly bazaar collection of 30 historic buildings, many of which are crammed full of wonderful antique and priceless collectibles. Wood chipped paths connect the buildings under a canopy of hard-woods with the chirping of songbirds rounding out the atmosphere.

More than 75 antique dealers offer a general line of antiques. Green Top is a popular stop for travelers moving between Detroit and Chicago and a great place for bargains. Many of the village buildings have "diamonds in the rough" where do-it-yourselfers can keep busy for months. You'll find lots of oak furniture, glassware, Victorian furniture, small things, and large furniture.

Wise shoppers often acclaim the Green Top Antique mall as a down-to-earth mall with good prices and a rapid turnover of merchandise.

Particulars: Green Top Antique Mall is a half mile west of Allen on US-12. Hours are 10:30 a.m. to 5 p.m. daily. Free unless you buy something.

▼ Jonesville

GROSVENOR HOUSE MUSEUM
(517) 849-9596

The wonderfully restored Grosvenor House was designed by the Michigan state capital architect, Elijah Myers. The 1870s house was the home of Jonesville banker E.O. Grosvenor, a man of high Victorian taste. Elaborate motifs, wood surfaces, and artworks fill the 32-room mansion while upstairs is a room dedicated to the history of Jonesville history.

Particulars: From US-12, turn south on Maumee Street. The museum is at 211 Maumee. Open weekends from Mother's Day through September. Small admission.

JONESVILLE VILLAGE HALL
(517) 849-2104

FREE

Most travelers driving US-12 pass through Jonesville without knowing that one of the earliest Michigan automobile factories was located here. It was the Deal Motors Vehicle Company, a buggy factory that tried to keep up with the era of horseless carriages.

The company was famed for its car warranty; no matter where the car broke down, Deal Motors Vehicle Company would come out to fix it. Little wonder the manufacturer went out of business.

Today only two Deal autos are know to remain. One is in a private collection in Nevada. The other is on display at the Jonesville Village Hall.

Particulars: The Village Hall and the car are right on US-12. You can see the car from the street but for a closer look step inside the hall when it's open at 8 a.m. to 5 p.m. Monday through Friday. Free.

▼ Litchfield

LITCHFIELD COMMUNITY HAND TOOL COLLECTION

FREE

Near the heart of this picturesque village is the Litchfield Town Hall and featured in the front of its storefront windows is the Litchfield Community Hand Tool Collection. I kid you not. In one window there are 75 tools from the turn of the century, in another 63 and all are numbered to correspond to a list taped to the window of what they are and who donated them. More are in the windows above, but with out a good ladder, it's tough to see what they are much less read the list. Maybe someday the people of Litchfield will use them to build a museum for them.

Particulars: Litchfield is 14 miles north of Allen at the north end of M-49. The town hall is near where M-49 and M-99 merge together. You can peak in the window anytime and it's free.

HOUGHTON COUNTY

VISITOR INFORMATION

Keweenaw Peninsula Chamber of Commerce
326 Sheldon Avenue
Houghton, MI 49931
906-482-5240 or 866-304-5722
www.keweenaw.org
email: info@keweenaw.org

Houghton County

Houghton

A.E.. SEAMAN MINERALOGICAL MUSEUM
(906) 487-2572

FREE

Located on the campus of Michigan Technological University, is this dazzling collection of more than 19,000 minerals and rock specimens from around the world are exhibits of fluorescent minerals, crystalized copper and silver specimens. Perhaps most interesting to many visitors are the samples of volcanic bombs on display from the Mt. St. Helens eruption in Washington.

Particulars: From US-41, depart on to Cliff Drive to the Electrical Energy Resources
Center. The museum is on the fifth floor and hours 9 a.m. to 4:30 p.m. Monday through
Friday. Free.

NATIONAL PARK SERVICE VISITOR CENTER
(906) 482-9086

FREE

If you don't feel like hoisting a backpack and taking the ferry across Lake Superior to Isle Royale, you can always stop at the visitor's center. Inside you'll find a handful of displays and video that will orientate you to this special island national park as well as maps, books, and posters.

Arrive around 9 a.m. during summer and you can watch the Ranger III depart with a load of backpackers and visitors for a six-hour trip to the park. Watching the historical Portage Lake Lift Bridge rise its tuss-and-girder section in the middle for the park boat is an impressive sight.

Particulars: The visitor's center is located at the waterfront where the Ranger III is docked . From US-41 follow brown signs to 87 N. Ripley Street. Hours are 8 a.m. to 4:30 p.m. Monday through Friday. In the summer the center is also open Saturday. Free.

Hancock

QUINCY STREAM HOIST
(906) 482-3101

Winter sports in Houghton County are healthy and cheap activities.

One of the wonder of the mining world, the Nordberg hoist is the largest steam-powered mine hoist ever manufactured. The hoist weighs 1,765,000 pounds and could raise a load of ten tons of ore at a rope speed of 3,200 feet per minuteBor over 36 miles per hour. Zooooom! Tours are offered into the mine while a gift shop rounds out this interesting attraction.

Particulars: The mine is located off US-41 on top of Quincy Hill north of (and above) Hancock. It's open mid-June through Labor Day from 9:30 a.m. to 5 p.m. daily. The last tour departs at 4:30 p.m. Admission fee.

Calumet

CALUMET THEATER
(906) 337-2610

There are no cheap seats in the Calumet Theater.

The intimate theater is designed like a megaphone, even whispers from the stage gently float through the air to the back seat of the balcony. It was obviously built in the days before they had PA systems.

It was also somewhat of a whim. At the height of the Keweenaw Peninsula's copper production, when local mines were producing 90 percent of the national total, the city of

Calumet Theater, Houghton County

Calumet was incorporated in 1875. By 1898 Calumet was a city of almost 40,000 that had wealth, importance, (it was once considered as a new site for the state capital) and a peculiar problemBtoo much money.

Flush with contributions from the rich mines, the city fathers had already paved the streets and installed telephones when they decided to build an opera house, one that would rival the stages on the East Coast.

The theater was built the following year, as an addition to the existing town hall, and designed in an Italian Renaissance style. Inside it featured two balconies, private viewing chambers along the walls and rococo plaster, ornamental of gilt, cream and crimson.

Pretty fancy. The halls real claim to fame is it's near perfect acoustics. The long list of performers who have appeared and marveled at the sound quality include John Philip Sousa, Sarah Bernhardt and Douglas Fairbanks.

Particulars: The hall is located at the corner of 6th Street and Elm in the heart of downtown Calumet. Daily tours are offered year-round from 9 a.m. to 5 p.m. Monday through Friday. Tours are available for a small fee.

COPPERTOWN USA MUSEUM
(906) 337-4354

The museum features exhibits and displays that covers the evolution of copper mining from ancient mines through the boom years of the late 19th century. You can explore nearby rock piles and tailings for bits of copper ore and other interesting specimens.

Particulars: The museum is located on Red Jacket Road a mile from US-41. In June and September the hours are 10 a.m. to 4 p.m. Monday through Saturday. In July and August they are extended to 6 p.m. Admission fee.

Lake Linden

LINDELL'S CHOCOLATE SHOP
(906) 296-0793

Fast food restaurants serve only fast foods in a plastic environment. At Lindells, you'll find 20 high-back oak booths, marble counters, wooden ceiling fans, and generally an interior that has changed little since 1928.

They no longer make chocolate, but they do serve delicious homemade ice cream made in a 1943 ice cream maker proudly displayed in the storefront windows. You can rise at 4 a.m. and watch them make ice cream or come by at a more reasonable hour and enjoy a huge bowl.

Particulars: The shop is located in the heart of Lake Linden on Calumet Avenue. Hours are 7 a.m. to 7 p.m. Monday through Thursday and Saturday and 7 a.m. to 9 p.m. Friday.

HOUGHTON COUNTY HISTORICAL MUSEUM
Keweenaw Tourism Council
(906) 4682-2388

The old Calumet and Hecla Mill Office now houses displays of mining, logging and other aspects of Houghton County's past. Children will love the dolls and historical toys as well as a Lionel Train collection. Outside they'll find real caboose to climb all over.

Particulars: The museum is on M-26 near the entrance to the village of Lake Linden. Hours are 10 a.m. to 4 p.m. Monday through Saturday and 1-4 p.m. Sunday from early June through September. Admission fee.

HURON COUNTY

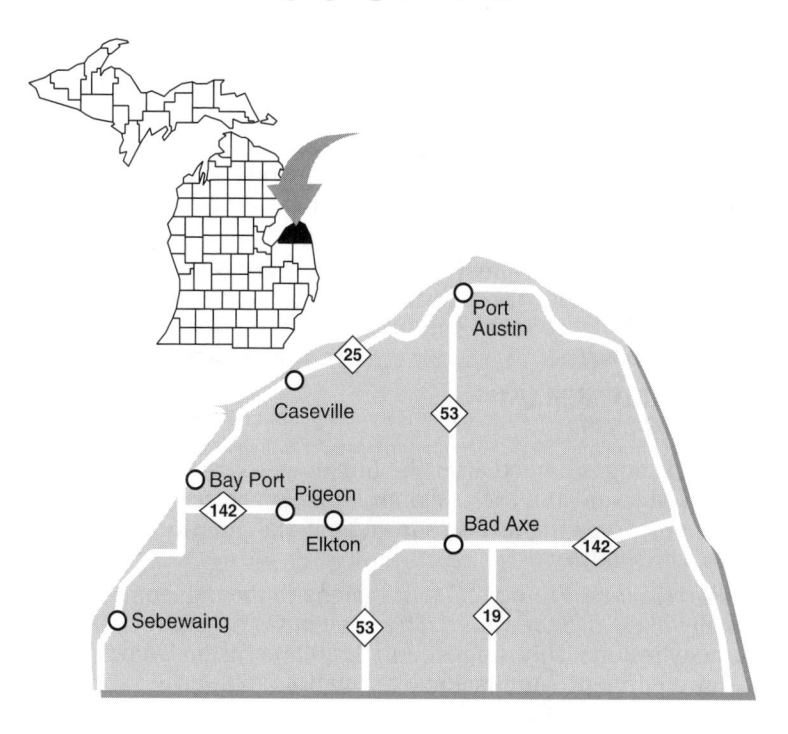

VISITOR INFORMATION

Bad Axe Chamber of Commerce
207 Van Dyke
P. O. Box 87
Bad Axe, MI 48413
989-269-9931

Huron County

Bad Axe

PIONEER LOG VILLAGE
(800) 35-THUMB

The Bad Axe Historical Society historical complex includes six small cabins ranging from a pioneer home, school, blacksmith shop and chapel to a general store and barn. Each one is filled with local artifacts. If you're in the marrying mood you can rent the chapel located in the colorful park.

Particulars: Pioneer Log Village is located in the Bad Axe City Park on S. Hanselman Street. Hours are 2-5 p.m. Sunday from Memorial Day through September.

Sebewaing

LUCKHARD MUSEUM
(989) 883-2539

Sebewaing is named after the Indian word that means "crooked river" and the Luckhard Museum in the heart of town preserves the artifacts from an Indian mission along with local history.

Particulars: From M-25 follow signs to the museum in the small village of Sebewaing. The museum is open the first Sunday in June, July, August and September from 2-4 p.m. or by appointment. Admission by donation.

Bay Port

BAY PORT FISH COMPANY
(989) 656-2121

FREE

From the 1880s, right past World War II, Bay Port was know as the "largest freshwater fishing port in the world." Carloads of fish were harvested and shipped to restaurants and markets throughout the country. Today, you can still buy fresh-caught fish right off the boat, if you are lucky enough to be at the docks when the boat is in.

Particulars: From M-25 in the heart of town, head for the water front docks where the company is posted. Hours are 9 a.m. to 5 p.m. daily during the summer. Free.

Pigeon

PIGEON HISTORICAL MUSEUM
(989) 453-3864

The historical Pigeon Depot has been fully restored and is now a museum that is listed on register of Michigan Historical Sites. It's packed with local artifacts from the railroading days of this town. The camera collection along is worth the sidetrip off of M-25.

Particulars: In the heart of town, just a block of Pigeon Road along the tracks (no kidding!). The museum is open mid-June through August 10 a.m. to 1 p.m. Saturday and 2-4 p.m. Sunday. Admission is by donation.

Port Austin

Port Crescent State Park
(989) 738-8663

The only true sand dunes along Lake Huron are found in this 569-acre state park that borders Saginaw Bay. You won't get them confused with those along Lake Michigan but kids will still love to romp through the sand.

There is also a scenic three-mile trail system through the dunes, the most beautiful beach on Saginaw Bay, fishing piers and a modern campground with beach-front sites.

Particulars: The park is off M-25, five miles west of Port Austin. A vehicle permit or an annual state park pass is required to enter.

Port Hope

LIGHTHOUSE PARK
(989) 428-4749

One of the eastern side of the state most picturesque lights is located between Port Hope and Port Austin just off M-25. It features a small museum that's on the first floor of the classic lighthouse, which was built in 1857 and is still used by the US Coast Guard to guide ships.

The lighthouse actually overlooks two parks: the county park around it features 74 campsites on a bluff, a beach, picnic areas, boat launch and a popular breakwall where campers can cast for yellow perch in the evening. Out in Lake Huron is another park. It's underwater. The Thumb Area Bottomland Preserve that the state established in 1985 to protect the 102 known shipwrecks that silently rest on the

Lighthouse Park, Huron County

bottom of the lake. Some of the ships include Chickmauga-Barge, J. Bertschy, Philadelphia, Iron Chief, Albany. The tiny museum displays many of the artifacts divers have found in the bottomland preserve.

Particulars: From M-25 between Port Hope and Port Austin, turn east onto Lighthouse Road to the park's entrance. The park is open year-round but the lighthouse is open only weekends from Memorial Day to Labor Day from noon to 4 p.m. Admission is by donations.

Harbor Beach

**GRICE MUSEUM
(989) 479-6093**

Three buildings make up the museum and include a farmhouse from the late 1800s, a barn and a rural school. The house features displays and artifacts from the local area. Nearby is the Harbor Beach Marina, where in the evening you can watch the fishing boats come in or talk to anglers along the breakwall fishing for perch.

Particulars: The museum is north of Harbor Beach off M-25 at the edge of the marina. It's open Memorial Day through

Labor Day from 9 a.m. to 5 p.m. Tuesday through Saturday and noon to 5 p.m. Sunday. Free.

MURPHY MUSEUM *FREE*
(989) 479-9664

For another trip back in time in Huron County visit Gov. Frank Murphy's birthplace. Murphy, the governor who paved the way for collective bargaining in the Michigan-based auto industry, was born in Harbor Beach and his home is a museum complete with potbelly stove and plain wood chairs in his father's office. Murphy used the home extensively and today shelves of books and historical souvenirs and photographs remain.

Particulars: The museum is right on M-23 in downtown Harbor Beach at 142 S. Huron. The museum is open June through September and hours are 10 a.m. to 5 p.m. Tuesday through Saturday, 8 a.m. to 4:30 p.m. Monday and 11 a.m. to 4 p.m. Sunday. Free.

Ruth

ST. MARY'S HISTORICAL MUSEUM *FREE*
(989) 479-6393

The small museum contains many Indian relics, antiques and other artifacts from the surrounding area.

Particulars: Located north of the Parisville Catholic Church at 4190 Parisville Rd. It's open only a few times each summer. Call ahead. Free.

White Rock

White Rock School Museum *FREE*

Hey kids, let's visit a one room schoolhouse. Well, maybe you'll get a yuck or two, but the small museum is a neat stop for families with school-age children that think they have it sooooooo rough. Built in 1909, the schoolhouse was used for students in kindergarten through eighth grade until 1968

Today it has lots of original books, desks of various sizes, charts, and teaching aids of an era that is quickly being forgotten. There's also a restored horse barn nearby where teacher housed her carriage and horse.

Particulars: From M-25, 10 miles south of Harbor Beach, turn west onto White Rock Road. Hours vary to say the least. Free if you are ever there when it's open.

INGHAM COUNTY

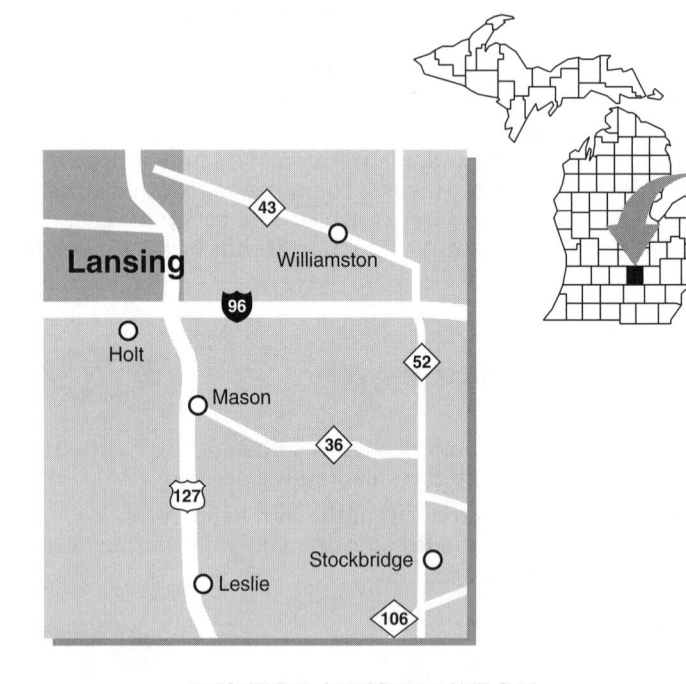

VISITOR INFORMATION

Greater Lansing Convention & Visitors Bureau
P. O. Box 15066
Lansing, MI 48901
866-377-1404

Ingham County

Okemos

NOKOMIS LEARNING CENTER
(517) 349-5777

We need more Native American cultural centers that focus on woodland Indians of the Great Lakes. The Nokomis Center features information, classes, and programs on Ojibwa, Ottawa and Potawatomi tribe known as the People of the Three Fires.

Particulars: From Grand River, turn north on Marsh Road. The center is at 5153 Marsh. Hours are 10 a.m. to 5 p.m. Tuesday through Friday and noon to 5 p.m. Saturday. Admission fee.

East Lansing

KRESGE ART MUSEUM *FREE*
(517) 355-7631

There are lots of classics permanently hanging in the Kresge center and that's good. But maybe more fun is the constantly changing exhibits that are often the work of local artist and artists from around the Great Lakes region.

Particulars: The museum is on Michigan State University Campus at Auditorium and Physics Road. During the school year the gallery is open 9:30 a.m. to 4:30 p.m. Monday through Wednesday and Friday and noon to 8 p.m. Thursday.

On Saturday and Sunday it's open 1-4 p.m. Summer hours may vary. Free.

CYCLOTRON LABORATORY *FREE*
(517) 353-9586

Those pesky atoms. Scientists can make all kinds of useful things from them including nuclear reactors, nuclear bombs, nuclear medicine, and panty liners. The guys at the national Super Conducting Cyclotron Laboratory, one of the nation's outstanding research facilities, are conducting basic research into mysteries of the nucleus of the atom and underarm odor.

Actually the MSU machine is also responsible for the world's first medical cyclotron to be used for treatment of cancer. Somehow this contraption can also magnify the smallest atom particles over one million times. The IRS is also looking at the machine to see if it can be used to collect taxes.

Particulars: The lab is also on the MSU campus at the corner of Shaw Lane and Bogue Street. Free tours are available but for groups only that call in advance. Tours will be given from 8 a.m. to 5 p.m. Monday through Friday.

MSU MUSEUM
(517) 355-2370

FREE

There are over two million objects and specimens in the football field size museum complex. Three floors of exhibits and displays, of things to touch, dioramas to study, historical antidotes to chuckle over, and natural phenomenons to ponder.

Founded in 1857, the MSU Museum was one of the first to be established in the Midwest on a college campus. It was actually being planned when the university was being created as a land grant college and originally occupied a space in Old College Hall, MSU's very first building.

Moved twice over the years, its been in its current home since 1952 and by then was recognized as the states finest museum of natural history and cultural history. In fact, the quality of the facility is the main reason Detroit never developed a natural history museum like Chicago, Cleveland, and other major cities.

The museum is a series of halls, each having its own theme and interpretive brochure or other information. On the main level of the museum is the Hall of Michigan Vertebrates which displays the state's amazing diversity in birds, reptiles and mammals, many of the dioramas depict their natural settings.

Heritage Hall is Michigan history. Displayed are a 19th-century print shop, Stanley's Crossroads Store that sells only "Fine Groceries," an authentic fur trader's cabin and tinsmith shop. The second level features the popular Hall of Elephants where a massive skeleton of a six-ton African elephant is shown. The tusks of an extinct mammoth are also interpreted. Did you know that a full grown elephant eats 600 pounds daily, drinks 40 gallons of water and can weigh 250 pounds at birth?

The North American Habitat Hall has life size dioramas of boreal forests, tundra, and other habitats, while in the middle of the rooms are complete mounted skeletons of two dinosaurs: Allosaurus and Stegosaurus, you can even touch a dinosaur bone.

This is one of the great Cheap and Free recommendations!

Particulars: The museum is located in the heart of the MSU campus, off West Circle Drive across from the library. Hours are 9 a.m. to 5 p.m. Monday through Wednesday and Friday, 9 a.m. to 9 p.m. Thursday, 10 a.m. to 5 p.m. Saturday and 9 a.m. to 1 p.m. Sunday. Free.

Lansing

POTTER PARK ZOO
(517) 483-4222

The Potter Park Zoo is one of the best in the state featuring 125 species and over 350 specimens in the 30-acre facility which attracts nearly 400,000 visitors annually. Began as a pony and camel ride in 1921 and now conducts significant breeding programs, and exhibits...everything from albadra tortoises to zebras.

Potter Park is one of the best bargains in the book while the entire family will enjoy the exhibit houses, rare black rhinos, and a river overlook. Lion tigers and penguins are also on exhibit and part of the facilities educational programming. The newest large exhibit houses, Feline and Primate House, is a renovated Victorian Building that is brightly lit and colorful. Filled with vegetation and a small waterfall, the featured attraction of this house is the ceiling-high gibbon cage. Monkey-like gibbons are lightening quick acrobats as they swing from one end of their large toy-filled cage to the other.

Particulars: From I-96 head downtown on I-496 and then exit south onto Pennsylvania Avenue for a quarter mile. The zoo is open daily 9 a.m. to 7 p.m. Admission fee.

MICHIGAN LIBRARY HISTORICAL CENTER
(517) 373-3559

FREE

Nationally recognized for its design, the museum includes 12 permanent galleries featuring lifelike facades of a lumber barons mansion and Michigan's first territorial capitol; a walk-through replica of a northern Michigan copper mine, geology interesting lake information, guides, and sound effects. Michigan's role in various wars and its place in industrial history is also highlighted.

Michiganians are proud of their state's rich past, which stretches back to the time when massive glaciers covered most of the upper Great Lakes region. As you walk through museum galleries, you are transformed to the wilderness as it was first seen by the French explorers of the late 17th century; our quest for statehood in the 1830s; the often

Michigan Women's Historical Center, Ingham County

dangerous life of an 1860s U.P. miner; and to the opulent 1889 mansion of a wealthy Muskegon lumber baron. A self-guided tour brochure is available.

Downstairs the Michigan Library (517-373-5400) houses archives, 27 miles of shelves, 5.6 million items and Glovebox Guidebooks.

Particulars: The museum is in the heart of downtown Lansing at 717 West Allegan. Hours are 9 a.m. to 4 p.m. Monday through Friday , 10 a.m. to 4 p.m. Saturday and 1-5 p.m. Free.

MICHIGAN STATE CAPITOL
(517) 335-1483

FREE

Government, the same folks that gave us swine shots, and who just gave a $5,000 pay raise to state legislators, offers one fine attraction: the recently renovated capital building. Probably funded by some slight-of-hand accounting miracle, the like-new building is adorned with refinished woodwork, new carpet fancy wall coverings, and plush fixtures from ceiling to cellar.

Some of the most humble politicians have actually been seen taking their shoes off at the door, but you won't have to, you own it. Guided tours are "complimentary" and offered daily, year-round. The best times to go is when the legislature is in session, Tuesday through Thursday, when you might, if you are lucky, see a fist fight.

Particulars: Located in the heart of downtown Lansing at the end of Michigan Avenue, you can't miss it. The 40-minute tour is offered on demand Monday through Friday from 9 a.m. to 4 p.m., Saturday from 10 a.m. to 4 p.m. and Sunday noon to 3:30 p.m. Free.

MICHIGAN MUSEUM OF SURVEYING
(517) 484-6605

Thrill to a bunch of survey stuff. Those tripod things, those little telescopes and long sticks with red painted numbers all make it exciting and cheap.

Seriously, surveying is important and the second oldest profession in the world (after you know what) as boundaries and property lines have been needed since the beginning of civilization. Only after quality surveying could the world - or Michigan, for that matter - be accurately divided into townships, villages, and cities.

Surveyors like William Burt, who was famous for building the first American typewriter and inventing the solar compass, also is credited with discovering the rich Marquette iron range.

The museum does a good job of explaining the contributions of individual surveyors and how the profession measures and helps bring order to our open spaces, cities, and personal property.

Particulars: From Michigan Avenue turn south on Museum Drive where you'll find the museum next door to Impressions Five. Hours are 10 a.m. to 3 p.m. weekdays. Admission fee.

MICHIGAN WOMEN'S HISTORICAL CENTER (517) 484-1880   *FREE*

Sadly, I, and many students, never learned in school what the Michigan Women's Historical Center is teaching. Happily, the center is a major success and they and others are having a significant impact on education curriculums.

Realizing that history did not fully represent the contributions of women, the Michigan Women's Studies Association was founded in 1973 to upgrade and elaborate what was being taught in public schools and universities. In 1979, the association took its idea a step further when it began planning for a public museum that would be dedicated to women.

After years of fund raising and careful renovation of the century-old Cooley Haze House, that once served as the Governor's mansion, the Historical Center and Hall of Fame was opened in 1987.

It had an immediate impact on womenBand men.

The center isn't flashy and it doesn't have elaborate exhibits and hands-on displays. But it does tell a side of history few of us have ever heard before The museum itself is two rooms, one is entitled, "Earning a Living" and illustrates the struggle women went through to earn a right to hold a job outside the home. Displays include the artifacts of early careers of women as teachers, telephone operators, librarians and nurses while voice box recounts the opposition trade unions put up in the early 1900s to keep "women at home and not in the work force."

The second exhibit room features the struggle of Michigan women to gain the right to vote. It took the suffragists 70 years to win that right but never did they resort to violence. Instead they waged a war of education.

The Center, which is surrounded by the Cooley Gardens, also includes an art gallery that features changing exhibits of Michigan women artists and photographers. But the most

Women's Hall of Fame, Ingham County

impressive part of the facility is the hall of fame located in the East Gallery. Within the sun room are pictures and stories of more than 40 Michigan women. They range from such notable figures as Rosa Parks and Betty Ford to Patricia Hill Burnett, a former Miss Michigan and runner-up in the Miss America pageant who later became instrumental in setting up Michigan's chapter of the National Organization For Women.

Particulars: The center is six blocks south of the State Capital. From I-496, depart at the Downtown/Capital Avenue Exit but head south of the interstate to Main Street where you'll find it at 213 W. Main. Hours are noon to 5 p.m. Wednesday through Friday and 2-4 p.m. on Sunday. Admission fee.

R.E. OLDS TRANSPORTATION MUSEUM
(517) 372-0422

More than just a bunch of old cars, this museum is a tribute to both the auto industry and one of Lansing's most prominent citizen's R.E. Olds. Among the exhibits is the very first Oldsmobile memorabilia from the horseless carriage days.

Particulars: Located near Impressions 5 Museum south of Michigan Avenue at 240 Museum Drive. Hours are 10 a.m. to 5 p.m. Monday through Friday. Admission fee.

RIVERFRONT PARK AREA
(517) 483-4277

FREE

Splitting Lansing in half, the Grand River and the adjacent greenbelt along the waterway stretches more than three miles offering board-walks, bridges, fountains, museums, dozens of attractions and the best view of the State Capital building. In fact, government never looked so good, especially when viewed at dusk when the lighted dome reflects in the quiet river waters.

The busy riverwalk offers bargain-minded travelers with an entire day of budget activities including side trip to the R.E. Old Museum, potter Park Zoo, Turner-Dodge Historical Mansion, campus of MSU, Impression 5 Museum, fish ladder, Sun Bowl Amphitheater, North Lansing Dam, and its also the site of many special events, parades, and community activities.

Particulars: You can pick up the boardwalk from many locations along the Grand River, including where it dips below Michigan Avenue. Walking is free.

TELEPHONE PIONEER MUSEUM
(517) 372-1400

FREE

The facility is dedicated to preserving typical telephone equipment used in homes and offices over the last 100 years.

Among the displays are rare photos documenting the phone industry in the 1800s.

Particulars: The museum is located at 221 N. Washington Square on the west side of Capitol Avenue. Hours are 10 a.m. to 2 p.m. Tuesday and Thursday. Free.

IONIA COUNTY

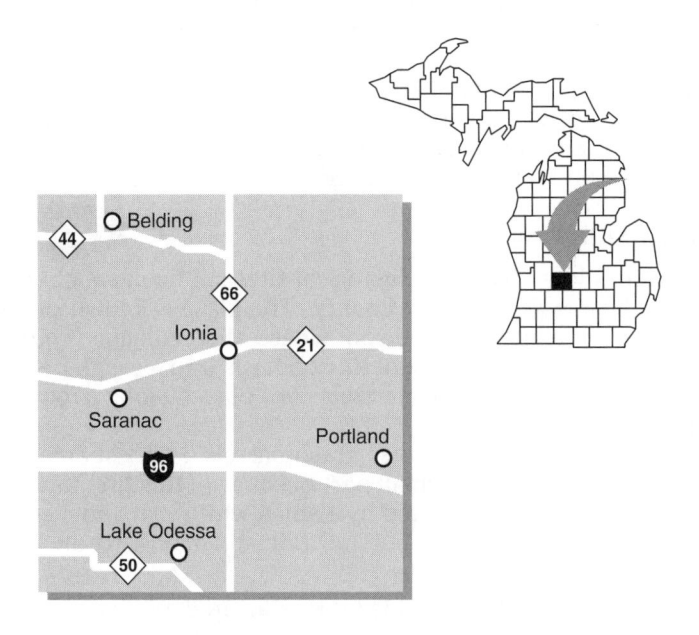

VISITOR INFORMATION

Ionia Area Chamber of Commerce
439 W. Main Street
Ionia, MI 48846-1553
616-527-2560

Ionia County

Belding

GUS MACKER BASKETBALL

Belding is the birth place of three-on-three basketball tournaments that now draw ten of thousands of three-man teams for tournaments conducted around the country. The small community of Belding still hosts a whopper of a tournament each summer. The family fun events attracts fans and old gizzer players trying to relive their youth as they rattle around taped-off courts located on city streets.

ROADSIDE TABLE   *FREE*

There's lots of obscure historical sites in Michigan, but one of the best is here in Ionia County. The place is known simply as "The Roadside Table," a spot where Allen Williams, county engineer, recycled a stack of thick boards into a rough picnic table, the first public picnic table ever placed along a road right-of-way.

Today, thousands of tables, trash barrels, and rest areas grace our roadways in small part because of this first table. The tiny site is only marked by a small white sign and a green historical narrative marker. The state still maintains the area, bring your picnic basket.

Particulars: The roadside table is located at the corner of Morrison Lake Road and Grand River Avenue, south of Saranac. Free.

COVERED BRIDGE   *FREE*

Michigan road maps have an average of three-zagged blue lines, four wiggly red lines, and dozens of tiny dots that have no bearing whatsoever to the road system, geography, or the location of stuff I'm interested in. But I'm learning.

Whatever the maps may says, portions of southern Michigan are becoming increasingly popular areas for fall color touring. One of the best drives a 15-mile route that is lined by towering hardwoods, rolling farm fields and crosses three covered bridges, including the oldest in the state, White's Covered Bridge.

Built in 1867 by J.N. Braze for under $2,000, the White's

Grand River is a terrific bass fishery, Ionia County.

bridge is nestled in a wooded area and spans the gentle Flat River. This is a classic wooden bridge with trusses hand-hewed and secured with two inch wooden pegs and square wrought nails. The bridge is only 14-foot wide, and less than 120 feet in total length, and you can drive your car over it, or park and walk for a more intimate look.

The bridge is found by driving from Smyrna (five miles southwest of Belding) and then going south on White's Bridge Road.

Continue southward on White's Bridge Road for nearly 4 miles, and turn west onto potters Road to Fallasburg Bridge Road, which will lead you over another covered bridge at the county park, just inside Kent County. The energetic Braze also built this bridge which is very similar to the White's bridge. His high construction standards have allowed both of these bridges to continue to be enjoyed more than 100 years later. The nearby county park that is situated along the Flat River is a great place for a picnic.

From the Fallasburg County Park, take Lincoln Lake Avenue south into the town of Lowell (home of the huge Flat River Antique Mall) and head west on M-21 to Grand River until you cross into the town of Ada, also in Kent County, where you'll find the often photographed Ada Covered Bridge.

The first Ada bridge was constructed by Will Homes in 1867 and sadly burned in 1980. But within about a year the area residents did a fund raiser and rebuilt the bridge which is now for pedestrians only.

Particulars: The bridges are open year-round and passage across them is free.

IOSCO COUNTY

VISITOR INFORMATION

Tawas Bay Tourist & Convention Bureau
P. O. Box 10
Tawas City, MI 48764-0010
877-TO-TAWAS

www.tawasbay.com
email: info@tawasbay.com

Iosco County

Tawas City

TAWAS HISTORICAL INDIAN MUSEUM
(989) 362-5885

The museum, located in an impressive home along lake Huron contains a terrific collection of North American artifacts along with flourescent rocks and prehistoric tools.

Particulars: Located at 1702 S. US-23 along Lake Huron. During the summer the museum is open from Thursday through Tuesday 1-4 p.m. and the rest of the year 1-4 p.m. Saturday and Sunday only. Admission is by donation.

LUMBERMEN'S MONUMENT
U.S. Forest Service
(989) 362-4477

FREE

Once this area was a vast wilderness, then the shouts of lumbermen filled the air, axes swung, and trees fell to be driven to the Au Sable for the float to market. Men known as river rats and bank beavers poked and sorted huge logs as they made their passage from the wilderness to downstate mill towns. The land still aches from the slashing cuts of another era.

Today, downstaters travel the same river and beaten path, especially during fall color time and now admires the trees' colors rather than the size of their trunks. Visitors can relive the logging era at the Lumbermen's Monument Visitor Center and learn what a bank beaver did, or try their hand at rolling a log with a heavy peavey.

The mighty bronze statue of loggers stands proudly and prominently, surrounded with the very trees they make a living cutting down. Nearby is the interpretive area and museum which details the logging era, the difficult life, the colorful stories and wisdom gained.

Learn that logger, even Paul Bunyan, was viewed as cheap labor making only $2 for a twelve hour day of sawing, sweating, and freezing wet feet. Little wonder that by the time most loggers turned 35 years old, they were too worn out or too sick to continue their trade.

The view of the Au Sable from the overlook area and a walk to Cooke Dam Pond is great. it's the walk back up the 260 steps that's a killer.

Particulars: From Tawas City, head west on M-55 for a mile then turn north (right) onto Wilber Road to reach Monument Road. Head north on Monument Road until it ends at River Road where the monument is a half mile east. The interpretive center is open from the third week of May to late October and daily from mid-June. Hours during the summer are 10 a.m. to 7 p.m. Free.

CANOE RACE MONUMENT
U.S. Forest Service
(989) 362-4477

FREE

Just to the west of the monument is another; the Canoe Race Monument. This spot honors Jerry Curley, who died practicing for the Au Sable River Marathon, often called the world's toughest canoe race. The monument, topped with two paddles, offers strength and honors all racers that attempt the 240-mile annual event. It also provides a great view of the Au Sable while nearby is an eagle's nest.

Particulars: The monument is 1.5 miles west of Lumbermen's Monument right off River Road. Free.

LARGO SPRINGS
U.S. Forest Service
(989) 362-4477

FREE

Still further on River Road is largo Springs, largo is the Chippewa Indian word for A"many waters" and this was a favorite spot for members of the tribe who were traveling along Saginaw-Mackinaw Trail. The springs are over 300 steps downward but along the way there are eight rest benches.

At the bottom is a pleasant and tranquil spot as the springs gurgle out of moss-laden bluffs and into Au Sable River under the canopy of towering pines.

Particulars: The springs are a one-mile west of Canoe Race Monument, where you'll find a picnic area, parking and the stairway to the river. Free.

Oscoda

PACK HOUSE
(989) 739-0454

This unusual house was constructed with yellow pine, without knots, and was declared Asound and flawless, A upon completion in the late 1800's. Now, area residents restoring the structure and each year more hours and programs will be added. The home represents a unique history of milling and lumbering along the Huron shoreline.

Particulars: The Pack House is located at 5014 North US-23.

PAUL BUNYAN
Oscoda-Au Sable Chamber of Commerce
(989) 739-7322

FREE

You can't miss him downtown. Paul Bunyan is the tallest thing in Oscoda. The huge statue is a tribute to Oscoda's favorite son James MacGillivery, author of the Paul Bunyan tales.

Particulars: The statue is off US-23 in downtown Oscoda.

IRON COUNTY

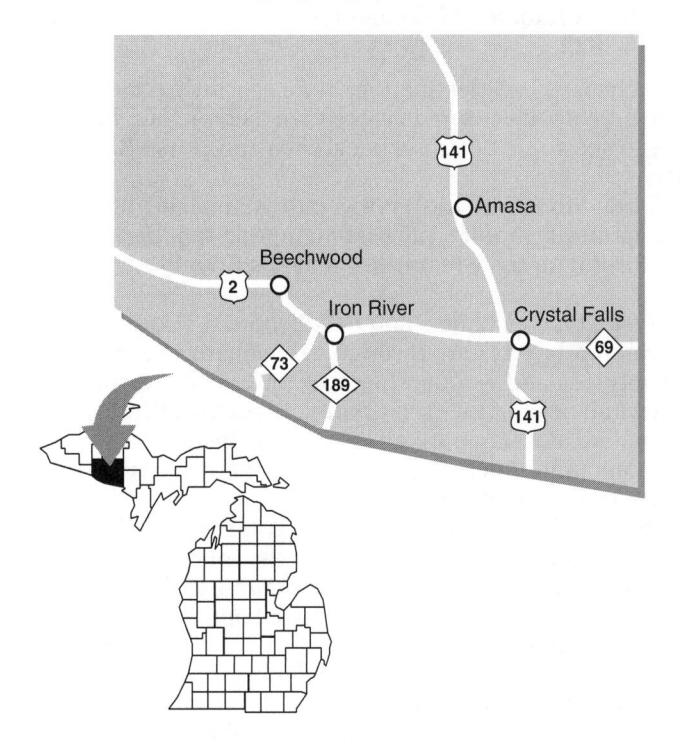

VISITOR INFORMATION

**Iron County Tourism Council
One E. Genesee Street
Iron River, MI 49935
906-265-3822**

Iron County

▼ Crystal Falls

HORSE RACE RAPIDS
Iron County Chamber of Commerce
(906) 265-3822

Some cheap travel destinations require a little patience and exploring. This adventure is more than a color tour, but a chance to see some beautiful backroads and Horse Race Rapids.

From Iron Mountain, head north into Wisconsin. It's not posted, naturally, but it's the first main road that departs east after returning to the Great Lakes state, is County Airport Road.

Go ahead, take a chance, and head left on it. Continue on the gravel road to its end, through a thick natural area of distance ridges and woods where the only sign of civilization are the windsocks of the Iron County airport. In three miles you dead end at a tiny parking lot by Wisconsin Electric and Power Company, which also built the stairway and trail that descends to Horse Race Rapids.

It's about a quarter-mile walk to the gorge on the Paint River where boulders are so huge and the rocky bluffs that box in the rapids so steep and sheer-sided that the locals call it Aour little Grand Canyon. It is roughed and most splendid dressed in fall colors.

Also nearby is CHICAUGON FALLS: Accessible by Bewabic State Park. Get a map and information at the park and then head out for a rugged two-mile hike. BEWABIC STATE PARK is on US-2 4 miles west of Crystal Falls and offers a sandy beach, tennis, excellent picnic facilities and hiking. It's on the scenic Fortune Lakes Chain.

Particulars: Horse Race Rapids is at the end of County Airport Road, three miles north
of the Wisconsin boarder on US-2 Free.

SPLIT ROCK
Iron County Chamber of Commerce
(906) 265-3822

FREE

Back in the car, continue north to another interesting sight; Split Rock. Here a huge pine towers over a boulder that has been split in half by the force of the tree's roots. I knew you'd love this attraction.

Particulars: Split rock is located across from the junction of US-2 and CR-424. Free.

Pine Mountain Ski Jump Dickinson County

▼ Caspian
Iron County Museum
(906) 265-2617

The Upper Peninsula's largest museum is also the least known. Yet the complex has 50 major exhibits and many small interpretive dioramas, a miniature working mine, and what is believed to be the largest miniature logging display in the world showing every aspect of logging operations using more than 2,000 pieces.

The grounds include almost 22 buildings, many over 100 years old, including a 1921 mining head frame. Stager depot is a 1890 railroad station, logs barns, pioneer cabin, nature center, logging camp, a sleigh barn and many other buildings all featuring artifacts representative of the era.

The main museum is the former engine house, which has been considerably enlarged and today is a maze of displays and three-dimensional exhibits. The renovated saloon, blacksmith shops, schoolroom, and a handcarved model of a logging camp fills an 80-foot display case with hundreds of figures and artifacts.

The Cultural Center was added in 1986/87 as part of the observance of Michigan Sesquicentennial. The admissions desk and the gift shop are near the main entrance. As an introduction, 32 woodcuts by artist, Mary Kale illustrate different aspects of Iron County History. The stage permits numerous types of programs: ethnic festivals, style shows, concerts, plays, lectures and many expanded exhibitions. The center itself can seat as many as 500 people and is used for large exhibitions such as quilt shows, art shows, hobby shows and conferences. Three galleries are part of the building and are specifically for Pioneer exhibits, Art exhibits and Humanities honorees.

Not as slick as Greenfield VillageBbut every bit as interesting at a fraction of the price.

This is an excellent destination for UP travelers.

Particulars: The museum is on County Road 424, two-miles south of US-2 and Iron River. Open daily from May through September. Hours are 9 a.m. to 5 p.m. Monday - Saturday and 1-5 p.m. on Sunday. Admission is $2.50 for adults and $1.50 for children.

ISABELLA COUNTY

VISITOR INFORMATION

**Mount Pleasant
Convention & Visitors Bureau**
114 E. Broadway
Mount Pleasant, MI 48858
888-772-2022

visitor@mountpleasantwow.com

Isabella County

▼ Mt. Pleasant

Center for Cultural and Natural History *FREE*
(989) 774-3829

Located on the campus of Central Michigan University, the center is a large gallery that features a variety of displays and interpretive exhibits ranging from anthropology and natural history to general history. You won't forget the 420-pound Petosky stone that's on display.

Particulars: From US-27, follow Business US-27 into Mt. Pleasant and onto the CMU campus. The center is in Rowe Hall. Hours are 8 a.m. to 5 p.m. Monday through Friday. Free.

Gerald L. Poor Museum *FREE*
(989) 774-3829

This one-room schoolhouse, administered by the Center for Cultural and Natural History, has displays pertaining to education in days gone by.

Particulars: Located on the edge of the campus, this museum has no regular hours.

Call ahead if you're just dying to see it. Free.

Michigan High School Coaches Hall of Fame *FREE*
(989) 774-7474

From around the state, from tiny Upper Peninsula communities to the largest metro areas, hundreds of high school coaches are in the Michigan High School Coaches Hall of Fame. Find your favorite high school coach and then guess why he was selected. The plaques simply contain the coach's name, his school and the year he coached. There is nothing on his accomplishments or the "big win."

Particulars: Head for the Hall of Fame room in the Bovee University Center on the
CMU campus. Hours are 8 a.m. to 5 p.m. Monday through Friday. Free.

University Art Gallery
Franklin and Preston
Mt. Pleasant
517-774-3800

This Gallery, located on the CMU campus, is the site of many media events, special exhibitions and college student shows from the Central Michigan University community.

Rock Climbing Wall & High Ropes Course
The A Wall: 32-foot indoor climbing wall and high ropes course located in Finch 112 on CMU's campus (989) 774-7307

Skate Park
Located in the south end of Island Park this 17,000 square foot skate park with ramps and jumps, is designed for bikers, skate boarders and inline skaters of all ages and skill levels. With two half pipes, a variety of quarter pipes, fun boxes, bank ramps, grind boxes and a pyramid with integrated rails. Seasonal operations. (989) 779-5331

Loafers Glory-Village of Yesteryear
Restored historical 1800's hardware store featuring handmade crafts from the local Amish settlements; collections of country, folk and Victorian art; antique treasures and delightful eateries. Seasonal hours. Blanchard, (989) 561-2020

Old Fence Rider's Historical Center:
Located in Edmore on M-46, 35 minutes southwest of Mount Pleasant. Displays of historic headlines from the past, Historical Flags of the United States, Barbed Wire Fence collection, The Life and Times of Will Rogers, Hats that covered America and speaking programs available from the "Old Fence Rider" himself, Carm Drain. Open Wednesday through Sunday, 9 - 11am & 1 - 4pm; Thursday evenings from 6:30 – 8 p.m. Individual, family and group rates. Call (989) 427-5222.

JACKSON COUNTY

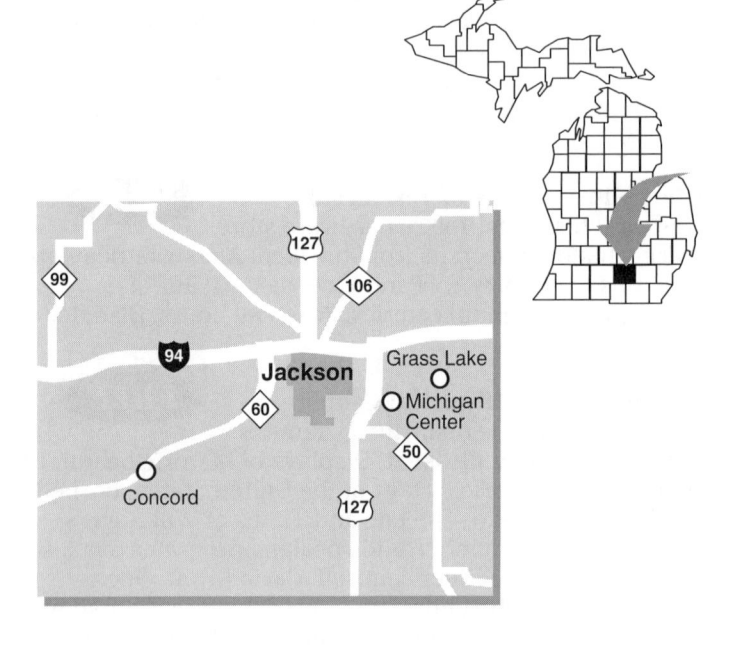

VISITOR INFORMATION

Jackson County Convention & Visitors Bureau
P.O. Box 80
Jackson, MI 49204
517-764-4440 or 800-245-5282
I-94, Exit 138 (Inside Jackson Crossing Mall)

www.jackson-mich.org

Jackson County

▼ Jackson

Cascades
(517) 788-4320

If it's a windy night you'll feel both the pulsing music and the fine spray from the dancing fountain as it goes through the nightly performance that has been ongoing since 1932. Visitors can watch the dancing lights and listen to the beautiful music from comfortable seats, while the more energetic can climb 129 steps to the top of the six giant fountains that are often billed as the world's largest manmade waterfalls.

Also nearby are paddle-boat rides, miniature golf, cascades museum and gift shop. 465-acre park.

Particulars: From I-94, depart at exit 138 head south for three miles. Signs will point the way to The Cascades located on South Brown Street. The falls operate nightly from 7:30 p.m. to 11 p.m. Memorial Day thru Labor Day. Admission is $3. Children five and under are free.

Under the Oaks – Republican Museum – Birthplace of the Republican Party

Following the passage of the Kansas-Nebraska Act (which would have greatly expanded the hated practice of slavery) citizens from across the Midwest came together "under the oaks" in Jackson, Michigan, to officially establish a new party which had been commonly conceived in towns like Ripon (WI), Exeter (NH), and Crawfordsville(IA).

On JULY 6th, 1854 - The REPUBLICAN PARTY WAS BORN. It was in Jackson that the party name, "Republican," was formally adopted. A political platform (the soul of a party) was passed, and a slate of candidates was chosen for elected office. Though the Party's conception may have happened elsewhere, its place of birth is certain.

Jackson, Michigan, is honored to be the party's birthplace and the beginning of the end of slavery.

Particulars: 501 W. Franklin St. Call (517) 841-6671

Ella Sharp Museum
(517) 787-2320

Hillside, once a busy family farm in the late 1800s, is now Jackson's finest cultural and recreational resource. Willed to the people of Jackson by Ella Merriman Sharp in 1912, these 530 acres contain a complex of historic buildings, a modern exhibit gallery, recreational areas for swimming, biking, soccer, baseball, golf and tennis. In addition, there are picnic facilities, playgrounds, formal gardens and natural areas.

Near the Merriman-Sharp family farmhouse, which is the main focus of the museum, is Farm Lane where the distinctive Tower Barn is located. Farm Lane displays carriages and farm implements, a General Store Complex, typical Victorian Print Shop and Doctor's Office. The General Store is packed with goods and items of the past where today's families can easily imagine what a "trip to town" must have been like.

Galleries include Heritage Hall, where exhibits reflect the history of the Jackson County area; Discovery Gallery, where the excitement of hands-on experiences relate the elements of art and science; the Exhibition and Graphic Arts Galleries which offer regularly changing art exhibits.

Each Sunday during the summer at 3 p.m. the Peter F. Hurst Planetarium, located
within the museum complex, presents programs to the public. Nearby is the Granary Restaurant with its excellent homestyle foods. The restored Ice Cream Soda Fountain offers snacks and ice cream desserts.

The newest building, the Mildred I. Hadwin Center is the main entrance to the museum complex, and contains a welcoming reception foyer and information center.

Particulars: From US-127, depart at M-50 and head west. Follow McDevitt Road west to Hinkley Boulevard and then turn north on Stonewall Road to the entrance of Sharp Park where the museum is located. Hours are 10 a.m. to 4 p.m. Tuesday through Friday and 11 a.m. to 4 p.m. on Saturday and Sunday. Admission for adults is $4, and $3 for children.

Indian Brook Farms

Artesian Wells - FREE Water, FREE wagon rides during the u-pick pumpkin season.

View 200,000 tons of pumpkins, low-cost family outings, feed the ducks and fish. This is an educational farm that features and demonstrates agriculture and aquaculture.

Kids and adults can see rainbow trout from the egg stage to large fish. Spring & Summer: Annual bedding plants, hanging baskets and gardening supplies. Company picnics, corporate campfires, parties, hayrides, fee fishing and nature walks.

Particulars: Seasonal. Open from mid-April to November.

Carnegie Library

The Library is on the National Register of Historic Places and on the State of Michigan Register of Historic Sites. With a grant from Andrew Carnegie, the building was designed and built in 1906 in the Neo-Classical Style. The inlaid terrazzo floors of the main hall, the Carrara white marble staircase, the white plaster and intricately detailed ceiling moldings that adorn both floors are beautifully maintained. The Andrew Carnegie Room features original Gold Oak woodwork and paneling six feet high, an arched ceiling with detailed plaster beams, hand-carved oak shields above the fireplace, windows and door, and a hammered copper canopy on the fireplace. Among the art works that may be seen are those of St. Gaudens, Ralph Alber Blakelock, George Innes, Leland Beaman, Adolph Behn, George Ames Aldrich, T. Echena, Luigi Scaffi.

Particulars: 244 West Michigan Avenue, Jackson, Michigan 49201, 517-788-4087

▼ Grass Lake

Michigan Whitetail Hall of Fame Museum, Grass Lake

More than 50 Boone And Crockett World record buck racks are on display with Michigan's record buck. Open seven days year round. See and feed the live deer. Call (517) 522-3354.

▼ Hanover

Lee Conklin Antique Organ Museum
(517) 563-2311

The converted school in Hanover, located south of Jackson, has 76 restored and working pump organs that wheeze and creak and produce music. Some date back to the Civil War and include parlor, cottage and church organs and melodeons. Organists gather on these days and warm-up the old machines to produce both old and new tunes. Guest enjoy the selections and occasional special events.

Particulars: From M-60, southwest of Jackson, depart south on Moscow Road and then west on Hanover where the museum is located at 105 Fairview St. The museum is open the first and third Sundays of each month from April through October from 1-5 p.m. Admission is $4 for adults, $2 for senior citizens, or there is a family rate available.

Childs Buffalo Ranch, Hanover
12770 Rountree Road
Hanover, MI 49241
517-563-8249

Take a hayride to feed and see buffalo in their natural state. The buffalo herd is the largest in southern Michigan. Visit the general store for learning information about bison. While you're there try a buffalo burger. Come to the annual Buffalo Rendezvous in May. Also visit in July for the Rodeo adventure. Pheasant hunts and buffalo hunts available to adults.

Eddy Geology Center
Waterloo Recreation Center
(734) 475-8307

Located amidst the 20,000 acres of rolling hills in Waterloo Recreation Area, the Gerald E. Eddy Geology Center, named for the former chief of the state's Geological Survey Division and is a tribute to his career in geology and education.

Often undersold, the geology of Michigan is among the most interesting in the Midwest, featuring sparkling minerals and crystals, glacial formations, fossils, and mining. Displays, hands-on exhibits and a nine-projector slide show presentation tells the story of our earth and of our state and plays an important part of the visitors experience at the center. The center also has a gift shop, classroom and exhibits on Native Americans and wildlife.

There are 30 miles of nearby hiking trails, including the Bog Trail where floating boardwalk and deck allow you to walk across a bog and closely inspect pitcher plants and other insect-chopping vegetation.

Particulars: From I-94, depart at exit 157 and head north along Pierce Road. Follow the park signs to the center. Hours are 9 a.m. to 5 p.m. Tuesday through Sunday and admission is a $4 vehicle entry permit or a $20 state park pass.

▼ Stockbridge

Waterloo Area Farm Museum
(517) 596-2254

In 1844, a young Jacob Ruehle emigrated from Germany with his mother, sister, and stepfather. They bought some rolling farmland in Jackson County and moved into a small log cabin that was located on the property. Years later, a frisky Jacob, married Catherine Archenbronn and they raised seven children and built the farm that today is preserved as the Waterloo Area Farm Museum.

There are a number of outbuildings and period buildings located on the farm that includes a one-room cabin with fireplace and authentic furnishings, a ten room farmhouse, barn workshop, bake hours which is an outdoor brick oven, mild cellar, windmill and ice house.

Particulars: From I-94, depart at exit 153 and head north on Clear Lake Road. In the hamlet of Waterloo, continue north on Waterloo-Munith to the farm museum at 9998 Waterloo Rd. The museum is open June through August and hours are 1-5 p.m. Wednesday through Sunday 1-4 p.m. Admission for adults is $3.00. Group tours are available.

▼ Tipton

Hidden Lake Gardens, Tipton

This 670 acre landscaped horticulture garden features a variety of hiking trails, a greenhouse - conservatory, and a visitor's center. 517-431-2060

▼ Concord

Mann House
(517) 524-8943

Concord is scenic and a historical village in the southwest corner of Jackson County and its crowning jewel is the Mann House. The Michigan Historical Museum is a 110-year-old Victorian-era home maintained as if the Mann sisters, Jessie and Mary Ida, had just stepped out for a moment. The table is set for dinner and upstairs seasonal clothing is laid out on the beds.

Family heirlooms and late 19th century Eastlake furniture, purchased when the home was built in 1883 by Daniel and Ella Mann, fill each room. The Manns' daughters continued to live in the home until they bequeathed to the state in 1969. Also on the grounds are a Victorian barn, large flower beds and formal herb garden.

Particulars: The home is off Michigan-60 at 205 Hanover in Concord. It is open April
through September from 10:00 a.m. to 4:00 p.m. Daily. Free.

KALAMAZOO COUNTY

VISITOR INFORMATION

Kalamazoo County Convention & Visitors Bureau

346 W. Michigan Avenue
Kalamazoo, MI 49007

269-381-4003 or 800-530-9192

www.discoverkalamazoo.com

Kalamazoo County

▼ Portage

Celery Flats Interpretive Center
(269) 329-4522

The Celery Flats Interpretive Center is not a zoo, not a nature center, but a unique facility that teaches the history of Dutch immigrants farming efforts to convert a wetlands area into one of the most productive celery growing areas in the world. From the 1890s to the 1930s, fields of green tipped celery covered Portage, Comstock and large tracts of Kalamazoo as, Afresh as dew from Kalamazoo.

The historic area, recently renovated, offers a 1856 one-room schoolhouse, 1931 grain elevator, and a great natural area perfect for bird watching or hiking. The nearby canoe rental offers visitors a low cost chance to explore the wetlands and winding Portage Creek by silently paddling and watching.

Particulars: The center is 2.5 miles south of I-94 and reached by departing at exit 76A and then heading a half mile east on South Westnedge Avenue. The center is near Cross Roads Mall at 7335 Garden Lane. Hours are noon to 5 p.m. Friday and 12 noon to 5 p.m. Sunday and 10 a.m. to 7 p.m. Saturday from May through September. Admission is $1.50 adults.

▼ Kalamazoo

Elvis in Kalamazoo

In 1988, for some reason, people all across America got the idea that The King wasn't dead, that he faked his death to get a little peace and quiet, and that he actually had spent those 11 years seducing fat waitresses and hanging out near Kalamazoo. Because we are trained journalists here at Glovebox Guidebooks, we have traveled the state looking for Elvis and are working hard trying to keep the Elvis Is Alive mania burning.

FREE

Particulars: Here are the locations, according to Vince Staten, author of "Unauthorized America" where Elvis has been sighted in Kalamazoo:
- J.C. Penney at the Crossroads Mall (probably buying some T-shirts)
- Columbia Plaza, 350 E. Michigan.
- Upjohn Pharmaceutical, 7171 Portage Rd.

He was also spotted in Vicksburg at Harding's grocery store, 120 W. Prairie, Kalamazoo.

Kal-Haven Trail
(269) 637-2788

FREE

Scenic 33.5 mile trail links Kalamazoo to South Haven. Cycling, hiking, snowmobiling, horseback riding, and cross-country skiing. Enter on 10th Street, west of Kalamazoo. Hours: 8 a.m. - 10 p.m., year-round. Free admission.

Echo Valley
8495 E. "H" Ave, Kalamazoo, MI 49004
(269) 349-3291

Tobogganing & ice skating. Eight 60 m.p.h. toboggan runs; toboggans furnished free. 43,000 sq. ft. outdoor skating rink, inner tubing hills, skate rentals, clubhouse with fireplace & snack bar. Excellent for groups and families. four miles northeast of the city.

Historic Districts

Kalamazoo County Visitors Bureau
(269) 381-4003

Many areas of Kalamazoo have historically noteworthy buildings and sites. Vine, Stuart and South Streets neighborhoods are designated historic districts and provide view of varied architectural styles, including Gothic, Italianate, Greek Revival, Sullivanesque, Queen Anne, Art Deco, and others. Home tours are occasionally offered.

Bronson Park, Haymarket and the Kalamazoo Mall areas feature examples of 19th and 20th century buildings. Frank Lloyd Wright designs can be seen in the county. Other historical attractions include the Underground Railway House in Schoolcraft, the John E. Gray Memorial Museum in Alamo Township and the State Theater in downtown Kalamazoo.

Particulars: Call the Kalamazoo County Visitors Bureau for dates and times of home
   tours or tour maps or brochures to the areas.

Kalamazoo Valley Public Museum

Kalamazoo Public Library
(269) 373-7990

General historical stuff is offered at the museum. What does the face of a 2,300-year old Egyptian woman look like? Did she have children? How did she get to Kalamazoo? Aided by the tools of science and the skills of scholars, these questions and more are answered in the Mystery of the Mummy exhibit.

Be a museum detective! Incorporate the evidence of artifacts, oral histories, written documents and images to step back in time. Using the themes of Land, Community and Work, learn how people of the past lived, worked and united. Figures literally emerge from the past to mingle together in the gallery's three-dimensional sculpture mural created by Kalamazoo artists Conrad Kaufman and Rod Homor. Come on in and stroll down a trail of history and discover for yourself! There is also a great weather display and information about Michigan's unique season.

Particulars: Located 230 N. Rose Hours are 9 a.m. to 5 p.m. Monday-Saturday, Sunday 1-5 p.m.

Kalamazoo Institute of Arts
(269) 349-7775

The significant collection at the institute includes over 200 prints, photos, and paintings in the downtown gallery.

Particulars: Two blocks west of the public museum at the corner of South and Park Street. Hours are 10 a.m. to 5 p.m. Tuesday through Saturday and 12 to 5 p.m. Sunday. Admission by donation.

Kalamazoo Nature Center
(269) 381-1574

Everywhere you look we see heating evidence that people are making a positive impact on mother Earth. In 1971, the Kalamazoo Nature Center, in an attempt to help compensate for some of the adverse effects happening to our wildlife, began it Wild Animal Care and Rehabilitation Programs, which had a goal of providing aid to injured and orphaned wildlife brought to the center. Each year 70 volunteers helped rehabilitate more than 2000 needy animals. This is just one of the many ways that the Kalamazoo Nature Center is helping educate and preserve our natural world.

The 800-acre nature center has an annual attendance of over 100,000 visitors, many of which are eager youngsters on naturalist-led outdoor education field trips. From winding trails to an ecology lab, the center has bird feeders, special programs and more than 30 specimens of wildlife on exhibit or under the care of the wildlife recovery team. Under the entrance deck are the cages where many animals are housed while they are being treated. Species include hawks, owls, bald eagles and turkey vultures.

There are also more than 40 floor-mounted display cases inside that detail a broad menu of issues including groundwater, bird mounts, ecology principals, geology, and much more.

Particulars: The center is located directly north of Kalamazoo at 7000 N. Westnedge. From US-131, head east on D Avenue and then south on Westnedge Avenue. Hours are 9 a.m. to 5 p.m. Monday through Saturday and 1-5 p.m. on Sunday. Admission is $5.50 for non-member adults, $4 for seniors, and $3.50 for children.

▼ Augusta

Kellogg Bird Sanctuary
(269) 671-2510

The Kellogg Bird Sanctuary was created in 1927 by cereal magnate W.K. Kellogg, of Frosted Flakes fame, after he visited a waterfowl refuge in Canada and wanted to duplicate it closer to home. Some years later Kellogg deeded the property to Michigan State University where they now manage the 2,000-acre tract of natural and research land.

The small 40-acre pond within the sanctuary is filled with Canada geese, black duck, pintail, mallards, trumpeter swans and many other migratory species during the spring and fall. Plagues, trails, and signs are welcome additions for visitors seeking a quality outdoor experience. But the biggest attraction for most visitors is the large pens where many injured avians are being rehabilitated.

A number of permanently injured birds including red-tailed hawk, barn owl, barred owl, Cooper's hawk, rough-legged hawk, broad-winged hawk, turkey vulture, American kestrel and a longtime resident American Bald eagle. Bring your camera for this close-up view.

Particulars: The sanctuary is halfway between Battle Creek and Kalamazoo, just east of Gull Lake. From Michigan-89 head north on 40th Street and then left on C Avenue to 12685 E. C Avenue. Watch for the green and while directional signs. Hours are 9 a.m. to 8 p.m. daily from May to October and 9 a.m. to 5 p.m. November through April. Admission is $1 for adults.

Kellogg Experimental Forest
(269) 731-4597

FREE

Kellogg Forest is actually a man-made forest. Once ravaged by poor farming and land-use techniques, W.K. Kellogg donated the scoured parcel of 280 acres to MSU in

1932. Hilly and abandoned, Kellogg wanted the state college to rehabilitate the land through tree plantings and innovative management practices.

Tree plantings have taken place every year since and today Kellogg Experimental Forest is 720 acres of towering Norway Spruce, white pine, sugar maple and hundreds of other species. There are dozens of non-native species, unique to Michigan, thriving for your pleasure.

The forest is the site of over 100 ongoing research projects and genetic experiments but it's also a recreation area that attracts 50,000 visitors annually. For the budget traveler, you can spend half-day motoring the area. Winding through the center is the "Learn Your Trees" drive, a 2.5 mile loop that takes visitors past 25 identified trees, everything from sassafras to Japanese red pine.

There's also a busy sugar bush that's operated early each spring. In fact, the March sugar bush and maple syrup programs are the most popular events of the year.

Particulars: From Michigan-89, east of Gull Lake and 10 miles west of Battle Creek,

head south on 42nd Street to the posted entrance. Hours are 8 a.m. to dark. Free.

▼ Mattawan

Michigan Fisheries Interpretive Center
Wolf Lake Fish Hatchery
(269) 668-2876

FREE

The 165-acre Wolf Lake State Fish Hatchery is for historians, naturalists, anglers, lovers of nature, biologists and families. Arguably the nation's most modern computerized and automated hatchery, the scientific facility is also action-packed and educational.

Indoors, the main tank building has many long raceway tanks used to rear millions of small fish until they are about two-inches in length. After the fry reach the correct size they are transplanted outdoors into large tanks, one offers a pedestrian walkway. The small fry often team to the surface, swirling the murky waters, creating tiny splashes for the visitors.

Aside from the modern building and pleasant landscapes, the facility has a millpond, the DNR Fisheries Lab, staff housing, and a pond with a long boardwalk overlook. In this pond are easy-to-spot steelhead, grayling, and lake sturgeon. Indoor displays offer a special opportunity to learn about stream habitats, fish anatomy and physiology, commercial fishing, fisheries management and species identification. Angling buffs will also enjoy the antique fishing tackle collection.

Particulars: From Kalamazoo head west for eight miles on Michigan-43 and follow signs to the entrance on Fish Hatchery Road. The center is open Memorial Day Through mid-November. Hours are 9 a.m. to 5 p.m. Monday through Friday; noon to 8 p.m. Sunday. Free.

Winery & Brewery Tours
Kalamazoo County Visitors Bureau
(269) 381-4003

FREE

Okay you rich BMW driving pretentious snots, here's all you need to know about tours of the increasingly improving Kalamazoo area wineries. You'll learn that the study of wine making called oenology, which sounds like a weird South Pacific sex act to me.

St. Julian Winery, 716 S. Kalamazoo, is north of I-94 on M-40 in PawPaw. Hours are 9 a.m. to 5 p.m., Monday through Saturday; noon to 5 p.m. on Sunday. Free. Call (269) 657-5568

Warner Vineyards, 706 S. Kalamazoo, is north of I-94 on M-40 in PawPaw. Hours 10 a.m. to 5 p.m., Monday through Saturday; noon to 5 p.m. on Sunday. Free. (269) 657-3165.

Peterson & Son Winery, 9375 East Park Ave., is south off of I-94 Exit 85, Galesburg. Hours are 10 a.m. to 6 p.m. Monday to Saturday; noon to 6 p.m. Sunday. Free. Call (269) 626-9755.

Kalamazoo Brewing Company is a micro-brewery at 315 Kalamazoo Avenue. Hours are 10 a.m. to 9 p.m. Monday through Saturday and 11 a.m. to 7 p.m. Sunday. Free. Call (269) 382-2338.

KALKASKA COUNTY

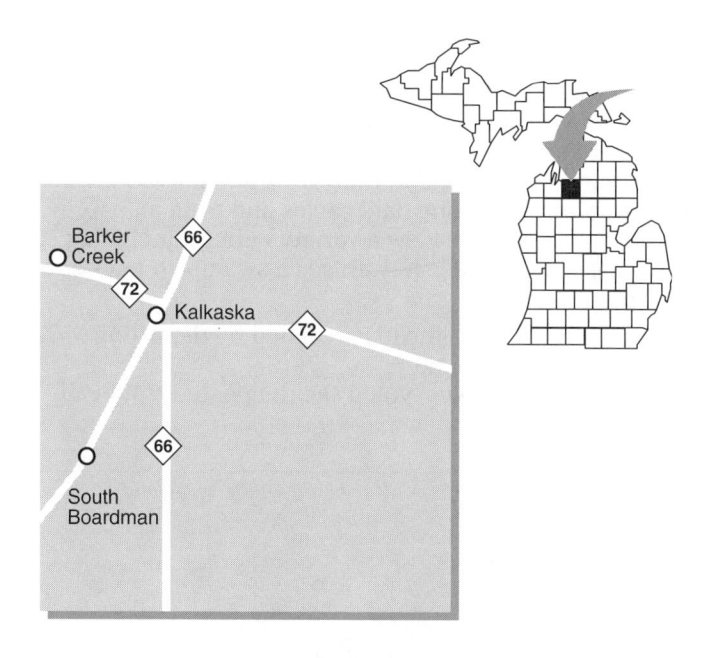

VISITOR INFORMATION

Greater Kalkaska Area Chamber of Commerce
353 Cedar Street
P. O. Box 291
Kalkaska, MI 49646
231-258-9103 or 800-487-6880
www.kalkaskami.com

Kalkaska County

▼ Rapid City

Skegemog Swamp
DNR Kalkaska Office
(231) 258-9471

FREE

One of the most scenic swamps in Michigan, and one of the driest trails too, it is located in the Skegemog Lake Wildlife Area, a preserve of 1,300 acres in the northwest corner of the county. From a parking lot, it's an easy one-mile walk through the woods to the edge of the swamp where a boardwalk lets you cross to an observation tower. From the top of the tower you can view the lake and in the spring and fall often view a variety of birds, including bald eagles and even an osprey.

In the summer, you'll view a variety of bugs, including some world-class mosquitoes. Hey, this is a swamp so pack some bug dope.

Particulars: The trailhead is reached by departing M-72 onto CR-597 toward Rapid

City. Within four miles, you'll see the posted trailhead. Free.

Skegomog Swamp Wildlife Area, Kalkaska County.

KENT COUNTY

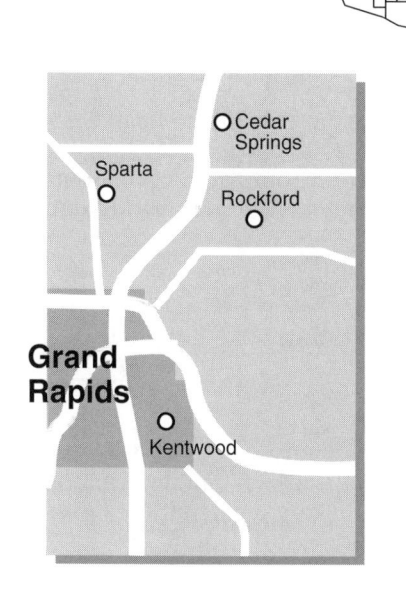

VISITOR INFORMATION

Grand Rapids - Kent County Convention & Visitors Bureau
140 Monroe Center St. N.W.
Grand Rapids, MI 49503
616-459-8287 or 800-678-9859
www.visitgrandrapids.org

Kent County

▼ Ada
Amway Tour
(616) 787-6701
FREE

Amway makes all kinds of products including cleaners, personal care items, and lots more using a unique sales and marketing network that takes its product to homes worldwide. A free one-hour tour features a look at the research lab, development area, and the corporate museum. Amway is a $3 billion per year business where among its ten pillars of economic wisdom is chiseled, "Let's just charge."

Particulars: From I-96, depart at exit 39 and head east on Fulton Street. The
corporation is at 7575 E. Fulton. Tours are on the hour from 8:30 a.m. to 5 p.m. Monday through Friday. There are not tours at noon. Free.

▼ Frennville
Fren Valley Vineyards – Free tasting
6130 122nd Ave.
Fennville, MI 49408
(269) 561-2396, (800) 432-6265
FREE

They offer free samples of distinctive wines that have garnered more than 300 regional, national and international awards since 1973. Video winemaking presentation and a picnic facility including gas grill.

▼ Grand Rapids
Blanford Nature Center
(616) 453-6192
FREE

Along with the historic buildings (blacksmith shop, log cabins, one-room schoolhouse, indoor live animal exhibits) located on the 143-acre nature center, the budget-minded travelers can observe wildlife that are under the care of the staff in the wildlife rehabilitation area behind the interpretive center. There are often a number of rapers, deer, and songbirds housed in the small area.

Particulars: From US-131, depart at exit 87 and head west on Leonard Street. Follow the signs to the nature center located at 1715 Hillbum NW. Hours are 9 a.m. to 5 p.m. Monday through Friday; Sat. and Sun. 1-5 p.m. Free.

Frederick Meijer's Sculpture Garden
This 125-acre attraction features the most comprehensive outdoor sculpture collection in the Midwest. It includes the monumental Leonardo da Vinci's Horse; largest tropical conservatory in the state; nature trails; and a farm garden. Its five-acre children's garden opened in 2004. Admission charged.

Particulars: 1000 East Beltline Ave. NE, Grand Rapids, MI 49525, (616) 957-1580,
(888) 957-1580.

Higher Ground Rock Climbing Center
Offering the finest in vertical entertainment, Higher Ground offers a 23-foot high artificial rock-climbing wall and a special bouldering room for your "above it all" experience.

Particulars: 851 Bond Ave. NW, Grand Rapids, MI 49503, call (616) 774-3100.

Meyer May House **FREE**
This 1908 masterpiece of the prairie-style design is one of the most complete restorations of a Frank Lloyd Wright house in existence. Admission free. Call 616-246-4821 for hours.

Particulars: 450 Madison Ave. S, Grand Rapids, MI 49503, Call (616) 246-4821

Jersey Junction Ice Cream Parlor
Jersey Junction celebrates 40 years as a favorite spot for ice cream treats. Recently restored, it offers ice cream, candy and sandwiches. Open everyday. Call for hours. Closed January and February.

Particulars: 652 Croswell Ave. SE, East Grand Rapids, MI 49506. Call (616) 458-4107.

Fish Ladder **FREE**
Grand Rapids Department of Parks
(616) 456-3696
In the 1960s the state began a massive program of rearing and stocking the Great Lakes with salmon and each year these spawning game fish attempt to spawn up the Grand River. But they couldn't get past the Sixth Street Dam until a ladder was built. The fish ladder was designed by local artist Joseph Kinnebrew and today it's a delightful stop along the city's River Walk.

Each fall, about early September through late October,

thousands of people visit the observation area to watch the single-mined salmon leap from step to step on their way upstream. The salmon jump completely out of the water as they climb the steps. Nearby anglers will crowd the area for the entire month of September trying to tempt the fish to their lure. The oft tangled lines of the shoulder-to-shoulder fishermen makes for a comical sight in itself.

Particulars: From US-131 depart at exit 85B, head east on Pearl Street and immediately turn north on Front Street. The ladder is at 606 Front. Free.

Gerald R. Ford Museum
(616) 254-0400

Shame on you for not knowing more about Jerry Ford. A fellow Michigander, and president, most of us have not taken the time to learn about or visit the Ford Museum. Well over 100,000 history buffs visit annually, but only a fraction are from Michigan. That's too bad. The museum is an interesting destination for budget travelers.

Opened in 1981, in pomp-filled ceremonies attended by Ford, then-President Reagan, and many other dignitaries, the two-story, triangular-shaped building features a 300-foot east wall of glass that reflects a stunning panorama of the nearby Grand River and bustling downtown Grand Rapids.

On the first floor, strategically located just beyond the admission counter and next to the elevator, is the auditorium where the award-winning film, "Gerald R. Ford: The Presidency Restored" film is shown every hour. The film will refresh your memory of those difficult years and set the stage for the rest of your visit.

Exhibits chronicle pre-White House days, Ford's childhood, his famous football career, and his first political campaign; the 1948 run for Congress. The museum also has a full-scale Oval Office, an exact replica in stark contrast to Ford's first office. The elaborate display of state gifts to the president give visitors a sense of the power and importance of Michigan's own president.

Particulars: From US-131, depart at exit 85B and head east on Pearl Street. The museum is at 303 Pearl and can be seen from the highway. Hours are 9 a.m. to 5 p.m. daily. Admission is $5 for adults, $4 for seniors, 15 years and under are free.

Grand Rapids Art Museum
(616) 831-1000.

Although it's a museum, the popular facility doesn't dwell on art of the past, they're too busy celebrating current arts and artists from Michigan and around the world. Their mission is to bring art to the people, actively providing the entire community with a vast spectrum of artistic viewpoints in painting, photography, sculpture, master prints, furniture, decorative arts, and terrific children's arts.

Particulars: From US-131, depart at exit 85B and head east on Pearl Street. Turn north on Ionia to the museum on the corner of Ionia and Lyon. The entrance is on Lyon. Hours are a bit complex, so call ahead. The museum is closed on Monday and major holidays. Admission for adults is $6.

John Ball Zoo
(616) 336-4301

In 1884, John Ball gave a 40-acre site to the city of Grand Rapids for recreational use. Reluctantly it was accepted by the city fathers in spite of being "too far out" of town. The zoo began with a pair of "bunnies" in 1891, but it didn't take long for the bunnies to make their own zoo, while other animals were added more slowly.

Today, the facility extends over a rolling 14-acre area, a far cry from the humble beginnings when many zoos of 1800s were little more than an animal curiosity shop. The John Ball Zoo is a delightful facility where the family can easily spend a half-day wandering, learning exploring all the exhibits, reading each sign, and examining up-close hundreds of animals.

The zoo is a bit difficult to navigate, I found myself walking in circles. Within a short time, after actually looking at the provided map, I was again oriented and rearing to go. Natural exhibits that teach visitors about man's role in nature is the primary function here.

Exhibits include snow leopards, big horned sheep, river otters, camels, foxes penguins, Nocturnal Exhibit, South American Exhibit, Siberian tigers, Monday Island, spider monkeys, children's petting area and dozens of others. Have a great day at this fine zoo, but remember, don't slip on the goat doots.

Particulars: From I-96, depart at exit 75 and head east on Fulton. The zoo is on the corner of Fulton and Valley Road. Open daily from 10 a.m. to 6 p.m. from mid-May to mid-September and 10 a.m. to 4 p.m. in the winter. Admission is $4 for adults and $2.50 for seniors and children.

Grand Rapids Public Museum
(616) 456-3977

The new museum Grand Rapids is building will no doubt

live up to the name of the river it overlooks. Perched on the bands of the Grand River, the Riverfront Museum is a $35 million project that, completed in the mid-1990s, will have 135,000 square feet of exhibits ranging from a two-story high Gaslight Village and a historic carousel that children will be able to ride to a 2,000-pipe Wurlitzer organ performing in its own riverside pavilion.

Just grand. But why wait?

The existing Public Museum of Grand Rapids is pretty good to begin with and very affordable as hundreds of families will find out when looking fro something to do. What began as a collection of odds and ends in a small room in 1845, today is what its staff claims to be Michigan's oldest and "largest general museum" with more than 300,00 artifacts on display. The heart of the Public Museum is its furniture collection, one of the top three in the country with more than 2,000 pieces from the early 1800s to the 1930 of which 150 are on display in period rooms on the second floor.

What children will delight in, however, are not sofas and dressers but lions and tigers. The Mammal Hall has a series of huge dioramas that depict life-size animals in their natural setting. There's a scene of Indians dressed in coyote skins sneaking up on a group of buffalo, a mountain lion with her cubs in the mountains and a pack of wolves sneaking up on their prey.

There's also the People of the Grand exhibition, a hall that begins with a small hunting party of Paleo-Indians stalking a mastodon and continues through history of the river. You wind past the Indian burial sites along the Grand being built, the arrival of French trappers and end in a one-room log schoolhouse.

There's a Gaslight Village where you wander down cobblestone streets past the fire station, dentist's office and 14 other shops of Grand Rapids in the 1890s.

Particulars: From US-131, depart at the Pearl Street exit, head east and follow signs. The museum is just north of Pear Street at 54 Jefferson Street. Hours are 9 a.m. to 5 p.m. Tuesday through Saturday. Admission is $7 per adult, $2.50 for children, and $6.50 for seniors.

Heritage Hill Walking Tour
Grand Rapids Visitors Bureau
(616) 459-8950

Heritage Hill is a long, narrow rectangle of historic homes only steps from the
  downtown area. Within the area are more than 60

architectural styles while 38 homes are detailed in a walking brochure that also provides a map to some really impressive exterior designs. There are two tours, the North Tour passes by 20 significant homes and takes about one and one-half hours, while the South Tour takes about one hour.

Two of the more noted homes are a Prairie Style design by Frank Lloyd Wright is located at 450 Madison Ave. SE. while a smaller Wright design can be seen at 226 Prospect north of Lyon.

Particulars: Near the public museum, the North Tour begins at Fulton and Prospect. The South Tour begins at College and Cherry. You can pick up the brochure at the Grand Rapids Visitor Bureau at 245 Monroe N.W. Free.

Voigt House
(616) 456-4600

The one home you can enter in the Heritage Hill Historical District is the Voigt House, donated to the city in 1974 and today maintained by the Grand Rapids Public Museum. Built in 1896, the home today reflects every facet of day-to-day life in the late 19th century. Every room is furnished and open to visitors, who will see the beautifully carved woodwork, inlaid parquet floors and stained glass windows as stunning as the collection of furnishings.

Particulars: From I-96, take the College exit south. Voigt House is the second one on College Avenue south of Washington Street. Tours are held every Tuesday from 11 a.m. to 3 p.m. as well as the second and fourth Sunday of the month from 1-3 p.m. Admission is $3 for adults and $2 for students and seniors.

▼ Rockford

Rosie's Diner
(616) 696-FOOD

There's only a handful of diners left in Michigan where you can squeeze in the door, wince at gleaming stainless steel, and spin on a counter seat while a gum-snapping waitress serves up the best in road food.

Named after the Bounty paper towel commercial's famed waitress, owner Jerry Berta rescued the diner which he discovered in New Jersey, still using classic thick coffee mugs and pleasing menu boards.

Particulars: The diner is five miles north of Rockford, and a half-mile east of US-131 on M-57. Hours are 5:30 a.m. to 9 p.m. daily. Water is free.

Corner Bar
(616) 866-9866

Welcome to the Hot Dog Hall of Fame, where hungry patrons sometimes try to break the record of 43 hot dogs eaten in an hour. Others try to eat 12 hot dogs in an hour and win a t-shirt. It's a challenge, if you can stomach it.

From the outside, the Corner Bar looks like your average neighborhood tavern. But inside the walls are covered with more than 5,000 brass name -plates, sports memorabilia, wacky newspaper clippings, and all types of hot dog history. Most of all there's brass name plates, more than 5,000 inscribed, honoring those who could consume 12 hot dogs in an hour.

The Hall of Fame began after a few members of the Detroit Lions football team challenged each other to an eating contest of an even dozen dogs. Who holds the record of 42.5 hot dogs? A huge lineman from the Lions? A brawny construction worker? A circus fat man? Nope, a 5-foot-3 and 110-pound area resident named Sharon Scholten, who had the crowd on their feet as she ate half of the 43rd frank.

Wow!

Particulars: Downtown Rockford is reached from US-131 by departing at exit 97 and following 10 Mile Road east. The Corner Bar in on the corner of Northland and Main Street. Hours are 10 a.m. to midnight Monday through Wednesday, 10 a.m. to 2 a.m. Thursday through Saturday and noon to 8 p.m. Sunday. Hot dogs begin at 85 cents apiece.

KEWEENAW COUNTY

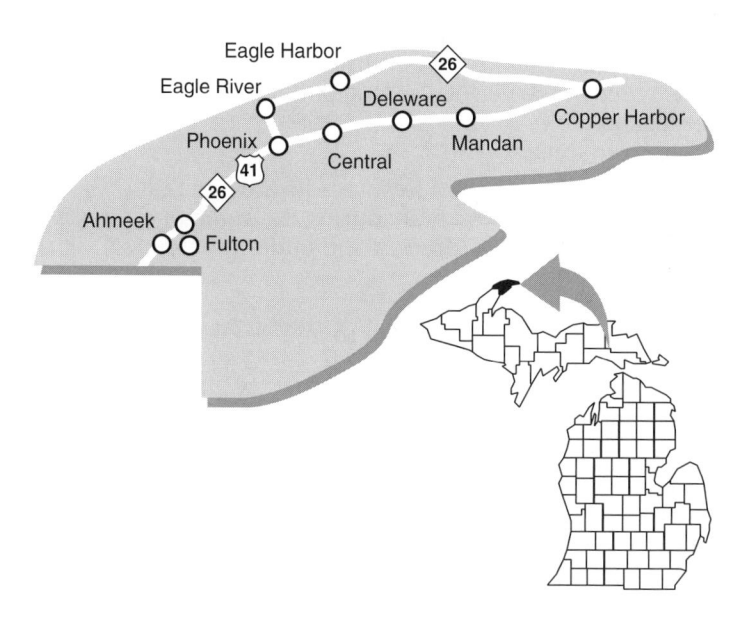

VISITOR INFORMATION

Keweenaw Tourism Council
326 Sheldon Ave.
Houghton, MI 49931
906-337-4579

www.keweenaw.info

Keweenaw County

▼ Copper Harbor

Astor House Museum
Minnetonka Resort
(906) 289-4449

Located at the Minnetonka Resort is one of the Midwest's largest collection of antique bisque and china dolls, old toys and Native American artifacts. Other collections on display include relics of the copper mining boom days, rock and minerals and Civil
War memorabilia.

Particulars: Minnetonka Resort is located just off US-41. Hours are 9 a.m. to 6 p.m. daily during the summer. Admission is $2 for adults while children 12 and under are free.

Delaware Copper Mine

US-41. 289-4688. Open mid-May to mid-Oct. May, June, Sept. & Oct.: 10 am to 5 pm; July & Aug.: 10 am to 6 pm. Adults $8.50, children 6 - 12 $4.50, 5 & under free. Antique engine display, indoor & outdoor train displays & mining equipment displays. Pet deer, pet skunk & baby goats. Not so cheap, sorry.

Keweenaw National Historic Park

US-41. 289-4688. Open mid-May to mid-Oct. May, June, Sept. & Oct.: 10 am to 5 pm; July & Aug.: 10 am to 6 pm. Adults $8.50; children 6 – 12, $4.50; five years and under free. Antique engine display, indoor & outdoor train displays & mining equipment displays. Pet deer, pet skunk & baby goats.

Keweenaw Water Falls:

FREE

EAGLE RIVER FALLS - Eagle River. At the bridge on M-26 in Eagle River.

SILVER RIVER FALLS - Silver River. 4.5 mi. east of Eagle Harbor along M-26.

MANGANESE FALLS - Manganese Creek. Turn right (south) immediately past the Copper Harbor Community Building on the Lake Manganese Rd and go approx .7 mi. The falls are about 100' from the road, on the left.

HUNGARIAN FALLS - Hungarian Creek. In Tamarack City, turn north off of M-26 on 6th St (the sign says Calumet Golf Course) & go 2 blocks to a fork. Take the left fork & drive uphill to the 2nd trail road on the left. Turn left & go .2 mi. to a fork. The right fork goes to the upper falls, the left fork to the lower falls

COPPER FALLS - Owl Creek. From Eagle Harbor take the cut-off road to US-41 about 3 mi to Owl Creek. Cross Owl Creek & take the second trail to the left ½ mi. to its end. Falls are about 30' directly ahead. These falls are best viewed during spring run-off.

UPPER & LOWER FALLS OF THE GRATIOT RIVER - Take the 5 Mile Point Road north from Ahmeek 2.3 mi. to the Farmers Block Rd. Turn left and go straight, a little over 1 mile, to a trail road. Continue on this trail road approx ½ mi to a gate. Park here & follow the path to the left to the Upper Falls. The Lower Falls, more a series of rapids downstream, is much harder to access as there is no formal trail.

JACOB'S FALLS - Jacob's Creek, 3 miles NorthEast of Eagle River on M-26.

UNNAMED FALLS - Silver Creek. Take the 5 Mile Point Rd west from Eagle River 1.7 miles to Silver Creek. Following the creek, the falls are approx. ¼ mi. upstream.

UPPER & LOWER FALLS OF THE MONTREAL RIVER - On the Bete Grise Road go east from Lac La Belle approx 2.8 mi to a trail road on the left. Take the right fork of this trail to Smith Fisheries. (This is a 4-wheel drive road.) A walk of approx 2 miles, one way, is then necessary.

HAVEN FALLS — Haven Creek. From US-41, just beyond Delaware, take the Lac La Belle Rd. south approx 4.5 mi.. Turn right at the fork at the bottom of the hill and go about ½ mi. to Haven Park on the right.

REDRIDGE DAM - Salmon Trout River. From M-26 in Houghton take the Houghton Canal Road approx 4.8 mi. to the road marked Redridge. Drive west 5.8 mi. to the dam, on the left.

RIPLEY FALLS - Ripley Creek. From Hancock take M-26 east to Ripley. Park behind the old Ripley School and follow the trail to the falls. These falls are best viewed during spring run-off.

WYANDOTTE FALLS - Misery River. 1.5 miles southwest of the Twin Lakes State Park, turn west off of M-26 onto the Wyandotte Hills Golf Course Road to a parking area .8 mi. down on the left. The falls are about 250 yards from this parking area.

Fort Wilkins
(906) 289-4215

Located on the rugged and scenic shore of Lake Superior, nearly 600 miles northwest of Detroit, Fort Wilkins was built to keep the peace in Michigan's lively Copper County. Things were rowdy and rampageous at the beginning of America's copper rush in the late 1940s. The government, as wise then as now, thought there was going to be major friction and fights between the Native Americans and the newcomers who were seeking their fortunes. Happily they were wrong and the fort closed two years later, the first cold war that ended peacefully.

The small fort was a typical 19th-century garrison, and one of the most northern in the county's history. What you'll find at the fort today is eleven historic buildings surrounded by a wooden stockade where visitors can explore the daily routine of military service, experience of soldier's families, the hardships of frontier isolation and discover the lifestyles of another era. From bakery, hospital, and company quarters to mess kitchen, a bookstore, and theater area, visitors will be immersed in living history of the fledgling era.

Particulars: The forest is located in Fort Wilkins State Park at the end of US-41. The park is open year-round but the fort is staffed only from May to mid-October. Hours are 8 a.m. to duck daily. Admission into the state park is $4 daily vehicle permit or a $20 state park pass.

Scenic Drives

Keweenaw Tourism Council
(906) 482-5240

FREE

Keweenaw County is the smallest, but most agree, the most scenic county in the U.P. You'll get a real buzz in your shorts as you explore any number of byways that traverse shorelines and forests, ridges, rocky coasts, and the sparkling cold waters of Lake Superior. It doesn't get any prettier than this, cheap and free fans!

Brockway Mountain Drive: A thousand feet above Lake Superior, the spectacular Brockway Drive, built by Depression-era laborer, is the highest above-sea-level scenic drive between the Rockies and the eastern Alleghenies. The 10-mile drive offers a riveting view of the rocky shoreline and islands below, while you are actually driving in an Alpine habitat surrounded by mountain-like flora. Plan at least an hour to drive and stop along the stretch. The million dollar sunset can be viewed from just about anywhere along the drive.

Sand Dune Drive: Less traveled but almost as scenic in its own ways is Sand Dune

Drive between Eagle River and Eagle Harbor. From Eagle River this portion of M-26 heads westward skirting the frothing Lake Superior shoreline, climbing above the water along sandy bluffs. The narrow road offers broad vistas, views of the Great Lakes on the horizon and the sandy, cold beach below. The best turnoff is to Great Sand Bay. The road returns to the lake level at Cat Harbor, a wonderful beach for sunning, family outings and fast dips in the cold waters of Superior.

The road then swings through Eagle Harbor and heads eastward, passing the junction of Brockway Mountain Drive, before being drawn, like a magnet, back to Lake Superior. Here the Great Lake shoreline is reddish and carved into unusual rock formations caused by the pounding surf for more than 10,000 years. Stop at Devil's Wash Tub, a large etched-out depression in the shoreline that echoes the waves that crash upon the sandstone.

Eagle Harbor Lightstation
(906) 289-4990

The Keweenaw County Historical Society is located in the Eagle Harbor Lightstation. The harbor was a crucial port for miners in the mid to late 1800s as men and supplies were unloaded here and replaced with copper ore and lumber. The lighthouse was built in 1871 and consigned to the historical society in 1981 after the U.S. Coast Guard automated. Inside the first floor has been restored and furnished as a 19th century lightkeeper's home. But it's the red lighthouse perched above the picturesque harbor that draws most people here. On clear afternoons, photographers have a field day shooting the historical structure.

Particulars: The lighthouse is in Eagle Harbor, just off M-26. Museum grounds are open daily, the light keeper's quarters is opened on the weekends May through
October. Admission is $3 for adults.

LAKE COUNTY

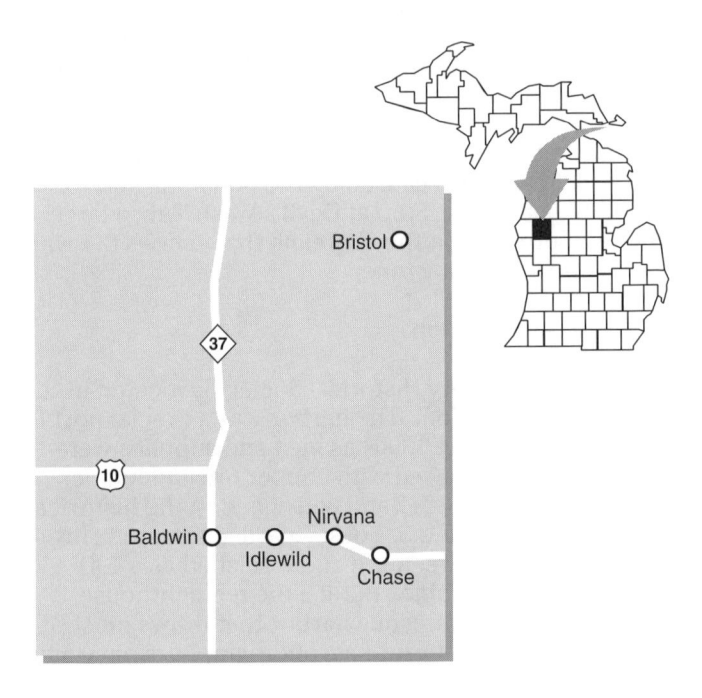

VISITOR INFORMATION

**Lake County
Chamber of Commerce & Tourist Center**
911 Michigan Avenue
P.O. Box 130
Baldwin, MI 49304
231-745-4331 or 800-245-3240
www.lakecountymichigan.com

Lake County

▼ Baldwin

Shrine of the Pines
(231) 745-7892

This historical log-hunting lodge is a unique museum situated on a high bank overlooking the Pere Marquette River, the designated national and scenic river. The shrine is dedicated to the great white pine lumbering days of Lake and Newaygo counties in the mid-1800s and guided tours take you pass the world's only collection of white pine handcrafted furniture (or so they say, how are we suppose to verify something like that!!).

The furniture is made from the pine stumps and roots left by the lumberjacks, which include a 700-pound stump table and a pine-root rocking chair. Surrounding the shrine is a 30-acre sanctuary with nature trails winding through the wooded area.

The North County Trail, Lake County.

Particulars: Located on M-37 two miles south of Baldwin on the banks of the Pere Marquette. Tours are offered from 10 a.m. to 6 p.m. daily May through October.

Admission is $3.50 for adults.

LAPEER COUNTY

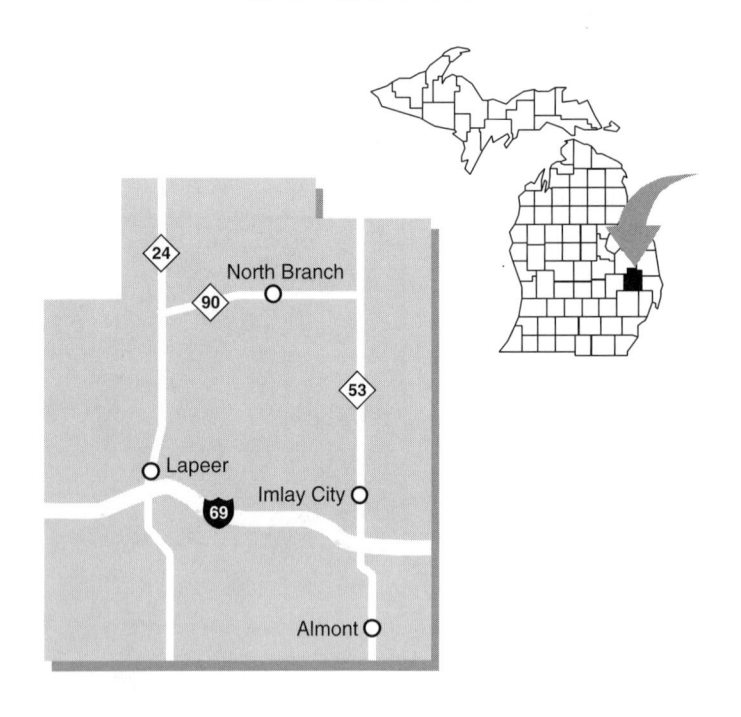

VISITOR INFORMATION

**Lapeer Area
Chamber of Commerce**
N. 431 Court Street
Lapeer, MI 48446
810-664-6641
www.lapeerareachamber.org

Lapeer County

Lapeer County Courthouse
(810) 664-4196

Settlers began arriving in Lapeer, a town of about 7,000 and the county seat in 1828 and borrowed their village name from "la pieree," the French translation of the Indian name for Flint River, which flows nearby. Lapeer became the county seat in 1831, and eight years later the county courthouse was built in the town common.

Lapeer is still bustling and the hub of government and the Lapeer County Courthouse still stands shaded by towering trees and viewed by thousands annually. It's a really an impressive building, featuring a Greek Revival style with four fluted Doric Columns and a large porch. It's topped by a three-tiered tower and a Roman dome and is noted as the Aoldest courthouse still being used in Michigan today, even though the county has long since built a newer, all-brick building across the street. The elder courthouse keeps its title because every summer the good judge, the jury, and a bunch of history buffs take-up court in the old building for a few days.

On the first floor of the aging courthouse is a well-organized museum operated by the Lapeer Historical Society that chronicles the county history and maintains a number of exhibits.

Particulars: The courthouse is located in the heart of Lapeer at Court and Nepessing Street. It's open from early June to mid-November from 1-5 p.m. Tuesday through Friday. A small admission fee is charged.

LEELANAU COUNTY

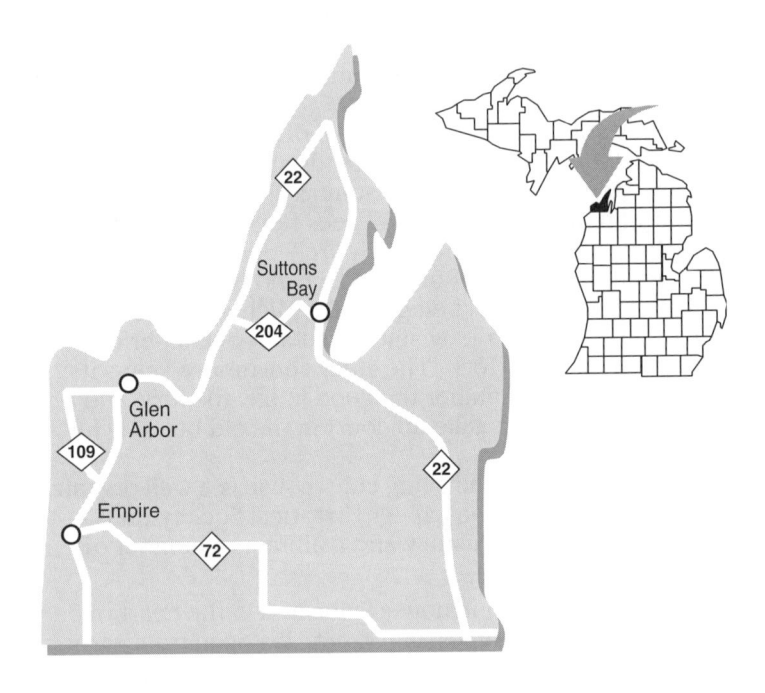

VISITOR INFORMATION

**Traverse City
Convention & Visitors Bureau**
101 W. Grandview Parkway
Traverse City, MI 49684
231-947-1120 or 800-940-1120
www.mytraversecity.com

Leelanau County

Wineries in Leelanau County

Bel Lago Vineyards and Winery
6530 South Lake Shore Drive, • Cedar, MI 49621
231-228-4800

Black Star Farms
10844 E. Revold Rd. • Suttons Bay, MI 49682
231-271-4882 (Winery)/ 231-271-4884 (Tasting Room) • Fax: 231-271-4883

Boskydel Vineyard
7501 E. Otto Rd • Lake Leelanau, MI 49653
231-256-7272

Good Harbor Vineyards
44 S. Manitou Tr • Lake Leelanau, MI 49653
231-256-7165

L. Mawby Vineyards
4519 S. Elm Valley Rd • Suttons Bay, MI 49682
231-271-3522

Shady Lane Cellars
9580 Shady Lane, • Suttons Bay, MI 49682
231-947-8865

▼ Empire

**Empire Museum
(231) 326-5181**

So, you've been racing about northwest Michigan, climbing a couple of sand dunes, hitting the beach, shopping and sightseeing, and you're ready for a break. There's this great little saloon you can stop at just down the road in Empire.

It has a terrific polished wooden bar, a honky-tonk piano in the corner and a smiling bartender, who doesn't talk your ear off. In fact, he doesn't say a word. From the tin ceiling to the glass cabinets, this is a colorful place to water-down that thirst. The only problem is they won't serve you a beer or even a glass of water. That's because the bartender is a mannequin and this saloon has been dry since the Empire Museum opened in its new location in 1987.

In scenic Empire, the history they preserved best is how the town drank its beer in the 19th century. The museum has its start in 1972 when the Empire Heritage Group formed to display historical pictures in the town's Masonic Temple. But the Roen Saloon dates back to 1892 when Andrew Roen opened his doors and poured the first mug of beer. It quickly became the community's beloved watering hole until closing up in the mid-1300s.

Roen had five children and when the last two sons died in 1986 and the family estate was auctioned off, the local historical group purchased the dismantled saloon. With lots of help they restored the saloon as the focus of the museum. Today the Empire Museum features more than just shot glasses and beer taps. In the basement, the focus in on transportation and you'll find a 1898 firehouse cart and a horse-drawn mail cart among other items. There's also a 19th century parlor and kitchen on the main floor while outside you wander through a furnished one-room schoolhouse and carriage barn.

But the most popular and charming aspect of this museum is where locals used to tip their glass. The humble saloon was re-constructed in the front section of the building and no detail was overlooked. The bar itself is complete with a polished foot rail and several spittoons placed within an easy shot of any drinker. The exhibit is complete with original two-tiered tables and chairs, a tobacco cabinet with tins of cut plugs, a Packer's one-cent gum dispenser on the wall and potbelly stove to keep patrons warm during the winter.

Particulars: The saloon is located just off M-22 in Empire and open daily from 8 a.m. to 10 p.m. during from Memorial Day to Labor day and then on the weekends during fall colors. Admission is by donations.

Sleeping Bear Dunes Visitor Center
(231) 326-5134

FREE

This unusual center for the National Park Service with its 50-foot high tower is a conspicuous landmark that visitors can home in on from miles around and then upon reaching it, come inside for displays and information about the Sleeping Bear Dunes National Lakeshore. Various historical buildings influence the design of the center, including early pioneer fort, forest fire lookouts and even an old school in Empire Today locals refer to it as Fort Empire.

Inside there's more than just restrooms. There are exhibits on how glaciers carved the Lake Michigan shoreline, the ecology of sand dunes, a look at the U.S. Lifesaving Service and the wildlife and hiking opportunities in the park. In the middle of the exhibit room is the lens from the North Manitou Shoal Light while nearby is a small theater that shows the usual National Park type video presentations.

Particulars: The center is in Empire on the corner of M-22 and M-72. Hours are 9 a.m. to 4 p.m. daily. During the summer the hours are 9 a.m. to 5 p.m. daily. Free.

Pierce Stocking Scenic Drive
(231) 326-5134

FREE

Pierce Stocking has already built many logging trails in this difficult terrain when he hatched the idea of a road that would wind along the top of the high dunes. His work began in the early 1960s and a mere seven years later the rambling road, then known as Sleeping Bear Dune Park, opened to the public.

He operated the byway, asking $2 per car, until his death in 1976. Only a year later the National Park Service obtained and renamed the road to honor Pierce Stocking. With a speed limit of only15 mph, this 7.4-mile loop, is mile-for-mile the most breathtaking route in the Great Lakes. The beauty of the dunes, placid Lake Michigan and surrounding forestland are unbeatable for the budget traveler.

The entrance is three miles north of Empire where you can pick up an interpretive brochure at a contact station. There are 12 numbered stops along the one-way road where drivers can safely pull over to read the related material. Stops allow you to examine the attractions, from a covered bridge that was once partly eaten by porcupines to a ridge that is appropriately named "Alligator Hill" and the intriguing aspects of dune ecology.

The most impressive stops are the high vistas along Lake Michigan. Stop No. 3 is "The Dune Overlook" from which you can see the green Manitou Islands on the distant horizon, Glen Lake to the east and dunes all around.

Particulars: From the Sleeping Bear Visitor Center in Empire, head northeast on M-22 and turn north onto M-109 where the entrance is posted. The road is closed in mid-November and by December becomes a favorite route for cross-country skiers. It's opened to vehicles in April. Free.

▼ Glen Arbor

Dune Climb
(231) 326-5134

FREE

This is it! The most famous dune in the

Midwest, the Dune Climb in the Sleeping Bear Dunes National Lakeshore. Every summer thousands upon thousands arrive here from across the country to do nothing more than kick off their shoes, struggle up the towering dune and then run wildly back down. Kids love to roll down, but you'll spend the next two weeks washing sand out of their hair.

Also located here are picnic tables, a small concession store and the trailhead to the Dunes Hiking Trail. Anybody can climb the dune but be forewarned it's a good four-mile trek to Lake Michigan and back that is not recommended for children under the age of seven.

Particulars: From the park visitor center in Empire head north on M-22 and then veer left onto M-109 to reach the Dune Climb in six miles. Free.

Sleeping Bear Coast Guard Station Museum **FREE**
(231) 326-5134

Pea soup fog, sudden and violent storms, and shallow shoals sank more than 80 vessels off the Sleeping Bear Dunes, the vast majority lumber ships that strayed too close to shore. So in 1901 the station was built by the United States Lifesaving Service, the forerunner to the U.S. Coast Guard.

An identical station was built across, the Manitou Passage on South Manitou Island because the channel, the favored shipping route between Chicago and the Straits of Mackinaw, was truly treacherous water.

When an accident occurred the six man crew from the station rushed to the rescue, but, amazingly, not in a lifeboat. Because most of the accidents were within range, the men pulled out a beach cart that hauled ropes, buoys, and a small cannon known as a "Lyle gun." The rescuers used the cannon to launch a light rope out to the stranded sailors which in turn was used to pull out successively heavier lines. The lengths of rope were anchored into the sand and the rescue crew rigged up the breeches buoy, a pair of canvas pants sewed into a life ring. They then could retrieve victims one-by-one without endangering themselves in the violent waters.

Helicopters, radios, and other technological tools eventually eliminated life-saving stations, but the excitement and romance remains alive at the museum. You'll see where the rescue crew lived, a Spartan lifestyle for sure, equipment used in their rescue efforts, maritime displays, artifacts, boat house, and surfboats.

Particulars: From the National Park Visitor Center in Empire, head northeast on M-22 for 2 miles and then north on

M-109 for five miles to Glen Haven. Turn west onto M-209 where the museum is posted. The complex is open from mid-May to mid-October. Hours are 10 a.m. to 5 p.m. daily in July and August but are reduced the rest of the time. Free.

▼ Leland

Fishtown
Leelanau Chamber of Commerce
(231) 271-9895

FREE

It still smells a little fishy, and that's good. Only slightly spoiled by the crush of tourism, the Fishtown area is a picturesque group of weathered old fishermen shanties that stand at attention along the dock. A small waterfall and dam, quaint shopping and commercial fishing makes this an interesting destination for budget-minded travelers.

Leelanau Historical Museum
(231) 256-7475

A delightful county museum that is small but well done. Exhibits trace the local history including cherry farming and shipwrecks of the Manitou Passage while also catering to special exhibits every summer.

Particulars: From M-22 in Leland, turn east on Cedar Street where the museum and library are located at 203 E. Cedar. The museum is open 10 a.m. to 4 p.m. Friday- Saturday during the winter and 10 a.m. to 4 p.m. Monday through Saturday and 1-4 p.m. Sunday from June to September. Admission is $2 for adults and $5 for a family.

Northport
Grand Traverse Lighthouse
(231) 386-7195

One of the most scenic spots in already very scenic peninsula can only be reached if you leave M-22, pass up more shops and cafes in the last town, Northport, and continue north along winding County Road 629. At the end of the pavement are the picnic grounds of Leelanau State Park, a rocky shoreline sprinkled with Petoskey stones, a watery view in almost every direction.

But the best reason to visit the park is to take in the light. In a state blessed with dozens of lighthouses and thus lighthouse museums. Actually there are two at the tip. The first was called Cat's Head Light and was ordered to be built by President Millard Fillmore in 1950, making it one of the first lighthouses on the Great Lakes. This light didn't last long.

The adjoining light keeper's house burnt down, the tower, threatened by erosion, was torn down and only the foundation, fenced off in the park's campground, remains.

Grand Traverse Lighthouse soon followed. Built in 1858, the structure featured a roof top tower and cupola sheathed in copper and was constructed on higher ground in a more secure spot at the tip. It survived and today its rooms are filled with the history and tales of schooners and steamships surviving one of the most wicked channels in the Great Lakes, the Manitou Passage just off shore.

The kitchen and several other rooms have been refurbished as a turn-of-the-century light keeper's home while other rooms display model ships or artifacts from area wrecks. But the most intriguing corner of the museum is devoted to tip's footnote in history. Its light was the only one on the Great Lakes to be attacked by pirates. Deputy U.S. Marshall Philo Beers was the first lightkeeper here when in 1852 "King" James Jesse Strang, who ruled the Mormon colony on Beaver Island 25 miles away, ordered his subjects to raid the remote facility. They did and in the unexpected sea attack, Beers lost provisions, fish nets and other equipment. But he managed to hang onto the most important thing in any lighthouse at the time; the imported Frensel Lens.

History aside, the real reason travelers find their way to the lighthouse at the tip is for the view. The tower is a short climb up and a tight squeeze through the trap door but once on top, the view is spectacular. You can see a chain of islands, from South Manitou to North Fox Island, floating on the blue horizon on Lake Michigan. You can watch freighters and sailboats glide past and dip into Grand Traverse Bay.

Particulars: The lighthouse is located in Leelanau State Park, eight miles north of Northport at the end of County Road 629. In July and August the lighthouse is open daily noon to 4 p.m. In June and from Labor Day to Oct. 15 the lighthouse is open daily 10 a.m. to 7 p.m. A $4 daily vehicle permit or a $20 state park pass is required to enter the park while museum is $2 for adults and $1 for children.

▼ Maple City

Sugar Shack
(231) 228-5835

FREE

In late winter, when the temperature raises above the freezing mark, the sap runs. My wife says the sap runs year-round.

That's maple sap, folks. Sap will actually run for about 15 hours after is thaws, then it waits for the next cycle to run again. The owners of the Sugar Shack, who offer free tours and tasting, eagerly await this annual rite so that they can collect and process gallon after gallon of the sweet sticky stuff.

Set in the rolling wooden hills south of Glen Lake, the farm consists of pumping stations, miles of tubing, the sugarhouse with its small country store at the front and buckets. On the mini-tour visitors are told that taps are inserted into trees to draw sap into hanging buckets where its later collected and boiled. Miles of tubing and a huge stainless steel evaporator helps boil 39 gallons of sap to make just one gallon of maple syrup.

Have you ever had real maple syrup? Check the label on the grocery store syrup, you soon learn there's not even a drop of real maple in its contents. See you there!

Particulars: The Sugar Shack is located 15 miles west of Traverse City. From M-72 turn north on Fritz Road and in a quarter mile turn west on Baatz Road where the farm is 1.5 miles on the left. During the syrup season and summer the store is open 9 a.m. to 5 p.m. Monday through Friday and until noon on Saturday. Tours and tasting are free.

Wineries of Leelanau County

Boskydel Vineyards
(231) 256-7272

FREE

A wine critic from the Chicago Tribune proclaimed (writers from the Tribune often "proclaim" things) that Boskydel is the country's most beautiful site for a winery. I proclaim it's also the most laid-back. No hype, no pressure, no marketing. I like that.

Bernie Rinke, a former Ohio farmboy, started testing grapes in 1965 and by 1971 he was planting hybrids from France. His dad would have liked it, too. Rinke says his father bootlegged plenty of wine in the early 1930s, often storing up to 50 barrels in his boyhood kitchen. Must be in the blood. Twisted vines grow in row after row towards the waters of Lake Leelanau and his 25 acres produce about 6,000 gallons a year, or about 2500 cases of reds, roses, and white wines. He doesn't stock his nectar in the stores, and bottles range in price from $4 to $10, so bargain-hunting travelers should try a couple of bottles.

Particulars: The vineyard is on a hillside at the corner of Country Road 641 and Otto

Road about 3.5 miles southeast of the town of Lake Leelanau. Hours are 1-6 p.m. daily throughout the year except holidays. The tasting rooms are free.

LIVINGSTON COUNTY

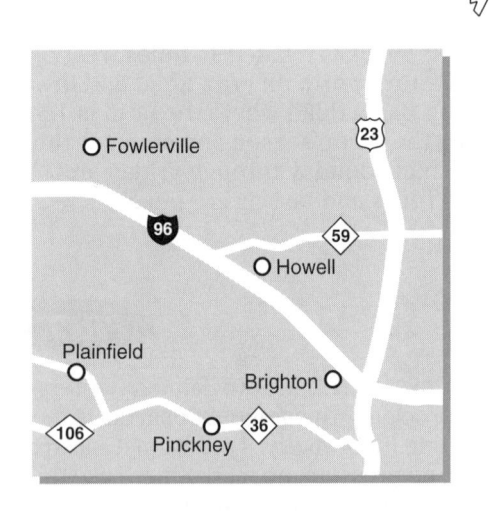

VISITOR INFORMATION

**Howell Area
Chamber of Commerce**
123 Washington Street
Howell, MI 48843
517 546-3920
www.howell.org

Livingston County

▼ Howell

Howell Nature Center
Wildlife Rehabilitation Center
(517) 546-0249

FREE

With the arrival of a red fox that lost its leg in a trapping mishap in 1982, the Howell Nature Center, operated by the Presbyters of Detroit, initiated the Wildlife Rehabilitation Program to assist native wildlife. Fully licensed as a rehabilitate facility, the program maintains a complex compound of more than 40 pens, flight cages and humane holding and treatment enclosures.

The mission of the program is to rescue, ill and orphaned wildlife and return then to their natural habitat once they are able to live independently. For animals with permanent handicaps, the program provides perpetual care at the rural facility. Yearly, over 400 wild birds and mammals will receive shelter, food, and medical attention through the volunteer organization. Concerned area folks actively provide skilled care to a wide variety of species and injury types.

The compound is only open to the public during certain periods, but clearly worth arranging a visit and offering a donation. One of the biggest wildlife rehabilitation operations in the state, the center has a membership program, training, and a massive job. A small pond and interpretive center is near the cages that are filled with raptors, coyote, various small mammals, and many other needy animals.

Particulars: The center is located five miles south of Howell at 1005 Triangle Rd. Call ahead to find out when it is open to the public and ask about upcoming special programs.

▼ Brighton

Gage House

This centennial farmhouse has 12 different rooms just chock full of Native American and Civil War items. Specialty rooms include children's rooms, kitchen with pantry, a milking room and washroom.

Particulars: 6440 Kensington Road, Brighton, (810) 437-1271

Spicer Orchards

Four generations of Spicers have been welcoming visitors

since the turn of the century. The current building was designed after an old Victorian carriage house that once stood on the farm. The building has storage for 10,000 bushels, a sorting machine, donut shop, bakery, cider mill, gift shop and farm market. Pick-your-own fruit fans will love picking a variety of fruits from July through October. Ask about the free hayrides to the orchard to pick apples on weekends during the fall. The roadside country store is open year-round, 9 a.m. 6 p.m. every day. Group tours are available.

Particulars: 10411 Clyde Road, Fenton, MI 48430, (810) 632-7692

LUCE COUNTY

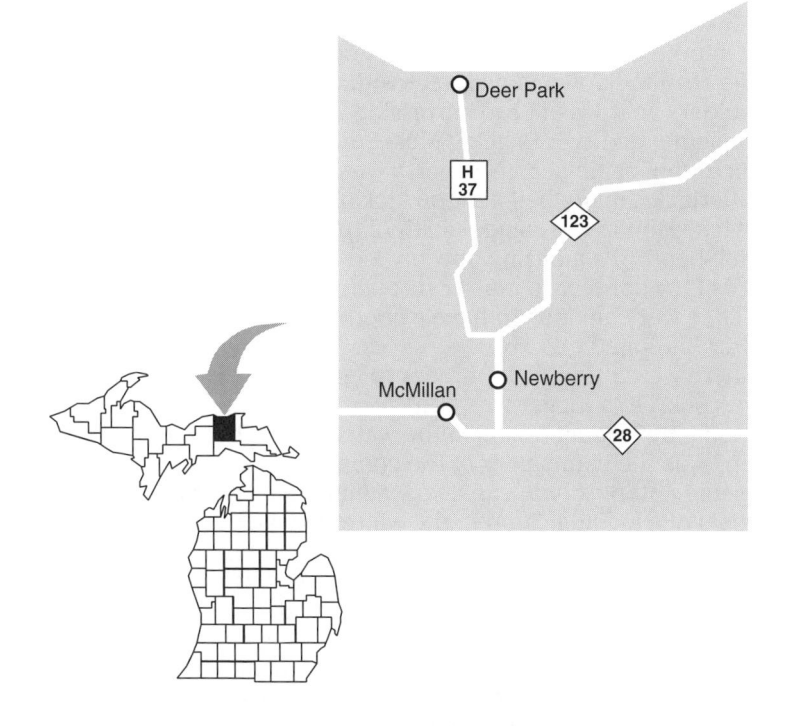

VISITOR INFORMATION

**Upper Penninsula
Travel & Recreation Association**
618 Stephenson Avenue
P. O. Box 400
Iron Mountain, MI 49801
906-774-5480 or 800-562-7134

www.uptravel.com

Luce County

▼ Newberry

**Tahquamenon River Logging Museum
(906) 293-3700**

Its been more than 70 years since they stopped floating timber down the Tahquamenon River but this Upper Peninsula town still has that rough-and-tumble character as if any minute a lumberjack in hi Mackinaw-checked shirt could some strolling down main street with a whip saw over his shoulder. So it wasn't too surprising while viewing the Tahquamenon River Logging Museum to read: During the peak of the logging ear, Newberry was a destination for lumberjacks, many hell-bent on kicking up their heels after a tough season in the camps north of town.

Hell-bent? It's amazing how my kid always catches my words I try hardest to mutter through quickly.

"They were anxious to have a good time after working all winter," I replied quickly.

There were other new phrases to learn as well. Like "livestock," to a logger was body lice, that "taking a drink standing up" meant falling in the water and a "boss of the rob shop" was the camp clerk at the company store. At this museum complex, you can also examine huge cross cut saws, models of a logging camp in the winter even a cookshack set up with red-checked table clothes and tin plates.

The museum complex is made up of the visitor's center, an original CCC building and authentic cookshack, all crammed with artifacts and memorabilia from the Newberry's logging era. Then you can leave the lumberjack lingo and the colorful era of bark eaters sawing down white pine by taking a stroll down the wood chip paths of the surrounding Tahquamenon River Nature Study Area.

The area contains 1.5 miles of foot trails, basically a pair of loops that eventually lead towards the banks of the Tahquamenon River. There are 22 interpretive posts along the trail that correspond to a brochure available at the visitor center. Fifteen of them point out a species of trees, from paper birch and American Elm to black ash and white pine, the tree that ultimately was responsible for Michigan's logging era.

But the highpoint of the short hike is arriving at post number 19. The trail eventually breaks out of woods to a long boardwalk overlooking the Tahquamenon River and ends at an observation deck.

Particulars: The museum is off of M-123 where the state highway crosses the Tahquamenon River 1.5 miles north of Newberry. The buildings are open Memorial Day through Labor Day from 9 a.m. to 5 p.m. daily. Admission is $3 per adult and $1.50 per child. Children five years old and younger are free.

Tahquamenon Logging Museum in Newberry.

▼ Deer Park

Muskallonge Lake State Park
(906) 658-3338

Muskallonge Lake State Park is basically a quarter-mile wide strip of land between its namesake lake, and Lake Superior. At one time, the park was the site of a bustling lumber town in the 1800s called Deer Park that included a hotel, store, doctor's office and, of course, a sawmill. Today all that remains of it are some dock pilings in Lake Superior.

The lumberjacks are gone but they have long since been replaced by rockhounds. From CO-H37, you descend a long wood stairway to the Great Lake shoreline where you will undoubtedly see a number of people carefully searching the pebbled beach for colorful agates. Don't know what to look for? There's a display of the rocks at the parking lot or just ask the rockhound you come to. They're usually more than happy to share their expertise.

Particulars: Muskallonge is 28 miles from Newberry and is reached by heading north on M-123 for four miles and turning west on H-37 and following it to the park entrance. A $4 daily vehicle permit or a $20 state park pass is required to enter. Camping is an additional fee.

▼ Paradise

Crisp Point Lighthouse

North of Newberry in the Upper Peninsula of Michigan Inaccessible for many years, Crisp Point Lighthouse can now be visited by car. A road has been opened all the way to the lighthouse. Crisp's Point Lighthouse is located on the deserted shore of Lake Superior, just 37 miles north of Newberry, Michigan. Crisp's Point Lighthouse is considered one of the most inaccessible and lonely mainland lighthouses in the Upper Peninsula, yet can be reached by taking a narrow country road through the Lake Superior State Forest.

Particulars: Paradise, MI 49768, (906) 492-3206.

MACKINAC COUNTY

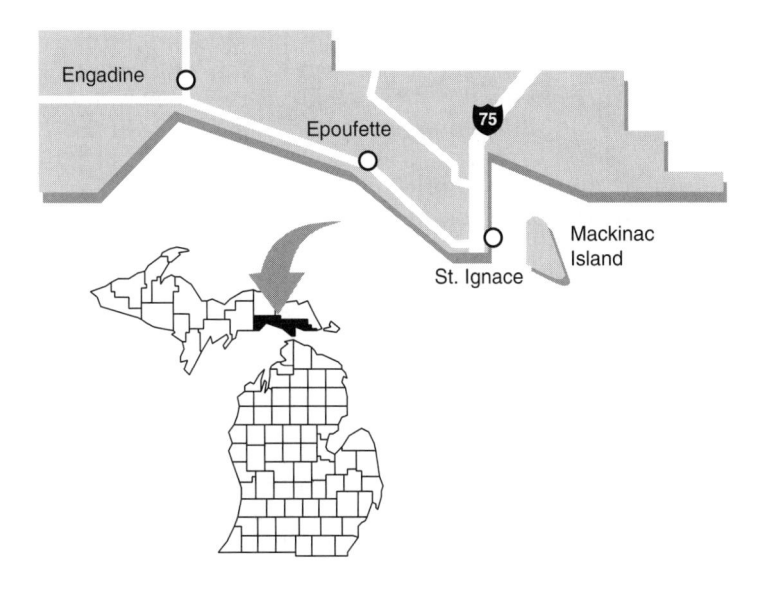

VISITOR INFORMATION

St. Ignance Convention & Visitors Bureau & Chamber of Commerce

560 N. State Street
St. Ignance, MI 49781

906-463-871 or 800-338-6660

www.stingnace.com

Mackinac County

▼ St. Ignace

Father Marquette National Memorial
Straits State Park
(906) 643-8620 Winter
(906) 643-9394 Summer

FREE

With the Mighty Mac looming in the background the end of the 5-mile span shimmers on hot days. If you look hard the cars and trucks in the distance twinkle as they slowly motor across the span with rubbernecked drivers soaking in the scenery. The best view of all is from the north shore at Father Marquette National Memorial just outside St. Ignace.

Father Marquette was a pretty popular guy back in the 1600s as eh paddled about the Great Lakes founding Sault Ste. Marie in 1668 and St. Ignace three years later. Modern day evangelists would have trouble keeping up with the explorer as he covered over 3000 miles by canoe accompanying Louis Jolliet on the trip that discovered the Mississippi River. The good Father also converted thousands of Native Americans to Christianity along the way.

To celebrate his work and explorations and tricentennial of Marquette's discovery of the Mississippi River, a presidential committee chose St. Ignace as the site of a permanent memorial which includes a small museum, park area, and telescope that gives a grand sweeping view of the bridge and surrounding waterways with boat bobbing and waves lapping the northern shoreline.

Particulars: From the bridge head west on US-2 and then look immediately for the signs pointing to the entrance of the park. The memorial is open from 9 a.m. to 8 p.m. daily June through Labor Day.

A $4 vehicle entry permit or a $20 state park pass is required to enter.

Museum of Ojibwa Culture
(906) 643-9161

Near the docks, this small but impressive museum interprets the lifestyles of the original inhabitants of the Upper Great Lakes region, and why Huron refugees came in 1671 to establish a village at this precise location. Outside the city-operated museum is ongoing reconstruction of the Huron Indian village while next door, in a small park, is Marquette's gravesite, marked by stone obelisk.

Particulars: The museum is at the north end of the St. Ignace downtown area at 500 N. State St. and is open from mid-May to October. In July and August hours are 10 a.m. to 8 p.m. Monday-Saturday, and 12 noon to 8 p.m. on Sunday. Admission is $2 for adults, $1 for children and $5 for the whole family.

Fort De Buade Museum
(906) 643-6622

Father Marquette arrived in 1671, but within 10 years the French had built a fort in St. Ignace in an effort to protect their profitable fur trade. The site is now occupied by the St. Ignace City Hall and is marked by a state historical marker. But nearby is Fort De Buade Museum, a private museum with its collection of artifacts and displays pertaining to those early French explorers and the Indians in the Mackinac Straits area.

Particulars: The museum is in downtown St. Ignace at 224 N. State Street. It's open
May through September. There is an admission fee.

Deer Ranch
(906) 643-7760

Just down the road from Mystery Spot, Deer Ranch sells deerskin products and U.P. novelties. Out back, enclosed in a wire pen are about 30 whitetail deer that you may pay a small admission fee to walk the tiny trail and observe.

Particulars: Deer Ranch is five miles west of the Mackinaw Bridge on US-2. Deer Ranch is open May through September from 10 a.m. to 6 p.m. until June and 9 a.m. daily after that. Admission to see the deer is $3.50 for adults and free for kids.

Hiawatha National Forest Ranger Station
(906) 643-7900

FREE

The Hiawatha National Forest is one of three in Michigan and offers an almost unlimited number of opportunities for hikers, canoeists, campers and skiers. The ranger station just west of the bridge is one of the best places to discover what to do and where to go. It's filled with maps, visitor's information, small gifts, guidebooks, and plenty of handouts on the national forest.

Particulars: The U.S. Forest center is next to Deer Ranch, five miles west of the bridge on US-2. It's from 8 a.m. to 4:30 p.m. Monday through Friday. Free.

Naubinway

Northernmost Point of Lake Michigan Upper Peninsula Travel and Recreation Association. (800) 562-7134

The 48-mile stretch of US-2, from the bridge to Naubinway, is a stunning drive with much of it skirting a high bluff that gives way to panoramas of Lake Michigan. There are almost a dozen rest areas and scenic pullovers along the route and one of the most popular is Cut River, where you can walk across the high bridge for a view into the steep gorge below.

But my favorite is the rest area just east of Naubinway, which marks the northernmost point of Lake Michigan. Big deal, you say? The geographical location has historical significance because Congress used it to mark the western boundary when it created the territory of Michigan in 1805. The boundary ran through the middle of Lake Michigan to its northern extremity. Everything east was Michigan. Everything west, including the half of the U.P. was considered part of Indiana Territory. That's right. At one time the U.P. was part of Indiana before the boundaries were re-adjusted in 1818. Besides its historical aspect, this rest area is a beautiful spot with picnic tables, scenic views and even a pleasant beach where the kids can go swimming.

MACOMB COUNTY

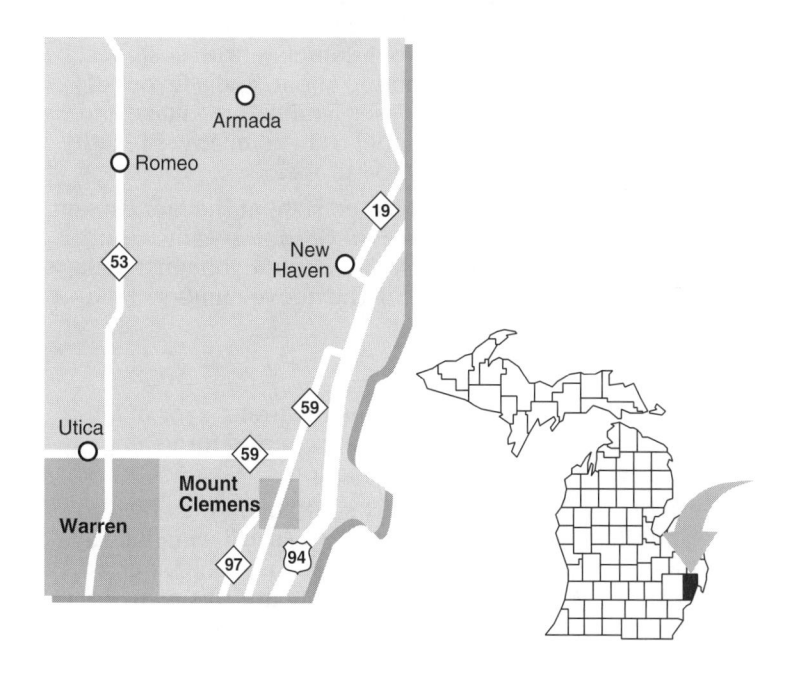

VISITOR INFORMATION

Central Macomb County Chamber of Commerce
49 Macomb Place
Mount Clemens, MI 48043
586-493-7600
www.central-macomb.com

Macomb County

▼ Mt. Clemens

Lionel Trains Visitor Center
(586) 949-4100, ext. 1211

FREE

Lionel Trains has created Lionelville, north of Mr. Clemens. Employees of the company volunteered time to build an impressive 560-square foot layout complete with switches, tiny depots, puffing engines tooting about, and a layout of 1,000 feet of track that crisscrosses a miniature village and mountains. The 91-year old model train company is healthy and importing the popular toy to Europe.

Particulars: The center is located right at the Lionel plant on 23 Mile Road, two blocks west of Gratiot Avenue. Tours are offered Wednesday through Sunday, but you must make a reservation in advance by calling the above number. Free.

Crocker House Museum
(586) 465-2488

Built in 1869 by Joshua Dickinson, the first mayor of Mt. Clemens, this Italianate house features period furnishing, historical artifacts and local information.

Particulars: From M-59, depart south on Romeo Plank Road and then east on Cass Avenue. Cass will wind its way into downtown Mt. Clemens. The museum is one block north of Cass and Gratiot at 15 Union St. Hours are 10 a.m. to 4 p.m. Tuesday through Friday and 1-4 p.m. first Sunday of the month. The museum is closed in January and February. Admission is $1 for adults and .50 cents for children.

Mr. Clemens Train
(586) 463-1863

We had a swell trip. About 45 minutes long the clanking Mr. Clemens train runs on the weekends during the summer taking visitors to the Military Air Museum at the Selfridge Air National Guard Base. The train ride has banjo music and the gentle swaying that enhance the short ride and jaunt over the Macomb County countryside.

Particulars: You purchase tickets in an old caboose located on Gratiot Avenue, just north of Joy Boulevard in Mt. Clemens. The train departs Sundays from mid-May to late September on the hour from 1-4 p.m. The train ride without the museum is $3 for adults and $1.75 for children. Kids four years old and younger are free.

Yates Cider Mill, Macomb County.

Michigan Transit Museum
(586) 463-1863

The museum is located in a restored Grand
Trunk Western Railroad Station that was built
in 1859 and is where Thomas Edison learned to use
a telegraph. Today it houses a variety of displays and
artifacts covering the age of railroads and trolleys in
southeast Michigan.

FREE

Particulars: From M-97, head a half mile east on Cass
Avenue to Grand Avenue where the depot is located at 200
Grand. The museum is open 1-4 p.m. on Saturday and Sunday
throughout the year. Free.

▼ Utica

Yates Cider Mill
(248) 651-8300

Crisp tart apples that are carefully squeezed and bottled to
make golden-colored cider is served each autumn out of the

1863 mill that is situated along the banks of the Clinton River. Its been a water-powered operation ever since, but in 1876 it began making cider and today the water wheel still powers the apple elevator, grinders, and press as well as generating electricity for the lights inside the buildings.

The handsome mill can produce about 300 gallons of cider per hour, all of which is needed in the fall to meet the demands of visitors who enjoy their treat around the huge red barn across the road from the Rochester-Utica state recreation area.

Particulars: The mill is on the Oakland and Macomb county border, west of Rochester on Avon Road (23 Mile Road). It's open daily from 9 a.m. to 7 p.m. from September through October and from 9 a.m. to 5 p.m. in November.

MANISTEE COUNTY

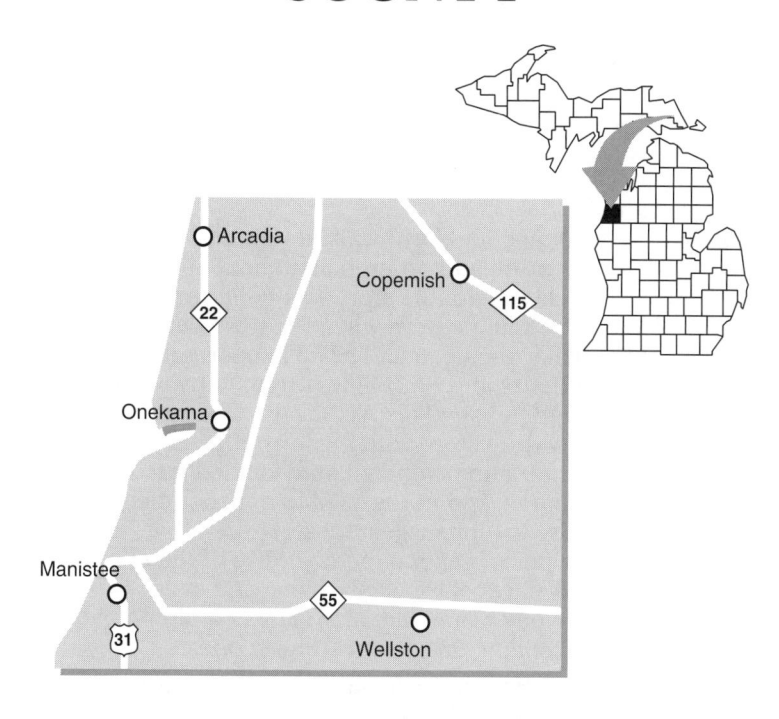

VISITOR INFORMATION

**Manistee County
Chamber of Commerce**
11 Cypress Street
Manistee, MI 49660
800-288-2286

www.manisteecountychamber.com

Manistee County

▼ **Manistee**

Lyman Building Museum
(231) 723-5531

There's a miracle cure for whatever ails you on the shelves of the old Lyman Drugstore in downtown Manistee. There's McLean's Liver and Kidney Balm that claims on the bottle that A$1 Will Buy Good Health. And there's May's Marshmallow Cream that is "unrivaled as a tonic in all wasting disorders or sustained nervous strain." There's even Dr. Thatcher's Blood Syrup, and many others that were mostly alcohol.

Fifty years ago you could have walked right in Manistee's most famous drug store and ordered just about any cure imaginable. The classic double store was built during the heyday of Manistee's lumber era when the town was the third busiest port on Lake Michigan and 32 mills operated in the area. The wood floors and tin ceiling is framed by a wrap-around balcony and polished display cases. One section is a replica of the early drug store with brass apothecary scales on top of the counter and behind kit gold-labeled jars still filled with roots, barks, and herbs used to concoct medicines.

The museum also exhibits a general store area that is stocked with all types of general merchandise of the era from fluting irons to cut plugs of tobacco, soaps, and even newspapers of the day. There are also cameras, old phones, a hand-sewn 1850 wedding dress, and stereoscopes.

Particulars: The building is located in downtown Manistee at 425 River St., five blocks west of US-31. The museum is open daily from 10 a.m. to 5 p.m. except Sunday. From October to June it is also closed Monday. Admission is by donations.

Old Water Works Building Museum
(231) 723-5531

Lyman Building isn't the only museum in Michigan's Victorian City. The Holly Water Works Building was built in 1882 and eventually became the county's first museum. Inside you'll find it overflowing with artifacts and memorabilia to Manistee's past. Some are displayed in exhibits, others are just piled up in the corner and they range from lumberjack tools and boats to an entire carriage once used by Louis Sand. The enjoyment here is just poking around the place to see what you can find.

Particulars: From US-31, head west on First Street to the museum at 540 First. Hours are 10 a.m. to 5 p.m. Tuesday through Saturday from Mid-June to Labor Day. Admission is by donation.

Manistee Fire Station
(231) 723-1549

FREE

Two other historical buildings along First Street include Ramsdell Theatre, built in 1902 and listed on the National Register of Historic Places, and the Manistee Fire Station, built in 1881 and listed on the Michigan Register of Historic Sites.

The fire station is the oldest continuously operating one in Michigan and its distinct architecture and red stone make it a favorite with photographers. You can wander inside where some old equipment and a few artifacts are along side the new stuff.

Particulars: From US-31 turn west on First Street to the fire station at 281 First. The first station is open daily to the public except during lunch and dinner hours. Tours are occasionally offered but it is best to call a head for times. Free.

▼ Stronach

Little Manistee Weir
(231) 775-9727

FREE

They were lively, they were leaping, they were big but more than anything else they were the stuff dreams were made of, at least the dreams of those of us who had gathered around the Little Manistee River Fish Weir. By the number of bulging eyes, you could tell there was more than one angler in the crowd that had gathered to watch biologists handle the big fish...very big fish.

Big as in 30-pound salmon, bigger than anything any of us had ever seen at the end of our line. Perhaps one of the most unusual fall rituals in Michigan is a drive out to the Little Manistee River fish weir in Manistee County to watch the salmon being harvested. Its been a ritual ever since 1966 when the state first planted salmon in Lake Michigan and shortly afterwards biologists began using the metal gate to collect eggs and sperm from the spawning fish.

The weir is first installed in April to collect the eggs of steelhead and brown trout, but that lasts only a couple weeks and the fish are not nearly as impressive, most of them ranging seven or eight pounds in weight. You want to see crowds, come in the fall when the fish average 12-pounds while 20-pounders are a pretty common sight.

Grates direct the fish into a pond where they are scooped out and funneled into the egg-taking building. Here a technician shoots oxygen into the salon and the eggs come flying out. The salmon harvest usually peaks around the first of October when the DNR staff will handle from 2,000 to 4,000 fish a day in removing two million eggs from them.

Particulars: From M-55, just east of Manistee, head south on Stronach Road for two miles then east on Old Stronach, which crosses the Little Manistee River. Continue following the dirt road east to the weir and egg-taking station to the left. The fall harvest takes place weekdays from mid-September to usually mid-October. Best time is the last week in September and first week in October from 10 a.m. to 2 p.m. Free.

▼ Kaleva

The Bottle House
(231) 362-3665 or 362-3344

Kaleva isn't exactly a haven for tour buses but there are two things in this small, out-of-the-way Manistee County village that you'd be hard pressed to find anywhere else in the Midwest. Stop at the Kaleva Phone Company in the center of town and out front you'll see a .10-cent pay phone. That's right, for only a dime, you can call any of the 445 residents of Kaleva.

And if you don't know anybody, then call Viola Jouppi of the Kaleva Historical Society and ask her to show you the Bottle House. Even more unique than a 10-cent pay phone is this home made out of bottles, more than 60,000 to be exact, that is on the National Register of Historical Places and today serves as the Kaleva Historical Museum. Why an exterior of bottles instead brick or aluminum siding?

The house was built by John Makinen and he operated a bottling company in town. In short, he just wanted to find a use for all his broken and chipped pop bottles. Call Makinen a recycler way before his time. After becoming swamped with glass, Makinen decided to build a plant storehouse out of bottles. He laid them on their side with the bottoms on the exterior, bound them together with mortar and on the inside covered the tops with plaster.

Makinen quickly discovered the air space in the bottles was excellent insulation. Even
on the coldest winter days he could safely store his capped soft drinks in the building and not worry about them freezing

and bursting.

In 1941, Makinen retired from his business and began building his bottle house in town at the age of 70. The walls of nine-room home were composed with the 60,000 bottles he had accumulated. Most of the bottoms say "Kaleva" indicating they were pop bottles from the plant. But not all. There are a few Hiram Walker whiskey bottles while others are small, square medicine bottles, beer bottles, what appears to be a milk bottle and a few electric insulators thrown in for good measure.

Inside the house is the typical small museum where rooms are filled with local artifacts, everything from the account file from the old Kaleva Mercantile Store to pre-Civil War washers and wringers that people have donated. The museum is open Saturdays during the summer but don't hesitate to stop any other day. There are a handful of curators who would live to take visitors though all you have to do first is call.

And in Kaleva it only costs a dime.

Particulars: From M-55, head north on High Bridge Road, just west of Wellston, and then east on Nine Mile Road. Once in town head a block north on Healy Lake Road and then a block east on Wuoksi Street. The house is on the corner of Wuoksi and Kauko. From Memorial Day to Labor Day the museum is open from noon to 4 p.m. on Saturday. The house can be seen other times by appointment. Admission is by donation.

Bottle House Museum, Manistee County.

MARQUETTE COUNTY

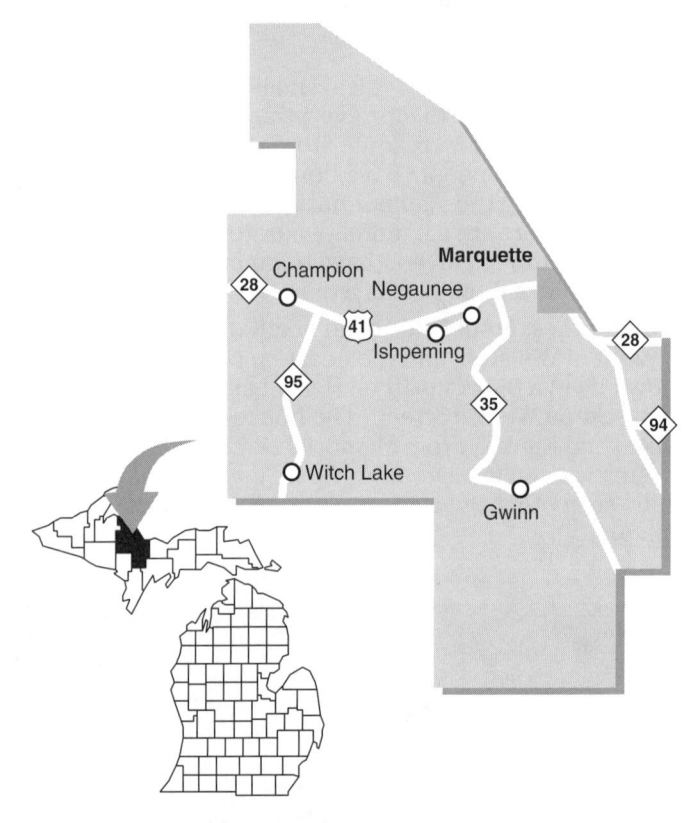

VISITOR INFORMATION

**Marquette County
Tourism Council**
501 S. Front Street
Marquette, MI 49855
906-228-7749 or 800-578-6489

www.marquette.org

Marquette County

▼ Lake Superior

Marquette County's crowned jewel, the pristine Superior, is the largest fresh water lake in the world, spanning 31,700 square miles and outlining Marquette County with 80 miles of shoreline. Comb the fine sand beaches for gemstones such as agates, amethyst and greenstone. Or venture onto the lake on a charter fishing boat, a sailboat, or a sea kayak; just a few of the ways to witness nature's awesome wonder in Superior. Try the free beaches that include South Beach is located off Lake Street and offers restrooms, volleyball courts and playground equipment. McCarty's Cove on scenic Lakeshore Drive has park benches, picnic tables, cooking grills, restrooms and playground equipment. Sandy beaches can also be found along M-28 east of the city of Marquette where state highway M-28 winds along Lake Superior. On County Road 550 heading to Big Bay, public beach areas are found at Little Presque Isle and Wetmore's Landing. At Big Bay, take in the breath taking view of the Big Bay Harbor at Squaw Beach.

Marquette County waterfalls

With more than a dozen waterfalls cascading through Marquette County, spend an entire day exploring these natural wonders. A few of the favorites are listed below.

Particulars: Black River Falls, off County Road 581 near Ishpeming, is a quick hike along a scenic path bordered by majestic pines. Black River Falls plunges 20 feet into an impressive waterfall that can be viewed at the center of the river from an island easily accessed by a footbridge.

Alder Falls, off County Road 550 near Big Bay, plunges 30 feet from a rock outcrop jutting out of a creek and continues to cascade over rocks lining the riverbed. The falls span about 15 feet across at their widest section.

Warner Falls are easily accessible and can be viewed from the road. The falls, located off M-35 near Palmer, plunge 20 feet into a still pool of water.

Unnamed Falls, the first of Twin Falls, will greet you with the roar of water plunging 20 feet into Morgan Creek. On a short hike to Carp River Falls, two consecutive falls drop 10 feet and pour rapidly over an intricate rock bed. These are located 2.5 miles south of Marquette off M-553.

"Moose Country," Marquette County.

The Moose are Loose.

In 1985 and 1987, 59 moose were re-introduced to Marquette County. Delivered by helicopter from Canada, these moose have reproduced and formed a new family that wanders miles and miles across the Peninsula. The largest percentage of reported sightings still centers around their drop off point along the Huron Grade near Michigamme. Adult moose can weigh up to 1,000 pounds. Their mating season occurs in September and October and caution is strongly advised during this time. Moose cows give birth in June to single or twin calves that weigh approximately 30 pounds.

Particulars: Many public trails can access great wildlife views. Marquette Maritime Museum (906) 226-2006

Colorful flags from ore carriers hang from the ceiling of the old Water Works Building where Great Lakes maritime history is interpreted and displayed. Only a few blocks from a lighthouse, the museum houses antique outboard motors, Finnish fishing equipment, iron mining history and samples of iron pellets that can also be found along many of the railroad tracks that crisscross the entire Upper Peninsula.

There is also a special area devoted to shipwrecks in the area while Marquette's turn-of-the-century waterfront has been re-created inside. Outside you'll find huge buoys and boats to admire.

Particulars: From US-41\M-28 continue into downtown Marquette on Front Street then turn right on Lake Shore Boulevard and follow it around the harbor to the museum. The museum is open Memorial Day to Labor Day daily from 10 a.m. to 5 p.m. Admission is $3 for adults, and $2 for students.

▼ Superior Dome
NMU Recreational Services
(906) 227-2850

In the middle of Marquette, the only town worthy to be called a city in the U.P., is the Superior Dome, the world's largest wooden dome. One is as impressive as the other.

Built in a whirlwind of controversy, pork barrel politics and a cost of $21 million, the dome was finally opened in August of 1991. From the outside it indeed looks like a giant bubble, whose perfect symmetry is broken only by the sharped peaked windows and doors protruding from it. Inside it's your best piece of dining room furniture. Or at least Marquette's.

For those who love the beauty of wood and appreciate a tight fitting tongue-and-groove joint, the Dome is a sight to behold on a scale you can't imagine until you stroll inside. It's located on the campus of Northern Michigan University and NMU officials best describe the interior as Astanding under a gigantic inverted wooden bowl. Looking up (way up as the ceiling is 156 feet above the floor or something close to a 14-story building) 781 Douglas Fur beams and arches crisscross above you. Between them is 108 miles of tongue-and-groove planking and even the catwalks are natural wood, appearing like a series of outdoor decks and boardwalks.

Even for the U.P., whose grandeur becomes common place with most residents, the Dome is still quite a structure, a place where at one end is the world's largest piece of movable artificial turf, waiting to be mechanically rolled out whenever the NMU football team takes the field.

But most people enter the structure with their gym bag in hand, even visitors to the city as area hotels are beginning to leave a pass to the Dome on your pillow instead of a chocolate mint. Open to the public, the Dome contains a 200-meter, six lane track, volleyball courts, tennis courts and basketball courts while its inside perimeter is used as a quarter-mile walking lane where you can power step pass four huge murals depicting sports in the U.P.

Particulars: From US-41\M-28 continue on Front Street into downtown Marquette and then left on Washington Avenue. Turn right ion Fourth St. Which becomes Presque Isle Avenue. The Dome is off Presque Isle Avenue on the NMU campus. The Dome's schedule varies according to events. But there is free walking from 8-11 a.m. Monday through Thursday. Otherwise a $5 guest pass must be purchased to use both the

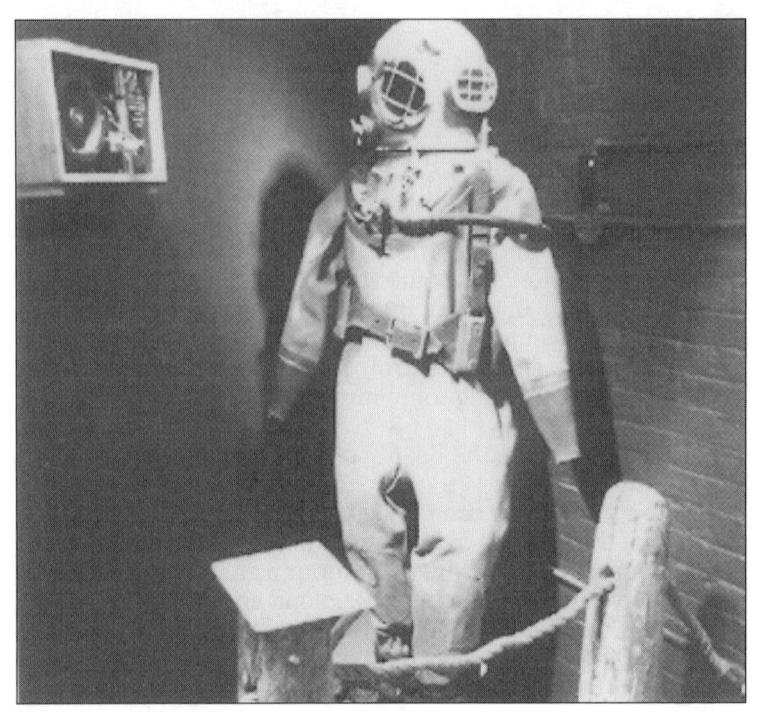

Maritime Museum, Marquette County.

Dome and adjoining recreation building.

Marquette County Historical Museum
(906) 226-3571

The museum features two floors and several galleries of exhibits that depict life in Marquette at the turn of the century. The collection of historical washing machines and irons alone will make you go home and hug your Matag.

Particulars: The museum is at 213 N. Front St., a block north of Washington Avenue. Hours are 10 a.m. to 5 p.m. Monday through Friday and 11 a.m. to 4 p.m. on Saturday. Admission is $3 for adults while senior citizens and children are free.

▼ Negaunee

FREE

Michigan Iron Museum
(906) 475-7857

In 1844, surveyor William Burt launched the mining era in upper Michigan after the compass he was using went erratic.

The needle swung wildly confusing the fastidious surveyor so he assigned his crew to find out why. The crew searched the ground and found huge deposits of pure iron protruding from the ground.

For Burt, it lead to two important things; the Michigan iron era and Burt's development of a solar compass. Because they could not survey the remaining area with a magnetic compass, the solar compass was used and is now enshrined right along with headlamps and hopper cars at the Michigan Iron Industry Museum located on the banks of the Carp River three miles from Negaunee.

Using skillfully crafted hands-on exhibits and static displays the museum spins the tale of Michigan's iron era that flourished for more than 125 years. The industry left a lasting impact on the Upper Peninsula and the location of this museum was no accident. After an Indian guide showed Philo Everett a fallen tree that had roots entwined with a large boulder of iron ore, the Jackson entrepreneur registered the first mining claim in 1845.

A visit to the museum begins in the 96-seat auditorium with short presentation on the iron era. From the theater you begin your stroll through the large exhibit area that chronicles explorations, mining technology, miner's lifestyles, ore processing and the impact of mining of future Michigan industry. You can also enter a re-created mining shaft.

Particulars: From US-41, turn south at M-35, 7.5 miles west of Marquette, and follow

the signs. From Negaunee, head south on CR-492 and follow signs. The center is open daily May through October from 9:30 a.m. to 4:30 p.m. Free.

▼ Ishpeming

U.S. Ski Hall of Fame
(906) 485-6323

In one exhibit at the U.S. Ski Hall of Fame there is a new high-tech Nordica downhill ski boot on display next to a Finnish travel ski with a fur binding which is next to an 1880 Lappland ski which is next to an inner tube binding that was used only a few decades ago by many Upper Peninsula youth. With a half twist of the head, you span 200 years of ski bindings and boots, going from fur to plastic and passing leather and an old bike tube along the way.

Nowhere is the evolution of skiing seen better than at this display and officials proudly proclaim nowhere is ski history better preserved than at their museum. The $1.7 million facility definitely slows down traffic on US-41. Its most impressive feature is not its size, rather the two-sided peaked roof at the front that looks all the world like a ski jump.

Today, Ishpeming is to skiing what Cooperstown is to baseball and football is to Canton, Ohio. From the lobby you pass a video theater that shows a 18-minute history of U.S. Ski Association and then enter the hall of fame itself with individual plaques on every member beginning with John "Snowshoe" Thompson who proved the value of skiing in the 18th century by using his equipment to deliver the mail.

From the plaques you proceed into "A Walk Through Ski History", starting with a replica of the 4,000 year-old ski pole found in a Swedish peat bog and moving onto a three-dimensional display of the famous Birkebeiners, the Norwegian soldiers who wrapped their legs in birch bark and skied 50 kilometers in saving King Sverre's infant son.

Particulars: The museum is right on US-41 in Ishpeming, 15 miles from Marquette. The Hall is open 10 a.m. to 5 p.m. year round. Admission is free.

MASON COUNTY

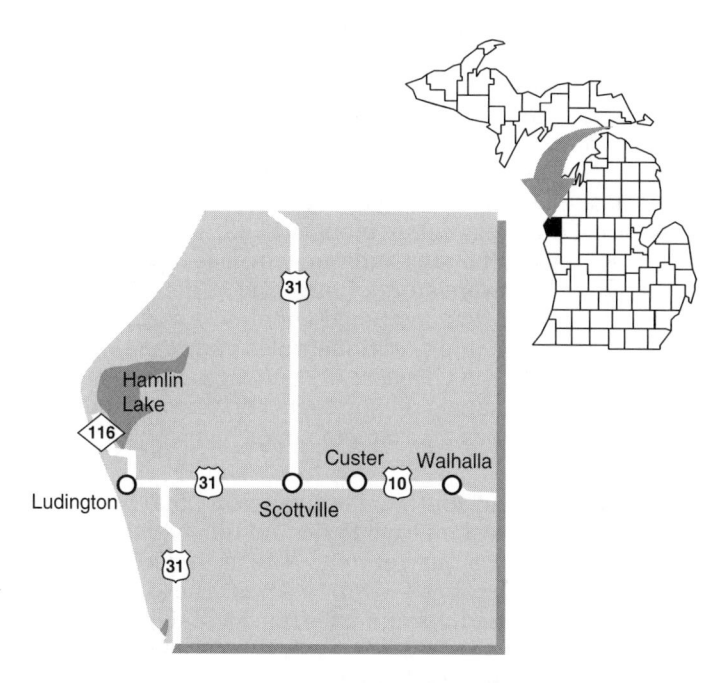

VISITOR INFORMATION

**Ludington Area
Convention & Visitors Bureau**
5300 West US-10
Ludington, MI 49431
877-420-6618

www.ludingtoncvb.com

Mason County

▼ Ludington

White Pine Village
(231) 843-4808

Aaron Burr Caswell built the first house in Mason County in 1849. Six years later the two-story home was still the only farm building in an area that was trying to organize itself into Michigan's newest county. Caswell offered the front portion of his humble house as the first courthouse and county seat.

Today, the marvelously preserved house is the focal point of the White Pine Village, a living history complex managed by the Mason County Historical Society. The small village has 20 historical buildings set up along streets. All of the old buildings are from the area and range from a 1840s trapper's log cabin to a hardware store of the early 1900s. During the summer season, period costumed volunteers roam and work in the village reenacting traditional roles and crafts.

Interaction with the village really enhances your experience. The chapel still conducts service on Sunday, while you can sit in as a jury member, or help cook a traditional meal.

Particulars: Head south of Ludington on US-31 and in three-miles head west on Irish Road and then north on South Lakeshore Drive for a quarter mile. The museum is open Memorial Day to October 11 a.m. to 5 p.m. Tuesday-Saturday. Admission is $6 for adults and children 5 and under are free.

Great Lakes Interpretive Center
Ludington State Park
(231) 843-8671

The largest state park along the shores of Lake Michigan and the second largest state park in the Lower Peninsula is Ludington. The 5,200-acre park has 5.5 miles of Great Lakes shoreline that is guarded by picturesque Point Sable Lighthouse, an impressive tower among the dunes that was built in 1867.

Tying one into the other is the Great Lakes Interpretive Center. Located on the south side of the Sable River is the Ludington State Park Nature Center, the center features slide shows, hands-on exhibits and displays that focus on the Great Lakes surrounding Michigan.

For the best view in the park of Lake Michigan and the surrounding dunes, climb the stairway to Skyline Trail adjacent to the interpretive center. It's a long climb to the top but the trail is well named, providing panorama of the Great Lake shoreline and Big Sable River.

Particulars: From Ludington, head north on M-116 to reach the park in 8.5 miles. The center is open during the summer months from 10 a.m. to 5 p.m. A $4 vehicle entry permit or a $20 state park pass is required to enter the park.

Amber Elk Ranch

See some of North America's finest elk, and visit the gift shop on 130 acres. See Tucker, the pot-bellied pig

Particulars: 2688 W. Conrad Road, Ludington, MI 49431, (231) 843-5355

Big Sable Point Lighthouse

TOWER TOUR DONATIONS: Adults $2, ages 6-12 $1, children 5 and under free.The gift shop, located in the original 1867 keeper's quarters, offers lighthouse models, books, t-shirts, sweatshirts and other lighthouse related item.

Particulars: From Ludington, follow signs to Ludington State Park. Park in Beach Cafe'
lot and walk north on beach 1.5 miles.

Father Marquette Shrine

Monument to Jacques Marquette and boat launch. South side of Pere Marquette Lake on Lakeshore Drive.

Bortell's Fisheries
(231) 843-3337

Traveling still cheers me up better than any major religion. Especially when you discover a backroads gem, a private destination away from the humbling freeway exits and tacky crowds. This is especially true when you're hungry. And, if you're hungry for a unique experience, head for Bortell's.

It ain't easy to find, but once you do it's awfully hard to pass it up. The front of the building is a colorful mural of perch and walleye swimming through the aquatic plants of northern waterways. In jumbo letters above them is the barbed hook that snares you from Lakeshore Drive: HOT FRIED FISH TO GO! Is your mouth watering yet?

According to David Bortell, his family held the first commercial fishing license ever issued in Michigan, and then, as if to reconfirm it, he shows you a wall of old photographs and points to a 1922 picture of his grandfather holding up tow huge whitefish. Along the way the family has successfully gone from catching to cooking.

For less than $5 you can pick out a trout or half-pound filet of walleye or tender whitefish and watch Bortell cook it to a golden crisp and then arrange it on a plate with a mound of creamy cole slaw and a pile of steaming French (or Freedom?) fries. The meal is best enjoyed across the street at Summit Park, where you'll find a dozen of picnic tables, all with a panoramic view of the breezy Lake Michigan shoreline.

Particulars: From US-31 turn west on Iris Road and then south on Lakeshore Drive to reach the shop in seven miles between Meisenheimer and Deren Roads. Bortell's is open May through September from 11 a.m. to 8 p.m. daily. Summit Park is open dawn to 10 p.m.

MECOSTA COUNTY

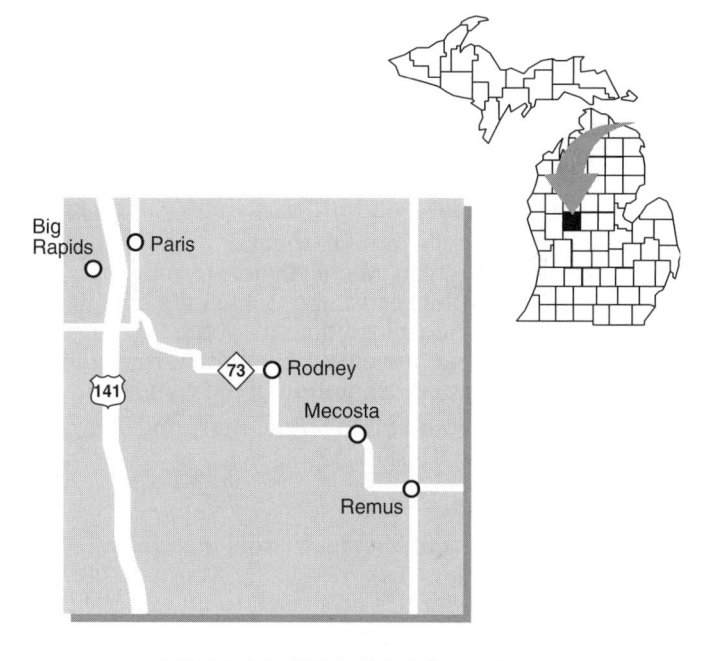

VISITOR INFORMATION

**Big Rapids
Convention & Visitors Bureau**
246 N. State St.
Big Rapids, MI 49307
231-796-7640 or 888-229-6697

Mecosta County

▼ Big Rapids

Jim Crow Museum of Racist Memorabilia
Come onto the campus of Ferris State University and visit this museum that houses over 4,000 pieces of memorabilia of racial items in a museum open to the public by appointment due to the nature of the museum Mr. Pilgrim wants to prepared those who enter and have a place where they can discuss some of the images they've seen.

Particulars: The Starr Building at Ferris State University, Big Rapids, MI 49307, (231) 591-5887

Michigan Art Walk - Free
This is a dynamic collection of original artwork created entirely by Michigan artists and installed throughout the Ferris State University campus. These works are the finest installments of the "Ferris Renaissance", a 20-year movement committed to furthering the beauty and cultural presentation of the campus.

Particulars: 901 South State Street, Big Rapids, MI 49307, (888) 378-0065, (231) 591-3815

Stickler's Family Farm
Located in the midst of Michigan's rolling farmland, visitors are welcome to learn and experience life "down on the farm." This third generation farm is now open to the general public for visiting from June through October. Get away from the hustle andbustle of every day life and experience the peaceful, unhurried life in the country. There is fun and adventure for people of all ages. The old granary is now decorated with rustic charm and filled with handmade items and specialty gifts for your shopping pleasure.

Particulars: 5394 50th Avenue, Remus, MI 49340, (989) 561-2033

Sawmill Canoe Livery
(231) 796-6408
Some fast water tubing or rafting is enough to make you wet your polyester pants, but not at the Sawmill Canoe Livery along the banks of the Muskegon River.

Along the Muskegon River, tubing isn't supposed to be death defying. It isn't even supposed to be hard. It's a

Tubing the Muskegon River, Mecosta County.

leisurely float down a river on a hot summer afternoon with one hand dragging in the water and the other wrapped around a cold beer. It's simple, it's relaxing, it's definitely one popular form of chilling out, and it's cheap.

More than 1,000 people float the river on a hot summer day and the Mecosta County Area Chamber of Commerce claims more than 35,000 float through downtown Big

Rapids every summer, the reason the city bills itself "the Tubing Capitol of Michigan."

Even though you actually tube through downtown Big Rapids, a community of 14,000 along with Ferris State University, you'll barely know it. Most of the way is lined with forested riverbanks, two parks, one bridge and five sets of rapids.

The first set of rapids is reached in only 15 minutes into the watery journey and from the shore it probably appears little more than a ripple. From a canoe it becomes "fast waters" and when you're half-stuck in an inner tube and waves are slapping at your face, it's all that most tubers want to handle.

You will have some control of the tube, paddle with your

hands and you can spin to and from. But mostly it's just an uncomplicated float, two hours of drifting along, socializing with the other tubers and soaking up the sun. At the Highbanks Park there's a big sign that instructs tubers to hit the shore and hop the bus, and if you're not too waterlogged, you can do it all over again.

Particulars: The livery is at 230 Baldwin St., at the north end of Big Rapids and just west of Business US-131. Tubes are rented daily from May to September. Cost of a tube and transportation is $6 per person.

▼ Paris

Paris Park Fish Hatchery
(231) 796-3420

Modern fish hatcheries located around the state rear and plant millions of sport fish into the Great Lakes providing the product that helps bring thousands of thrill-seeking anglers to the state. These facilities have control rooms, computer assisted techniques, special diets, pumping trucks and experienced biologists that scurry around making sure everything are working. The Paris Hatchery, built in 1881 was the second state hatchery.

The old-style hatchery, using concrete raceways and water pumped from the nearby Muskegon River, has raised literally millions of salmon and brown trout over the years supplying Michigan and neighboring states with stock for the waters. Closed in 1964, the Mecosta County Parks Commission reopened the facility to the public in 1976 as a visitor destination where youngsters can fish and trout fishermen can drool at the fat 24-inch lunkers that cruise the raceway.

The series of aging concrete raceways murmur a constant bubbling sound as you walk along the edge admiring the denizens that would look even better in a frying pan. Complete with shady benches and a miniature Eiffel Tower, the park also host art fairs and small performances each summer. Kids can fish in the pond, which is operated by a concessionaire. Recipe cards are available, just in case you catch a big one.

Particulars: The park is on old US-131 (Northland Drive), six miles north of Big Rapids. The trout fishing concession is open 10 a.m. to 6 p.m. Thursday through Sunday from June through August and weekends May and September. A $4 vehicle permit is needed to enter the park while the cost to fish is $.30 and inch for the trout you catch.

MENOMINEE COUNTY

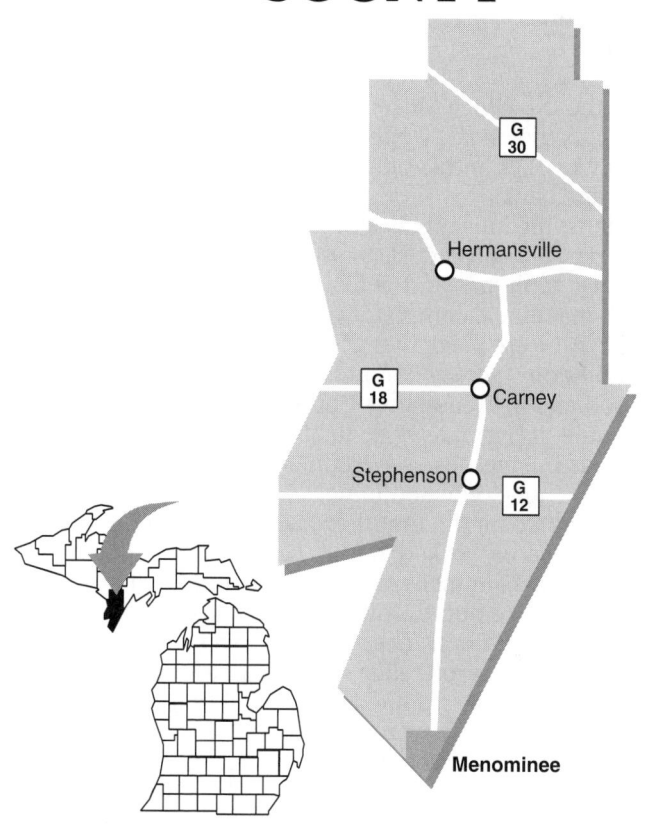

VISITOR INFORMATION

Menominee Area Chamber of Commerce
1005 Tenth Avenue
P. O. Box 427
Menominee, MI 49858
906-863-2679

MDOT Welcome Center
1343 10th Ave.
Menominee, MI 49858
906-863-6496

Menominee County

▼ Hermansville

IXL Office Museum
(906) 498-2181

For anybody who has worked in an office, and there's a lot us who has, the IXL Office Museum is probably the most remarkable museum in the Upper Peninsula. To put it simply, it's as if every worker in this office left for lunch a century and just never came back.

The Hermansville museum is a preserved 19th century office, from classic rolltop desks and a huge walk-in vault to typewriters, Dictaphones and one of the earliest A.B. Dicks mimeograph machines, complete with the original instructions. All were used after C.J. Meyer, who operated a large sash and door factory in Fond du Lac, Wis., purchased acres of woodland in Menominee County in 1870s and then set up a sawmill in Hermansville. In 1881-82, Meyer reorganized his businesses as Wisconsin Land & Lumber and constructed the huge office building.

The general office on the first floor, where two typists and a switchboard operator worked, if full of century-old equipment including an Edison's mimeograph, an early Burroughs adding machine and an office dumbwaiter used to ship records and memos to the second floor. There's the bookkeeper's department with its payroll teller's cage, eight-foot high vault and even some IXL dollars pinned to the wall that workers would use at the company store. Most of all there are records. On the top floor you can flip through boxes of old records and spread sheets that on Jan.17, 1887 Carl Lange was paid $9.36 for a week's worth of wages. Almost makes you appreciate your job or at least the office you work in.

Particulars: Hermansville is 24 miles west of Escanaba along US-2/41where signs direct you to the museum in the middle of the small town. The museum is open daily from June through Labor Day from 1-4 p.m. Admission is $1 per adult and $.50 per child.

▼ Menominee County Historical

Menominee Chamber of Commerce
(906) 863-9000

Located in the former John The Baptist Catholic Church, the museum offers a variety of exhibits on local history

IXL Office Museum, Menominee County.

including the world's largest grindstone (hey, there's a reason to drive 10 hours to the U.P.!) The museum does have an excellent exhibit of Indian artifacts, which ranges from an extensive arrowhead collection to a pair of wooden canoes that were hollowed out from trees 800 to 1,200 years ago. The church itself, built in 1921 with stunning stain glass windows, is an interesting building to view.

Particulars: The museum is at 904 11th Ave., just a block from US-41 in the downtown area of Menominee. It's open June 1 to Labor Day from 10 a.m. to 4:30 p.m. Monday through Saturday. Free.

Iron Mountain Iron Mine

All aboard the underground mine train to tour the Iron Mountain Iron Mine! See close up iron mining techniques and tools used in mining from 1870 to 1945. Skilled guides take you 2,600 feet into the mine and give demonstrations and insight about the long ago mining era. Tours last about 45 minutes. Tours daily from June 1 to October 15.

Particulars: 9 miles east of Iron Mountain on Hwy U.S. 2, Vulcan, MI 49892, (906) 563-8077.

▼ Wallace

DeYoung Family Zoo

Come view the exotic felines and get the opportunity to interact with these magnificent creatures. The zoo is unique because is a Hands-On and all of the animals are very responsive.   The zoo has tigers, wolfs and lions.

Particulars: North 5406, County Rd 577, Wallace, MI 49893, (906) 788-4093. 15 miles north of Menominee on US 41.

MIDLAND COUNTY

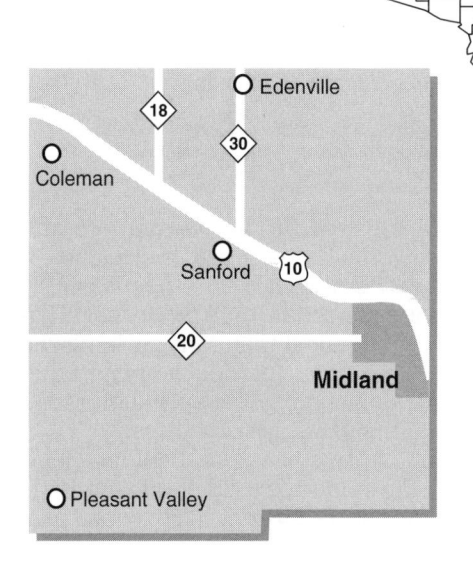

VISITOR INFORMATION

**Midland County
Convention & Visitors Bureau**
300 Rodd St.
Midland, MI 48640

989-839-9522 or 888-464-3526

www.midlandcvb.org

Midland County

▼ Midland

Dow Chemical Company Tours
Dow Visitor Center
(517) 636-8658

FREE

Have you recently wondered how Saran Wrap is made? Chemicals? Drugs? What exactly does Dow Chemical, one of the biggest in the business do? Well, they have a tour that will answer these and other pressing questions.

Particulars: The visitor center is at the corner of East Lyons Road and Bayliss Street. The tour is free, but you must register in advance.

Dow Gardens
(989) 631-2677

Spread over 66 acres, the colorful Dow Gardens combines flowers, lush shrubs, towering trees, grass, rocks, and cascades of water in a series of wonderful, eye-pleasing vistas. The Gardens were started in 1899 by Herbert Henry Dow, founder of the Dow Chemical Company, as landscaping for his "humble" home. Today, the garden is open to the public and thousands annually enjoy the spring blossoms, summer flowers, and colors of autumn.

The overall collection of plans is one of the finest anywhere in the country comprising some 1,200 different woody trees and shrubs and 500 different permanent herbaceous plants including perennial, wildflowers and unique ground covers.

Budget minded travelers will enjoy a million dollar view of outstanding displays of rhododendrons, crab apples, native trees, roses, herbs, 25,000 tulips and 10,000 bedding plants.

Particulars: The visitor entrance is located adjacent to the Midland Center for the Arts (corner of Eastman Rd. and W. St. Andrews Dr.) The gardens are open 9 a.m. to sunset daily, except major holidays. Admission is $5.00 for adults.

Midland Center for the Arts
(989) 631-5930

See works of art from around the world, stellar attractions in music, theater and dance, and have fun learning about science and history at one of America's most exciting centers fro arts and entertainment. The Midland Center for the Arts' massive red brick building with interlocking metal sculpture circles creating patterns of light over the entrance was designed by the celebrated architect Alden B. Dow. The wonderful complex includes a 1,500-seat auditorium-concert hall, a 426-seat theater, and art galleries, art studios and dining and meeting facilities. The core of the building combines elements of science, history, and art. At the entrance, a swinging Foucault pendulum demonstrates the rotation of the earth. Then, on three lives, active exhibits depict the geological history of the Midwest, how the earliest settlers developed tools to control nature and how people reached beyond mere survival to achieve a meaningful quality of life in science, technology, and medicine. The fourth level is a gallery of art, history, and science exhibits, with something new every two to three months.

Particulars: The center is located near the Dow Gardens, just at Business US-10 (Eastman) and W. St. Andrews Rd. Hours are 10 a.m. to 6 p.m. Monday through Friday. Admission is $4 for adults while children under 12 years of age are $1.

Herbert H. Dow Historical Museum
(989) 832-5319

The H.H. Dow Historical Museum, the newest to Midland's Historical Square, is a replica of the Evens Flour Mill, where the 240 year old Herbert Dow pioneered the experiments on the separation of bromine from natural brine by hydrolysis. This and several adjacent buildings are replicas of the Midland Chemical Company, forerunner of the Dow Chemical Company.

The museum is located adjacent to the Bradley House (a Victorian Era mansion furnished authentically) and Carriage House, both interesting restored homestead buildings.

Particulars: The museum is at the end of Emerson Park near the entrance of Northwood University on Crook Road. Hours are 10 a.m. to 4 p.m. Wednesday through Saturday and 1-5 p.m., Sunday. Admission is $4 for adults, $2 for children or $5 for the family allows you entrance into both the museum and the Bradley House.

MONROE COUNTY

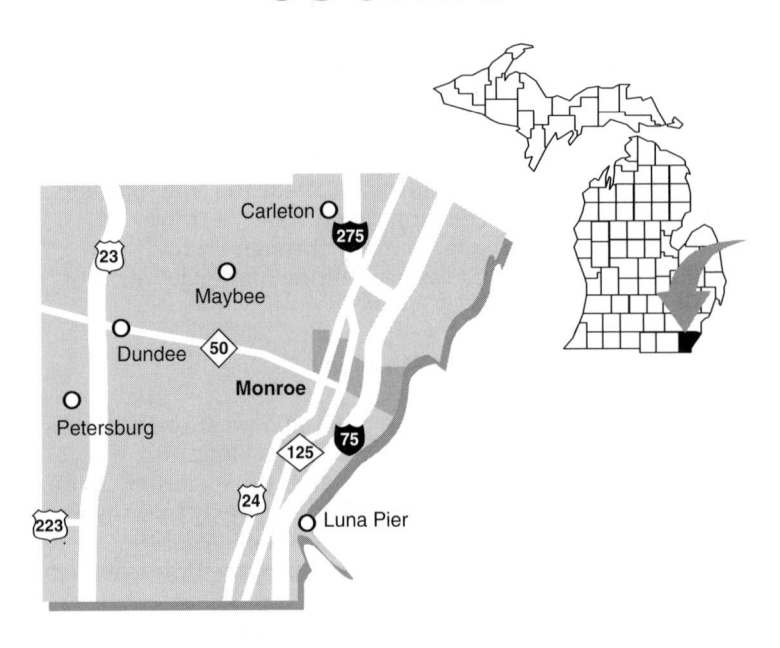

VISITOR INFORMATION

**Monroe County
Convention & Tourism Bureau**
106 W. Front Street
Monroe, MI 48161
800-252-3011

MDOT Welcome Center
I-75 Northbound at
10 mile marker
Monroe, MI 48161

MDOT Welcome Center
U.S. 23
Petersburg, MI 49270

www.monroeinfo.com

Monroe County

▼ Monroe

Battlefield Trail
Monroe County Historical Museum
(734) 240-7780

FREE

Near the banks of the River Raisin on Elm is a small battlefield interpretive center that details local battles and the intrigue of the War of 1812, which pitted the British and Indians against the Americans. With huge tracts of land at stake the battles were bloody and terrible.

Monroe, then called Frenchtown was almost completely destroyed by battle and massacre. The Monroe County Historical Museum has a fine interpretive brochure that details "Battlefield Trails," and areas of the region where you can visit and learn about the conflicts. Tours can be taken by walking or driving.

Particulars: From I-75 depart at the Elm Street exit and head right a quarter mile to the battlefield at 1403 East Elm. The center is open Saturday and Sunday from 10 a.m. to 6 p.m. Free.

George Custer Tour
Monroe County Historical Museum
(734) 240-7780

FREE

Though few people know it, George Custer's hometown is Monroe, the place where he grew up, fell in love, and spent this youth. The Monroe Library has even published a detailed brochure that traces much of Custer's life while in Monroe, detailing 15 sites in the city that the daring general frequented.

We all know where the gold-locked general died at Little Big Horn, but few people know of his life before his military career. The first stop, where the brochure can be obtained, is the Monroe County Historical Museum. The building, a former post office, was built in 1911 on the original site of Judge Daniel S. Bacon's residence. It was the judge's daughter, Elizabeth, who captured the heart of young Custer, and their romance flourished in the southeastern community. The museum features an entire room to their native son, featuring the largest collection of the dashing general's personal artifacts that trace his life and career all the way to his demise at Little Big Horn.

The museum has a considerable collection of Custer's

Custer's Statue, Monroe County.

papers, along with such artifacts such as his baby dress, cadet uniform from West Point, and a heavy buffalo coat that he wore during the winter of 1868. Visitors will also learn that Custer was the first Union officer to use a hot air balloon to survey and map Confederate positions and military movements during the Civil War.

The collection also interprets his non-military life, which includes a passion for hunting, taxidermy and the outdoors. His old Remington hunting rifle and mounts of his quarry are on display in the rooms.

From the galleries of the museum the tour travels through out the city to several interesting stops including the Custer statue that was unveiled in 1910 with President William Taft in attendance and, perhaps most interesting, the Nevin Custer Farm. Nevin Custer was the general's brother who was too sick to serve with him in the military and thus did not die at Little Big Horn. The farm eventually became the home of general's widow and was visited by such dignitaries as Buffalo Bill Cody and Annie Oakley.

Particulars: From I-75, depart at either Front Street (exit 11) or M-50 (exit 13) and head west into downtown Monroe. The museum is at 126 South Monroe Street in the heart of the city. Hours are 10 a.m. to 5 p.m. Wednesday through Sunday and daily during the summer. Free.

Fermi 2 Power Plant Tour
(734) 586-5228

FREE

Groups of heavily sedated suburbanites visit all types of attractions around the state tagging behind a guide listening attentively to canned speeches and a stream of facts. But this tour is different, much more exciting and it really does a good job of detailing our need for alternative energy sources, the marvels of nuclear energy and the safety standards that the Fermi 2 plant exceeds.

Fermi 2 supplies over 10 percent of Detroit Edison's Electricity. The tours combine a film of how nuclear energy is controlled and produced, and there is an adult-only tour that takes you by the turbine generators.

Particulars: From I-75, depart at exit 15 and head north on Dixie Highway to Enrico Fermi Drive. Group tours are free, but they must be scheduled in advance while individuals may join scheduled tours.

River Raisin Battlefield Museum

FREE

At 1403 East Elm Street on the Historic River Raisin. The battle fought here on Jan 22, 1813 was one of the largest engagements of the War of 1812. Of 934 Americans who fought here, only 33 escaped death or capture. The massacre of wounded soldiers the following day shocked and enraged Americans throughout the Old Northwest Territory. The display includes dioramas, full-size British and American soldiers, as well as a fiber-optic map presentation on the Battle of the River Raisin.

Particulars: Free admission. Call the Monroe County Historical Commission at (734) 240-7780 for hours and additional information.

Monroe Street (M-25) National Scenic Byway

FREE

Monroe Street is a unique reflection of more than 200 years of development, adaptation and growth. The route is two miles long. It is a cultural landscape that connects the community - from the oldest families to the newest residents; from the earliest French settlement to a period when the community, as a point of debarkation on Lake Erie, was poised for explosive growth; from elation as hometown to genuine war hero to the sorrow of his later demise - it's the story that's told along Monroe Street.

Driving, walking or cycling along Monroe Street provides the visitor with an unparalleled opportunity to enjoy a mix of residential, religious and commercial landmarks and structures, as well as natural resources such as the historic River Raisin, known by Native Americans as Numaseppee or River of Sturgeon. Monroe Street represents this community's history and culture. It reflects man's impressions upon nature and his willingness to modify, reshape and, in some cases, completely redo what he found, resulting in the creation of a cultural landscape that is uniquely Monroe.

Cabela's

FREE

Cabela's has helped Dundee and Monroe County become the #1 tourist destination in Michigan. It is expected that the outdoor retailer itself, will attract over six million visitors per year. A huge display of North American mammal mounts, special events.

Particulars: 110 Cabela Blvd. East, Dundee, MI 48131, Mon-Sat 8 a.m.-9 p.m., Sun 10 a.m.-6 p.m., 734-529-4700

MUSKEGON COUNTY

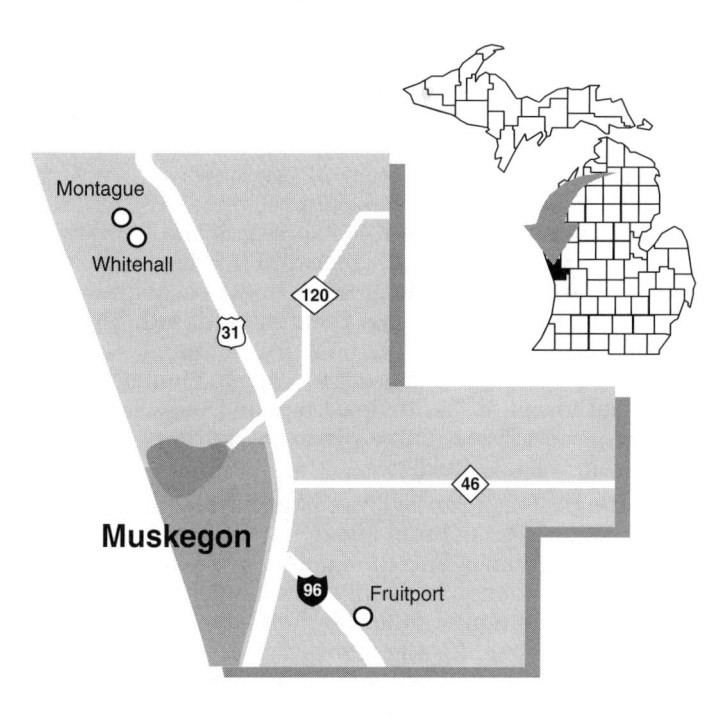

VISITOR INFORMATION

**Muskegon County
Convention & Visitors Bureau**
610 W. Western Avenue
Muskegon, MI 49440
231-724-33100 or 800-250-WAVE
www.visitmuskegon.org

Muskegon County

▼ Muskegon

Gillette Nature Center
(231) 798-3573

Occasionally a visitor will arrive at the Gillette Nature Center in P.J. Hoffmaster State Park and not know it's the Michigan Sand Dune Interpretive Center. They'll enter the split-level building, walk through the lobby then stop dead in their tracks at the huge glass wall on the north side. Framed in by the window is a steep, wind blown dune that towers over the center less then 20 yards away.

Built in the Bi-Centennial year of 1976, the Gillette Nature Center is in the heart of the 1,043-acre park and helps people understand the significance and fragile nature of Michigan's sand dunes. The story is told all around the center, beginning in the 83-seat theater, in the exhibit hall, and on the ground floor hands-on activity area.

The nature center does a great fob of explaining dune ecology, but for a first hand view take the Dune Climb Stairway up the 165 stairs to a platform on top of a dune 190 feet from the lake surface.

Particulars: The nature center is located within Hoffmaster State Park. From I-96 depart at exit 4 and head south on 148th Avenue and then immediately turn west onto Pontaluna Road, which ends in six miles at the park entrance. In the summer, hours from the center are 9 a.m. to 6 p.m. and 1-5 p.m. for the rest of the year. A $4 daily vehicle permit or an $20 annual pass is needed to enter the park.

Hackley and Hume Historical Site
(231) 722-0278

Sick and tired of cookie cutter architectural design? Boxie looking building of metal and glass, houses clad in aluminum or drywall. Never fear, the Hackley and Hume mansions will rescue you.

The homes were built side-by-side in 1889 by Charles H. Hackley and Thomas Hume, a pair of lumber barons and partners in business. They even shared the same carriage house located behind their homes. Today the homes are listed on the National Register of Historic Places and have been called two of the country's most outstanding examples of Victorian architecture.

Inside you see polished hardwood floors of contrasting light and dark wood, hand-carved coat racks, and monkeys and lions skillfully carved into the walls, with five races of mankind etched into the ceiling trim. Every piece of wood in every room is richly polished and lavishly carved displaying craftsmanship and the opulence of the 19th century golden era of Muskegon when the city was known as "the Lumber Queen of the World."

The homes aren't only castles of carved wood but also contains seven large fireplaces, each different from the other, imported ceramic tiles and hand stenciled ceilings and wall that are renovated as are the 15 Tiffany-type stained glass windows throughout the house.

Particulars: From US-31, depart onto Business US-31 into downtown Muskegon. The homes are at 484 W. Webster Ave. and open from mid-May through September as well as fro the Christmas season. Hours during the summer are noon to 4 p.m. Wednesday through Sunday. Admission is $3 for adults and children 12 years old and under is free

Muskegon Museum of Art
(231) 720-2570

FREE

People that really know about such thins consider the Muskegon Art Museum one of the finest small facilities in the Midwest. Why? In part, because monies from lumber barons compiled a collection of 19th century and 20th century American art. An extensive glass collection has also added to its reputations as a fine gallery offering ever-changing exhibits and educational programming.

Particulars: The museum is located in downtown Muskegon at 296 W. Webster Ave. Hours are 10 a.m. to 4 p.m. Wednesday and Friday, 9 a.m. to 5 p.m. on Saturday, noon to 4 p.m. on Tuesday, and noon to 8 p.m. on Thursday. Free.

Old Indian Cemetery
Muskegon County Visitor Bureau
(231) 724-3100

FREE

One of the oldest cemeteries in the state, both settlers and Indian graves dating back to 1750 and are well preserved.

Particulars: The cemetery is located in downtown Muskegon on Morris Avenue. Free.

Trolley Company
Muskegon County Visitor Bureau
(231) 724-3100

Take a ride on an old-fashioned electric car along three routes that run from Muskegon State Park, through downtown Muskegon and south to P.J. Hoffmaster State Park.

Particulars: The clanking cars rumble about daily Memorial Day to Labor Day from 11 a.m. to 6 p.m. Call the visitor's bureau for route maps and stops.

U.S.S. Silversides, Muskegon County.

U.S.S. Silversides
(231) 755-1230

The U.S.S. Silversides was commissioned into the Navy fleet just eight days after the historic attack on Pearl Harbor. After sinking 90,000 tons of enemy ships on 14 patrols of the Pacific, she now is a floating submarine museum, offering guided tours below decks to share the excitement and drama of underwater warfare.

From bow to stern, tours will show visitors the cramped engine room, sailor quarters, and torpedo tubes. The Silversides carried 72 crew members during 90-day patrols and ranked third among all U.S. subs during the war for sinking 23 ships.

Although there are two other subs open to the public in

Ohio and Wisconsin, the Silversides is the only one that offers overnight stays for groups. Organized groups may book an evening on the sub and sleep in cramped bunks while stowing their personal items in the tiny two-foot-by-two-foot lockers.

Particulars: From Business US-31, head west on Laketon Road and continue towards Lake Michigan on Lake Shore Drive. Lake Shore ends at Pere Marquette Park where the submarine is tied up. Below deck tours are offered daily May through September and Weekends in April and October. Hours are 10 a.m. to 5:30 p.m. Admission for adults is $5.50 and children five to 11 years old are $3.50. WWII veterans are free.

▼ Montague

Montague City Museum
(231) 894-6813

FREE

Open weekends only during the summer, the museum displays local logging era artifacts, including chain dogs and peaveys, a doll collection,sorry, no Barbie dolls, stone collection and lots of historic photographs.

Particulars: From Business US-31, turn west on Dowling just after crossing the White River. The museum is on the corner of Church and Main Street and open Saturday and Sunday from 1-5 p.m. June through September. Free.

World's Largest Weather Vane
(231) 894-8265

FREE

As we've already mentioned in this award-winning travel guidebook, damn near every town in the state has a world famous or world record something or other. Sebewaing has the "world's best walleye fishing," Hessel has the world's biggest antique boat show, and White Lake has the world's biggest weather vane.

Erected in 1984, the weather vane is 48 feet tall, weighs 3,500 pounds, has a 26-foot long arrow and directional letters that are 3 feet, 6 inches tall. It's topped off by a 14-foot-long schooner with a mast almost 12-feet nigh. There are few rooftops big enough to have this monster installed. Although weather vanes originally came from Europe, it was in America where they reached their fullest development and became works of art. In 1941, Whitehall Metal Studios set up shop in Montague and its main business was hand casting weather vanes. In fact, the company's reputation has spread to President Eisenhower's rooftop in Gettysburg, and President Ronald Reagan's ranch in California and now to Montague. Do only Republicans buy weather vanes?

Particulars: The weather vane is right off Business US-31 and the Whitehall Metal Studios are just up the street. The factory store of the studios is open Monday through Friday from 8:30 a.m. to 4:30 p.m. Free.

▼ White Lake

White River Light Station Museum
(231) 894-8265

The stately old building made of Michigan limestone and brick reverberates the character of its longest serving keeper, William Robinson. Robinson spent 47 years tending the light, crawling out onto a railing during snowstorms to wipe glycerine on the tower windows, or keeping wicks lit so ships may pass safely in the night. Today, the light is retired to museum status but its colorful past is preserved for the 4,000 annual visitors that climb the stairs and examine the artifacts from another era.

A variety of nautical devices are featured, including a binnacle, compasses, bilge pump, chronograph, sextant and other helmsman items. You can listen to a foghorn, look through the original Fresnel lens and climb the spiral stairs for a glimpse of Lake Michigan's unique sand dunes that stretch along the coastline. Despite its off-the-beaten path location, the yellow brick building with its black-capped tower and red roof is worth a tour.

Particulars: From US-31, depart west on White Lake Drive and then south on South Shore Drive to where it ends at the corner of Murray Road and Scenic Drive. Museum signs will direct you to the lighthouse at the end of Murray Road. The lighthouse is open June through August from 11 a.m. to 5 p.m. Tuesday through Friday and noon to 6 p.m. Saturday and Sunday. It is also open Memorial Day weekend and weekends in September. Admission is $1 for adults and 50 cents for kids.

NEWAYGO COUNTY

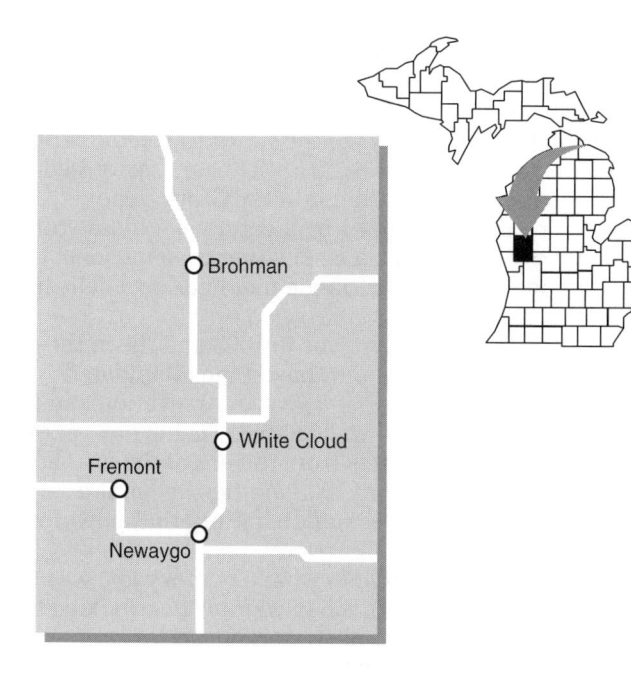

VISITOR INFORMATION

**White Cloud
Chamber of Commerce**
12 N. Charles
P.O. Box 2030
White Cloud, MI 49349
231-689-6607

Newaygo County

▼ Grant

Grant Depot Restaurant
(231) 834-7361

The most distinctive structure in Grant is its wooden water tower, the last one left in the state. Built in 1891, it's the classic Petticoat Junction water tower and driving down Main Street you half expect to see Uncle Joe and the rest of the cast from that zany television comedy.

Drive through the town to see the water tower, but stop because of its train depot. Chuck Zobel has transformed the once bustling passenger station into the Grant Depot Restaurant, one of the county's best eateries. Unless you're a railroad enthusiast, then it's a fascinating train museum that serves a very good lemon meringue pie that Zobel calls his "Mile High Lemon Pie."

The last ticket sold in Grant was in 1963 and the4n the depot sat vacant until Zobel purchased the dilapidated building in 1979. It took almost a year of renovation and in the process of tearing down walls and replacing floors Zobel turned up a variety of artifacts from the era of the iron horse; tickets and trains orders from 1903, bottles, telegrams, signs, even the remains of a copper sulfate battery that powered the telegraph before the age of electricity.

Today you can sit at a table in what a century ago was the passenger waiting room or in a bay window overlooking the tracks where a station agent once worked a telegraph. What was the baggage room is now the kitchen and next to the cashier counter is the original freight scale. Its never been moved. The walls of the restaurant are covered with memorabilia; everything from lanterns and oil cans to warning lights, passenger tickets and a engineer's manual on how to operate a locomotive. And beneath a model train that chugs along a ledge near the ceiling, you can order the Pere Marquette Chopped Sirloin, The Express Steak Dinner or just a cup of coffee and one of those cinnamon rolls that are almost as big as a boxcar.

Particulars: From I-96 in Grand Rapids, head north on M-37 (exit 30). Grant is reached in 24 miles and the Depot is right off M-37. The restaurant is open 7:30 a.m. to 8 p.m. Monday through Thursday, until 9 p.m. Friday and Saturday and from 11:30 to 3 p.m. Sunday.

Schoolhouse Youth Hotel.

▼ White Cloud

FREE

Loda Lake Wildflower Sanctuary
Baldwin/White Cloud Ranger District
(231) 745-4631

Most self-guiding nature trails point out things like trees or a bog, features that you can pretty much count on being there from year to year. At Loda Lake Wildflower Sanctuary interpretive posts mark the location of trillium, blueberries, swamp rose, insect eating sundew plans and fragrant water lily. AA Few yards to the right of post number 36, notes the trail map and guide, Aare birdfoot violets.

How much more accurate can you get?

The sanctuary was originally part of a 1000-acre private reserve, much of it farmed and then sold to the US. Forest Service. The wide variety of habitats in such a small area, where in less than a mile it's possible to pass through marshes, forests, skirt a lake or a grassy meadow, immediately attracted the attention of many. In 1938, rangers invited the Federated Garden Clubs of Michigan to help them create a sanctuary for native plants, including endangered and protective species to ensure their survival.

Although part of the Manistee national Forest, the preserve is still managed by the Federated Garden Clubs and over the years has evolved into an unique haven for botanists, wildflower enthusiasts and families like us who just want to know the difference between Michigan holly and Holly, Michigan (post number 19).

The trail guide is so important that it's best to either stop at the White Cloud ranger station or call ahead for one rather than trust your luck on the map box at the trailhead being stocked. The trail is a on-mile loop of easy hiking where you encounter the first numbered post in less than 20 feet. Before you return to the picnic you'll pass 39 posts and if you stop to examine every one, plan on a good hour or two for the adventure.

Particulars: From White Cloud head north on M-37 and then left on Five Mile Road where directional sign to Loda Lake is posted on the corner. Head a mile west and then turn right on Fletcher Road. The entrance to the sanctuary is a mile to the north. To obtain a trail guide stop at the U.S. Forest Service Ranger Station on M-37 in White Cloud, which has an information parlor open 24-hours a day. Free.

▼ Newaygo

Power House Museum
Newaygo County Tourist Council
(231) 294-0630

FREE

In 1900, a large powerhouse was built on the banks of the Muskegon River to supply power for the Portland Cement Company. Eventually its high ceiling and partitioned off rooms proved to be an ideal setting for the history of Newaygo and today the Power House is the largest museum in the county.

The tall red brick building features a number of exhibits on the logging era of Newaygo as well as the county's original inhabitants, the Ottawa Indians. Also inside you will find an old time pharmacy, country store, print shop, fire-fighting equipment, one-room school and other displays.

Particulars: The Power House is located just off M-37, where the state highway descends a hill to cross the

Loda Lake Wildflower Sanctuary, Newaygo County.

Muskegon River. Hours vary but it's always open on Saturday and Sunday afternoons in the summer. Admission is $1 for adults.

OAKLAND COUNTY

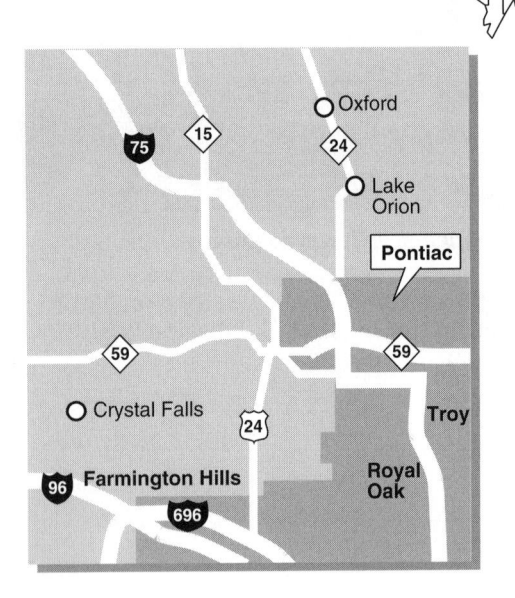

VISITOR INFORMATION

Farmington/Famington Hills Chamber of Commerce
30903 W. Ten Mile Rd. - Suite B
Farmington Hills, MI 48336
248-474-3440

www.ffhchamber.com

Oakland County

▶ Holly

Battle Alley
Holly Hotel
(248) 634-5208

On Aug. 29, 1908, Carry Nation, the protemperance leader known as the "Kansas City Saloon Smasher," and her supporters arrived in Holly and invaded the bars lining a red brick street on the town's seedier side known as Battle Alley, due to frequent fights among drunks. With umbrellas in hand, they went down the street clubbing patrons and smashing whiskey bottles until they reached the end of the short street where Nation entered the Holly Hotel. Inside the hotel's saloon, she unleashed the most fury that day attacking the painting of a flimsily draped lady above the bar.

Today you can walk the red bricks of Battle Alley, read a Michigan historical marker about the account or enter the Holly Hotel for a fine meal. And despite her determination, you can still get a beer or a shot of whiskey in this town.

Particulars: Depart I-75 at exit and head west on Grange Hall Road into town. Exploring Battle Alley is free but you'll find the hotel restaurant a bit pricey.

Seven Lakes Vineyard
(248) 629-5686

FREE

Located between Fenton and Holly, in the northwest corner of Oakland county, is the only bonded vineyard of southeast Michigan. What began as 25 acres of grapes in 1978, today is a vineyard of more than 100 acres that produces more than 20 types of wine from award winning whites to Cady Lake Apple, a sweet apple wine.

The winery also features a large tract of dense hardwood forest with some trees more than 200 years old. Winding through the stands of black walnut, white oak and maple is a network of hiking trails with picnic tables located along the paths. The winery offers both tasting and tours but the real charm of Seven Lakes is to bring a picnic, purchase a bottle and then enjoy it in the soothing quiet of the woodland trails.

Particulars: From I-75 depart at exit 101 and head west on Grange Hall Road then north on Fish Lake Road. Continue west on Tinsman Road to the winery at 1111 Tinsman. From US-23, depart at exit 79. Seven Lakes is open 10 a.m. to 5 p.m.

Monday through Saturday and noon to 5 p.m. Sunday by appointment only. Tasting is free.

▼ Oxford

Northeast Oakland Historical Museum
Oxford Chamber of Commerce
(248) 628-0410

Located in the heart of historical Oxford, a town with more than its share of Victorian homes, the museum is housed in the former Oxford Savings Bank. The imposing stone building was built in 1922 features a high ceiling, tile floor and a walk in steel safe that is so large it now serves as the curator's office.

The museum is best known as the home of the Radio Lone Ranger. Brace Beemer, the "masked stranger" who entertained the country through the air -waves in the 1920s and then lived in this corner of Oakland County until his death in the mid-1960s.

You'll also find an interesting collection of furniture, tools, home appliances and other items from the 19th century when this was a remote rural area of southeast Michigan. Along with the artifacts there is a delightful staff that dates back to the wood burning stoves and gramaphones and whose stories about growing up in the era of chamber pots and heated soapstones for your bed make this a charming place to visit.

Particulars: The museum is located right on M-24 in the heart of Oxford. Hours are 1-4 p.m. on Saturday and 1-4 p.m. on Wednesday June through August. Admission is by donation.

▼ Davisburg

Davisburg Candle Factory
(248) 634-4214

FREE

Watch them make candles in this enchanting 125-year-old factory, a three story rambling building in the hamlet of Davisburg. There is also a gift shop and its hard not to watch the taper being dipped time and time again and then leave without purchasing a dozen candles.

Particulars: From I-75, depart at exit 92 and head north on Dixie Highway. In two miles turn west on Bigelow Road and then continue west on Davisburg Road to the village. The factory is on 634 Davisburg Rd. and is open 10 a.m. to 5 p.m. Monday through Saturday. Free.

▼ Rochester Hills

Rochester Hills Museum
Van Hoosen Farm
(248) 656-4663

In 1851, Joshua Van Hoosen set off to make his fortune in the California gold fields, returning two years later to purchase the Taylor family farm and marry Sarah Taylor. Van Hoosen found success in farming as almost as easy as in gold panning and soon he was the major landholder in the Stony Creek area.

Van Hoosen raised his family in the 1840 farmhouse and eventually his granddaughter, Sarah Van Hoosen Jones, deeded the property to Michigan State University, which turned it over to Rochester Hills in 1979 to be used as a museum.

Much of the museum honors Bertha Van Hoosen, one of Van Hoosen's daughters who went on to become one of the first woman to graduate from the University of Michigan Medical School and became an internationally know surgeon. Visitors can also tour the farmhouse with changing exhibits as well as barns that are open during the summer.

Particulars: From the city of Rochester head north on Rochester Road and then northeast on Romeo to the museum at 1005 Van Hoosen Rd.

Hours are 1-4 p.m. Wednesday through Saturday. Admission is $5 for adults and $3 for senior citizens and children.

▼ Pontiac

Pine Grove Historical Museum
(248) 338-6732

The former Greek Revival Home of Governor Moses Wisner was built in 1845 and today serves as the Pine Grove Historical Museum dedicated to the history of Pontiac and the surrounding area. Rooms within the home have been restored and feature exhibits and displays while also on the grounds are several other buildings including a classic red carriage barn and a one-room schoolhouse from Dayton Plains.

During the summer guides in period customs lead tours of all the buildings and do a wonderful job explaining the history behind the displays.

Particulars: From Woodward Avenue continue north on Wid Track Drive, which merges into Oakland Avenue. The museum is at 405 Oakland Dr. Hours are 9 a.m. to 4 p.m. daily but the tours are held only Tuesday through Friday during the summer. The tours are $5 for adults $3 for senior citizens and $1.50 for children.

▼ Birmingham

The Hunter House
Birmingham Historical Society   *FREE*
(248) 642-2817

Built in 1822 and originally located on Woodward Avenue, the Hunter House has been moved several times but is still one of the oldest homes in Birmingham. Inside you'll find six rooms with period furnishings dating to the mid-1800s.

Particulars: Today the home is located in downtown Birmingham, just west of Hunter Avenue at 550 W. Maple. Hours are 1-4 p.m. Wednesday through Saturday. Admission is $2 for adults and $1 for seniors and students.

▼ Troy

Troy Historical Village   *FREE*
(248) 524-3570

Located at the site of the old city hall, The historical village includes the 1832 Caswell House, a log cabin built in the 1820s, a Village Print Shop, 1877 Poppleton School and a wagon repair shop. You'll also be able to wander through a blacksmith shop and the replicas of an 1870 general store and gazebo as well as a small museum.

Particulars: From I-75, depart at exit 69 and head east on Big Beaver Road and then immediately north on Livernois Road to Wattles Road. The village is west at 60 W. Wattles. Hours are 1- 4 p.m. Tuesday through Saturday and 1-5 p.m. on Sunday. Free.

▼ West Bloomfield

Holocaust Memorial Center   *FREE*
(248) 661-0840

Some museums entertain you. Some thrill you. Some leave you in wonderment. The Holocaust Memorial Center stuns you. The purpose of the center is to tell the story and teach the history of the Holocaust and it's a heart-wrenching experience the minute you step into the darkened hall.

Founded by Rabbi Charles Rosenzveig, a member of the group of survivors known as Shaarit Haplaytah (Saved Remnant), the $7 million center opened in 1984 as the

Holly Hotel, Oakland County.

country's first exclusively designed museum and research facility dedicated to the Holocaust. It attracts more than 100,000 visitors annually and 85 percent of the visitors are non-Jewish.

A journey back into the Holocaust begins in a darkened tunnel with the Roman Legion's conquest of Israel and the destruction of the Temple of Jerusalem that resulted in A a people with a long and rich history (being) dispersed. AWith a soft Yiddish lullaby playing in the background, you follow the Jews as they scattered across the world, particularly in Central Europe where they had settled in Germany 800 years before it became a nation.

Suddenly, the lullaby is shattered by a recording of Adolf Hitler ranting to a wildly cheering crowd. You have entered the section entitled A"The Gathering Storm" where exhibits detail how rampant inflation and food shortage of a post-World War I Germany lead to anti-Semitism and the raise of the Nazism and Hitler himself.

The heart of the center is perhaps one of the most emotional museum exhibits anywhere in Michigan. The walls change to rough wood and rusty corrugated steel while in front of you is barbed wire stretched across a barren field and a mural of a death camp on the background. Overhead roving spotlights search of escaped prisoners. Among the wire and the searching lights are five video monitors whose footage takes you step-by-step through the death camp experience. The first view how Jews were transported to camps, others look at their treatment on arrival, living conditions and deterioration of the camps. The final one is entitled "Extermination."

If that wasn't emotional enough, the center also has a small video theater in which Detroit-area survivors detail life in the camps, a gallery dedicated to the uprising in the Warsaw Ghetto, diorama of the bombing of Berlin and films of what greeted the Allied troops whey they liberated the camps.

Particulars: From I-696, exit at Orchard Lake Road and head north. Turn west on Maple Road and the Jewish Community Campus is on the corner of Maple and Drake Road. Signs on the campus will direct you to the center. The center is open 10 a.m. to 4 p.m. Sunday through Thursday. Free.

▼ Farmington

Farmington Historical Museum
(248) 473-7275

The Farmington Historical Museum is located in the Governor Warner Mansion, an 1867 Victorian Italianate home of Governor Fred Maltby Warner. Not only is the house restored, but so are other buildings and the gardens that landscape the grounds.

Particulars: The museum is located right off Grand River Avenue, just west of the downtown area of Farmington. Hours are 1-5 p.m. Wednesday and the first Sunday of each month.

▼ Milford

Mildord Historical Museum
(248) 685-7308

The 1853 Greek Revival home has since been restored into a museum featuring local history and artifacts. The upper floor is furnished as a home with period furnishings while the lower floor is used for theme displays.

Particulars: From M-59, east of US-23, head south on Milford Road into the downtown area and then east on Commerce Street. The home is at 124 E. Commerce. Hours are 1-4 p.m. Thursday, Friday, and Sunday except when the museum is closed from Christmas to the first Wednesday in February. Admission is $3 for adults and $2 for seniors and students.

OCEANA COUNTY

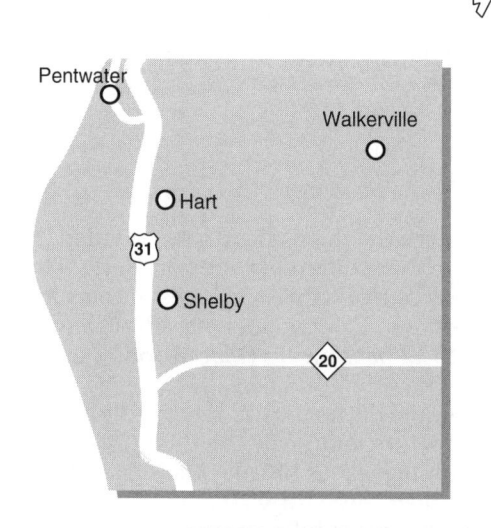

VISITOR INFORMATION

Hart-Silver Lake Area Chamber of Commerce
P. O. Box 69
Hart, MI 49420
800-870-9786

www.whitelake.org

Oceana County

▼ Shelby

Shelby Gem Stone Factory
(231) 861-2165

FREE

The Shelby Gemstone Factory is a one-of-a-kind in the United States in the production of man-made gems, including diamonds. A brief audio-visual program in a 50-seat theater and displays of Shelby gems and gem-producing equipment are highlights of a visit.

Particulars: From US-31, exit at Shelby Road and head east, following signs to the factory at 1330 Industrial Drive. Hours are 9 a.m. to 5:30 p.m. Monday through Friday and noon to 4 p.m. Free.

▼ Mears

Silver Lake State Park
(231) 873-3083

At Silver Lake State Park the dunes have been divided into three separate areas for three different types of users. The designated area south is one of only two places in the state where dune rides are offered in large open-air all-terrain vehicles that hold up to 12 passengers (Mac Woods Dunes Rides, call 616-873-2817).

The section is the middle of the park is reserved for foot-travelers only, where visitors may scale the mightily dunes and walk among the lapping waves of Lake Michigan. To the north is the ORV area, designated for virtually any type of four-wheeler, dune buggy, or dirt bike. Cheap and Free fans will enjoy the daredevil riders climb the dunes and throw rooster-tails of sand in every direction. The best view of the antics is from the first dunetop.

Particulars: From US-31, depart at Shelby Road but head west for six miles to CR-B15 (16th Avenue). Head north to pass the park headquarters where you can pick up a map of the state park. A $4 vehicle entry fee or a $20 state park pass is required to enter the park.

Little Sable Point Lighthouse –
Silver Lake State Park

The Little Sable Point Lighthouse was built in 1874 and once looked very similar to the Big Sable Point Lighthouse near Ludington. Both towers stood 107 feet tall, both were constructed of brick, and both had a third-order Fresnel lens. The Big Sable Point tower deteriorated and eventually was covered with steel plates, but the tower at Little Sable Point still looks much as it did 120 years ago.

Particulars: (231) 873-3083; Silver Lake Road, Silver Lake State Park, Mears, MI 49436.

ONTONAGON COUNTY

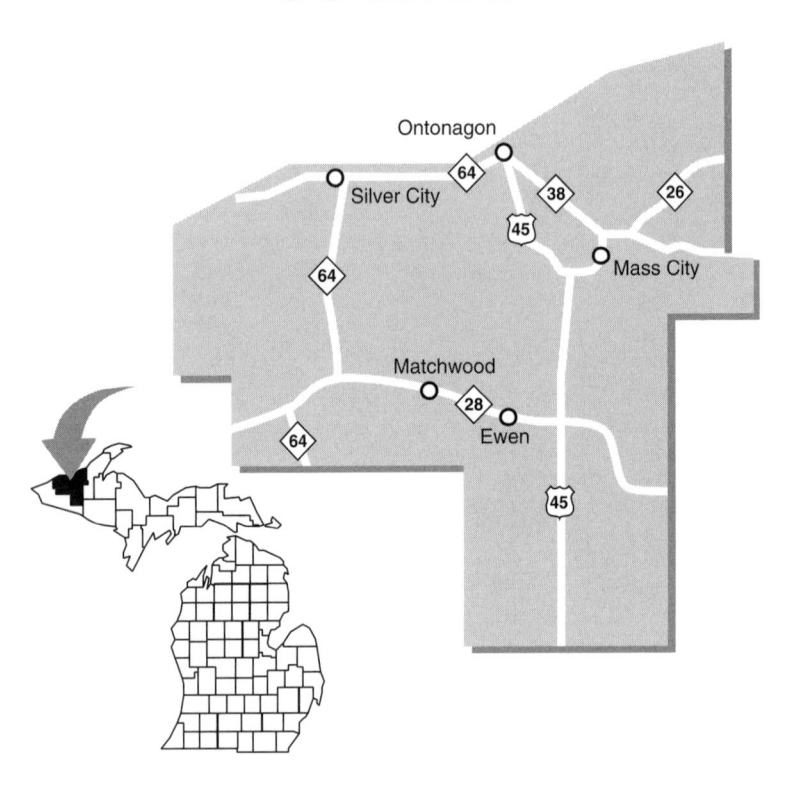

VISITOR INFORMATION

Ontonagon Tourism Council
600 River Road
P. O. Box 266
Ontonagon, MI 49953
906-884-4735

Ontonagon County

▼ Rockland

Old Victoria
Upper Peninsula Travel and Recreation Association
(800) 562-7134

There's a scattering of ghost towns around Michigan, many are merely rubble in the woods. One of the best however is Old Victoria. The Ontonagon County town was originally named Cushin and established in 1849 after the discovery of an ancient miner's pit that still contained a mass of copper. In 1858, a new group of investors came in renamed the Victoria and eventually the company town grew to more than 2,000 residents.

What remains today are several buildings of hand-hewed logs, ruins of a rock house, and mining equipment lying all over the place. The Society of the Restoration of Old Victoria has renovated four of the log cabins and offer guided tours of the entire town during the summer.

Particulars: Old Victoria is four miles west of Rockland with an entrance road clearly posted on US-45. Historical tours of the town are given daily from 9 a.m. to 6 p.m. Memorial Day through the fall colors in October. Admission is by donation.

▼ Ontonagon

Lake of the Clouds
Porcupine Mountains Wilderness State Park
(906) 885-5275

Without a doubt, the most photographed spot in the Upper Peninsula and possibly all of Michigan is from the lake of the Clouds overlook in Porcupine Mountains Wilderness State Park. Little wonder why. The panorama is stunning. The deep blue lake sits deep between two towering ridges that appear like mountain ranges. Over your shoulder is Lake Superior. The overlook is a short walk from the parking area that features picnic tables and toilets but no source of water. More views of the lake can be enjoyed from the 5-mile Escarpment Trail that ends further east along M-107. This is not a stroll for young children or those with flimsy shoes on.

More about the Porkies can be learned at the state park's visitor's center that features displays on wildlife, the mining history of the area and a video theater with an excellent

Victoria Ghost Town, Ontonagon County.

presentation on this 60,000-acre wilderness. But perhaps the most intriguing exhibit in the visitor center, especially for anybody planning to hike the 90-mile network of trails, is the relief map that clearly shows just how rugged the Porkies are.

Particulars: The park's east entrance is 17 miles west of Ontonagon, via M-64 and M-107 and the Lake of the Clouds overlook is at the west end of M-107. The visitor center is open from 10 a.m. to 6 p.m. daily from Memorial Day to mid-October. A $4 vehicle permit or a $20 state park pass is required to enter the park.

Waterfalls in Ontonagon County   *FREE*

Waterfalls abound! Big, small and famous, take your pick. Two of the most notable are the Bond and Agate falls. Bond Falls has been the backdrop for national ad campaigns for sport utility vehicles as well as for tourist snapshots. These falls are here for you to see just off Highways 28 and 45. A partial list of Water Falls: Overlooked & Greenstone Falls, Trap Falls, Union Gorge & Numerous Waterfalls, Cascade Falls, O Kun De Kun Falls, Bond Falls and Agate Falls. For waterfall information call (906) 884-4735.

OSCEOLA COUNTY

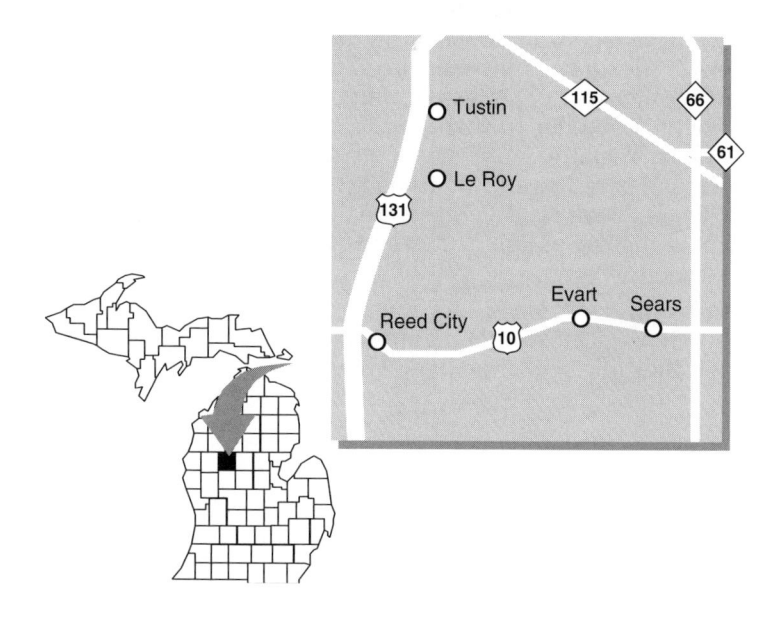

VISITOR INFORMATION

**Reed City Area
Chamber of Commerce**
P. O. Box 27
Reed City, MI 49677
231-743-9929

Osceola County

Osceola County
Cadillac Area Visitors Bureau
(800) 22-Lakes

Grove Hill Township Park

To those who want to stand on the highest point in the Lower Peninsula, head to the northeast corner of Osceola County. A view you can forget about at Grove Hill Township Park, but there is elevation.

The park is little more than a picnic table at the top of a hill in a stand of red pine. But, as an interpretive sign states, at 1,725 feet above sea level, you are officially on the highest point in the Lower Peninsula and to some people that's all they need.

Particulars: From M-115, southeast of Cadillac, turn south at 130th Avenue towards Dighton and in three-miles you will reach the entrance of the park. Free.

OSCODA COUNTY

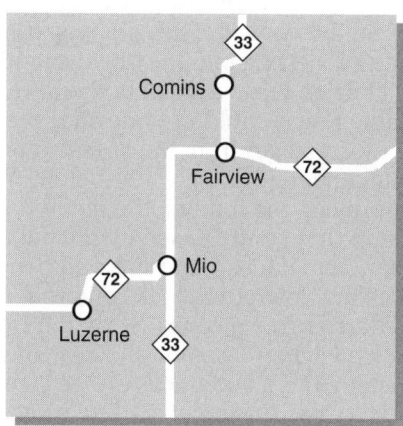

VISITOR INFORMATION

Oscoda Convention & Visitors Bureau
4440 North U.T. Route 23
989-739-7322 or 800-235-4625
www.oscoda.com

Oscoda County

▼ McKinley

O'Brien Lake Fishing Pier
Harrisville Ranger District
(989) 739-0728

FREE

When the Northeast Michigan Sportmen's Club proposed the O'Brien Lake fishing pier to US. Forest Service, the idea was simple. The club wanted to build Michigan's first and only "barrier-free fishing access in a primitive setting."

The members felt it wasn't enough just to put up a ramp and dock anywhere. Anglers in wheelchairs, older anglers, and anglers with disabilities enjoy the same aspects of fishing as anybody else. They enjoy getting away, and they like a natural setting and they love catching fish.

O'Brien Lake, a small body of water just north of the Au Sable River, could provide all three if only there was someway they could get from the Forest Service road down a 23-foot embankment to the water below. With the U.S. Forest Service supplying the lumber, the members built a 638-foot wooden ramp that gently descents the hill and ends at a 50-foot long pier. It includes handrails and benches to aid anybody walking down to the lake and that's the key word. Anybody.

Barrier free means just that; it is there for anybody; anglers in wheelchairs, senior citizens, and especially children. Fishing piers and docks are perfect for young anglers whose fidgety nature and short attention span is not well suited to spending an afternoon in a small boat. They can walk around the pier, lean over the railing and watch a crayfish in the shallows, run up and down the ramp until their little legs are dead tired. They can even try their hand fishing as O'Brien Lake is stocked with trout.

Particulars: From County Road 32 in McKinley, turn right on River Road and then an immediate left on Reed Road. Follow Reed Road for almost a mile where it merges into FR 4061. In another mile swing left on FR 4838 and stay on the main dirt road, avoiding all other tracks that swing off into the woods. In 1.2 miles FR 4838 ends at the parking area of O'Brien Lake. Free.

River Road National Forest Scenic Byway -

FREE

4.3 miles of M-65 and 17.7 miles of county roads near the south bank of the famed Au Sable River. Attractions along the way include Lumberman's

Monument Visitor Center, Eagle's Nest Overlook where you can see an eagle's nest that been in use for many years (bring your binoculars) and Iargo Springs which has been in use since the 1840s. Indians believed the springs held mystical powers.

OTSEGO COUNTY

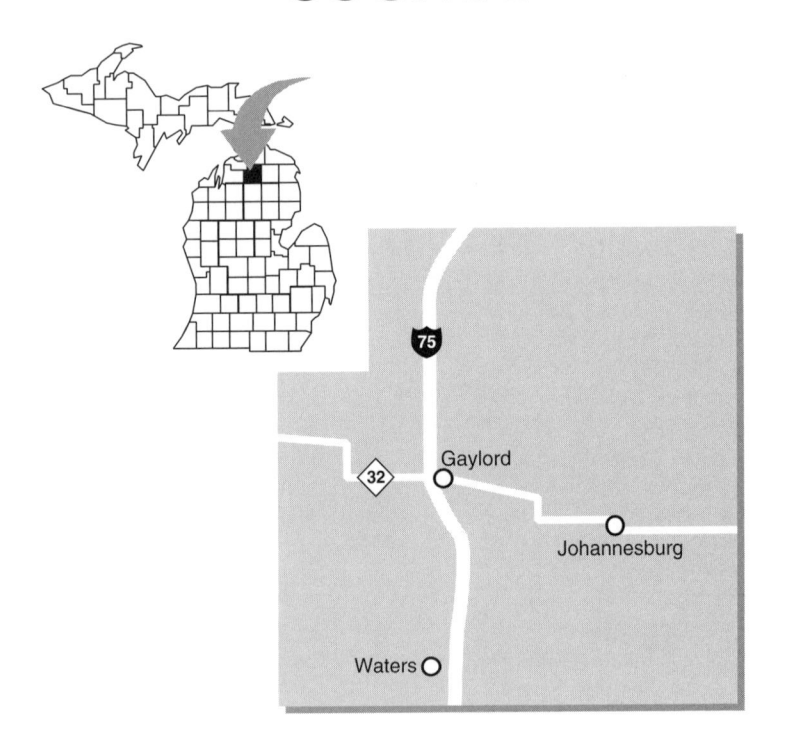

VISITOR INFORMATION

**Gaylord Area
Convention & Tourist Bureau**
101 W. Main Street
Gaylord, MI 49735
989-732-4000 or 800-345-8621
www.gaylord-mich.com

Otsego County

▼ Gaylord

Elk Park
Gaylord Chamber of Commerce
(989) 732-6333

FREE

You want to see an elk but have no desire to be swatting flies in the Pigeon River Country State Forest? Head over to this 40-acre park, Michigan's only elk park. Feed is put out in the partly wooded preserve, which attracts both elk and deer. No one will guarantee you seeing an elk here but your chances are pretty good.

Particulars: The park is on the east side of I-75 near K-Mart, behind the Elk Lodge off Grandview Boulevard. Gaylord is on the 45th parallel. Free.

Gaylord Car
Gaylord Chamber of Commerce
(989) 732-6333

FREE

Gaylord is no Detroit (thank goodness!) But the community did manufacture automobiles at one point and the remnants of the era, a 1911 Gaylord Car is housed in the Chamber of Commerce Building.

Particulars: The chamber building is in the downtown section of Gaylord, a block south of M-32, at the corner of South Otsego Avenue and First Street. The chamber is open 8 a.m. to 5 p.m. Monday through Friday but you can see the car through a picture window day or night. Free.

Otsego County Historical Museum
(989) 732-4568

FREE

Gaylord's newest museum is dedicated to the history of Otsego County and is filled with artifacts and local memorabilia.

Particulars: The museum is located in downtown Gaylord along M-32, northwest of the County-City Building. Being a relatively new museum the hours tend to change from season to season but in the winter they are usually 1-7 p.m. Tuesday and Saturday. Free.

▼ Vanderbilt

Elk Viewing
Pigeon River Country State Forest
(989) 983-4101

A bull elk can weigh close to 700 pounds, a mature cow about 350 pounds, they are big and impressive, sometimes noisy, often easily seen if you are patient during the month of October. Elk are native to Michigan and once roamed the forests throughout most of the state. But the intense logging of the 19th century removed their habitat and native elk disappeared in 1877.

In 1918, seven elk were transplanted from Yellowstone National Park to an area near Wolverine and within ten years the herd had multiplied to 500. At times the herd struggled but the 1980s there were more than 1,000, roaming a range that consisted of southern Cheboygan, northern Otsego and northern Montmorency counties. Although stray elk have wandered as far south as the high school football field in Mio, the heart of the range is the 98,000-acre Pigeon River County State Forest, whose headquarters is 13 miles east of Vanderbilt.

Although elk can be seen anytime of the year, they are most difficult to spot in the summer season when they head fro thick cover to escape the heat, while in the winter they tend to herd-up and find logging areas where clear cut areas offer young woody sprouts. Late September and early October are prime times to see and hear elk.

Remember, that grassy meadows are the focal points for elk during the rut and the best time to sight them is at dawn and especially at dusk in the final hour before dark. Bring your binoculars for a great budget-minded adventure along the backroads of Otsego County.

Particulars: There are fields and meadows scattered throughout the state forest but three are posted as designated ilk viewing areas:

1) Eight miles east of Vanderbilt on Sturgeon Valley Road, right before you cross the Pigeon River.

2) Along County Road 622, 18 miles east of Gaylord and a mile east of Meridian Road.

3) Along Osmun Road, four miles north of the new state forest headquarters and reached by going north from Sturgeon Valley Road onto Twin Lakes Road.

OTTAWA COUNTY

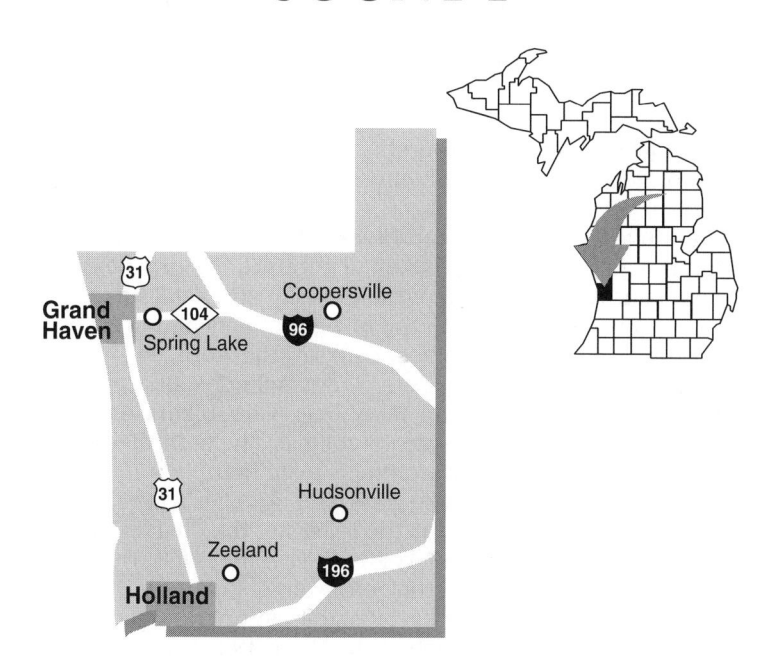

VISITOR INFORMATION

**Holland Area
Visitors & Convention Bureau**
76 E. 8th Street
Holland, MI 49423
**616-394-000
or 800-506-1299**
www.holland.org

Ottawa County

Grand Haven

Grand Haven Boardwalk
Grand Haven Visitors Bureau
(616) 842-4910

FREE

Government, the people that take our money in the form of taxes and spend it on wise stuff, also helps tourism and Grand Haven boardwalk is a prime example. It's one of the places where government, in partnership with the private sector, have created a bustling, high-energy strip, all near Lake Michigan.

The walk stretches for nearly two miles from the historical Grand Haven Lighthouse past small shops, outdoor cafes, a museum and sculpture in a park. Colorful characters from the early morning anglers to the beach bunnies and Chicago tourists, make it one of the best walks in the state. In between, there are rollerbladers clad in spandex, charter captains and clients cleaning salmon, joggers, bikers, and people licking dripping ice cream comes. The natural scenery is terrific, but the people watching is even better.

From the historic train, you pass Chinook Pier where crowds gather twice a day for the return of the charter fishing boats to view their catches. Then it's Tri-Cities Historical Museum, located in a century-old train depot, and Waterfront Stadium, where every night visitor and resident alike arrive for a performance of the "World's Largest Musical Fountain."

Continuing on, the boardwalk swings around Government Pond, home port for the local Coast Guard station and a spot where you can read about the cutter "Escanaba" that was sunk in World War II or learn the difference between a nun can and a flasher buoy.

The final stretch to the pier is Lighthouse Connector Park, a delightful blend of wooden planks, strips of beach grass and benches for idlers who want to take in the view of the lighthouse, the boat traffic heading out into Lake Michigan or people passing by. By the time you reach the pier, that was constructed in 1883, it could be early evening so pop down next to the angler fishing for perch and take in another Grand Haven tradition: sunset on the catwalk, and don't worry about finding your way back, the catwalk it lit, the only one lighted on Lake Michigan.

Particulars: You can pick up the boardwalk anywhere along the Grand River from Grand Haven State Park to Chinook Pier. Walking the boardwalk is free.

Harbor Trolleys
(616) 842-3200

Many Michigan shoreline communities have trolley rides and tours, but none have as good a view as the Grand Haven motorcade. There are two trolleys, each offering different excursions around the harbor town and adjoining area.

Particulars: You can pick up the trolleys at Chinook Pier near the corner of Washington Street and Harbor Avenue. The trolleys run from Memorial Day to Labor Day from 11 a.m. to 10 p.m. when the musical fountain performance is over. Admission is $1 for adult and 50 cents for children.

World's Largest Musical Fountain
(616) 842-2550

FREE

Located approximately one-third the distance up the sand dune known as Dewey Hill, the fountains basin is almost as long as a football field and one-half as wide. The huge speakers trumpet 20-minutes-worth of music and choreographed water dance nightly during the summer season to throngs of people that crowd to the water's edge.

Sprays of up to 125 feet are achieved by pumping 40,000 gallons of water through 1.5 miles of pipe. Nozzle sizes, which account for the various patterns and direction, range from 3/16 to 1 inch in diameter. Lighting for the fountain is equivalent to 125,000 watts, or enough to run a town of 10,000.

Particulars: The world's largest musical fountain, located in Waterfront Stadium is located at the corner of Washington Street and Harbor Avenue. The performances are held daily from June through August and begin at dusk or roughly between 9 a.m. and 9:30 p.m. Free.

Tri-Cities Historical Museum
(616) 842-0700

Located in a traditional restored Grand Trunk railroad depot near the waterfront stadium, the local museum displays lots of local artifacts and aged photographs that interpret the areas lumbering, shipping, railroad, Coast Guard station, and manufacturing.

The museum is also a maze of Victorian room arrangements, household objects, common tools, clothing samples from area industry, local-based mementoes, and considerable information about the Coast Guard.

Particulars: Head to the south end of the boardwalk where the museum is located at One Harbor Drive. The museum is open Memorial Day to Labor Day from 10 a.m. to 9:30 p.m. Tuesday through Saturday and noon to 9:30 p.m. Sunday. Admission is $1 for adults.

▼ Fennville

Crane's Pie Pantry Restaurant & Bakery

Specialties at this unique family restaurant include desserts made with fruit grown in Crane's Orchards. Light lunches on homemade buns and bread are served with a 10-cent glass of cider in an antique atmosphere. Fresh fruit is available in season. The average check is less than $5.

Particulars: 6054 124th Avenue (M-89), Fennville, MI 49408-9440. (269) 561-2297.

Blue Coast Artists   *FREE*

A group of eight unique rural professional artist studio/galleries. Various media include pottery, blown glass, painting, fiber art, papermaking and more. Regular hours are Fri, Sat & Sun, 11 am-5 pm or other times by appointment. Free admission.

Particulars: 6322 113th Ave, Fennville, MI 49408, (269) 236-9260. US 31 South to I-196 to exit 30 (Glenn). Blue Star Highway west to 114th, east to 66th, south to 113th, east to studio.

Fenn Valley Vineyards – Free tasting

Visit Fenn Valley Vineyards, family owned and operated since 1973, where you can enjoy complimentary samples of premium wines that have earned more than 200 awards.

Located on the sandy soils near Lake Michigan, our vineyards carpet the hills that surround the winery and produce the noble grapes used to create our classic wines and champagnes. Discover how our wines combine the art of old world winemaking with the benefits of modern technology. Self-guided tours are available and special events are held throughout the year.

Particulars: 6130 122nd Avenue, Fennville, MI 49408-9457. Call (269) 561-2396.

PRESQUE ISLE COUNTY

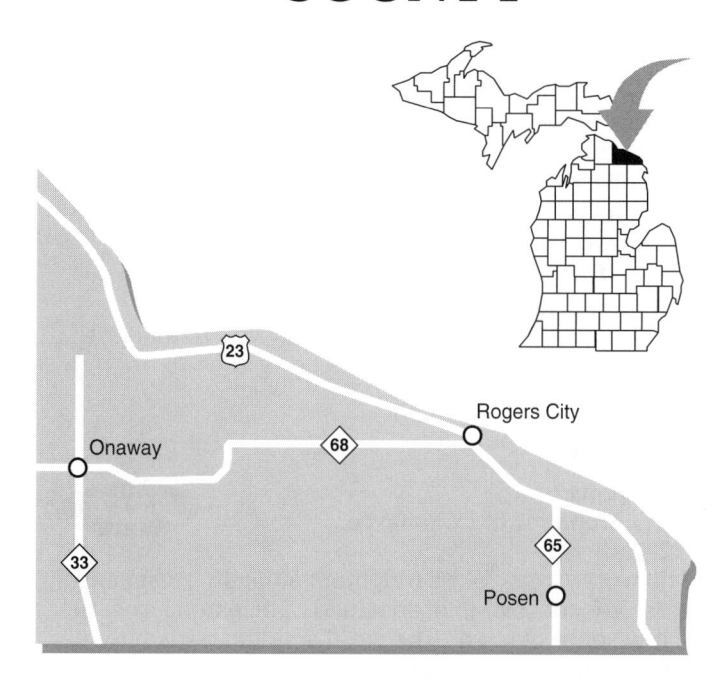

VISITOR INFORMATION

**Rogers City
Chamber of Commerce**
292 South Bradley Highway
Rogers City, MI 49779
989-734-2535 or 800-622-4148

www.rogerscitychamber.com

Presque Isle County

▼ Presque Isle

Old Presque Isle Lighthouse and Museum
(989) 595-9917

Designed by Jefferson Davis in 1840, this lighthouse was abandoned in 1870 when the new tower, the highest in the state at 113-feet, was built in 1870 just up the road. Visitors can climb the hand-hewn steps to the top of the tower for a panorama of the bay while the restored keeper's house features a collection of historic artifacts.

Particulars: From US-23, 23 miles north of Alpena, head east on Old State Road to
Grand Lake Road and then follow signs to the museum at the end of Grand Lake
Road. The light- house is open from mid-May to mid-Oct. From 9 a.m. to 6 p.m. daily.
Admission is $1.50 for adults.

▼ Rogers City

Limestone Quarry
Rogers City Chamber of Commerce
(800) 622-4148

FREE

More than 300 Great Lake's freighters annually steam into the Rogers City docks to take on a load of limestone from the huge quarry south of town. The 4,800-acre quarry is busy with heavy equipment mining the rock nearly 200 feet from the surface.

Particulars: There are two viewing points where budget-minded travelers can watch the action. Maybe the best view is from the observation turnout along Business US-23, while at a harbor viewing area you can see the rock being sorted, piled, and loaded. Free.

▼ Hammond Bay

Hammond Bay Biological Station
(989) 734-4768

FREE

Miles from nowhere, but the center of high-tech research and serious lamprey control, the Hammond Bay station is jointly funded by the United States and Canada. The station's mission is to find and maintain safe, effective lamprey control in the Great Lakes.

Sea lamprey, a snake-like creature, of the Atlantic Ocean gained entry to the Great Lakes via the Welland Canal and were first found about the Niagara Falls in 1921. Stream conditions and abundant foods in the upper lakes allowed the parasitic creatures to multiply quickly, reaching Lake Superior by 1938. Sea lamprey savagely attach themselves to fish with their sucking disk and horn-like teeth. Its sharp tongue rasps through the scales and skin as it feeds on body fluids, often killing the host fish. The lamprey was a major cause of the crash of the lake trout fishery in the 1940s and 1950s along with whitefish, chubs, and virtually all commercially viable species.

Particulars: The lab is just off US- 23, down a small gravel road (Bay Road) about 20 miles south of Cheboygan. Both group and individual tours are offered Monday through Friday from 1-3 p.m. The tour lasts about 20 minutes. Free.

▼ Onaway

Ocqueoc Falls
Onaway Chamber of Commerce
(989) 733-2874 (summer only)

Well, I was a bit disappointed. Ocqueoc Falls, the "biggest in waterfalls in Lower Michigan," is actually a series of rapids and small cascades that ripple over and around rocks and swirling into deep pools where travelers often cool off. The area also contains picnic tables and a seven-mile hiking trail, with the first loop, a three-mile hike, the most scenic by far.

Particulars: The scenic area is just off M-68, on Ocqueoc Falls Road. 12 miles west of Rogers City, Free.

ROSCOMMON COUNTY

VISITOR INFORMATION

**Houghton Lake
Chamber of Commerce**
1625 W. Houghton Lake Drive
Houghton Lake, MI 48629
989-366-5644 or 800-248-5253
www.houghtonlakemichigan.net

Roscommon County

▼ Higgins Lake

CCC Museum
North Higgins Lake State Park
(989) 821-6125

The key to the northwoods recovery, after the loggers had devastated the forests with their aces and saws, was the Civilian Conservation Corps. In 1933, President Franklin Roosevelt created the CCC with the Emergency Conservation Act in effort to put America to work. Michigan's response to the act was immediate. Within two months nearly 8,400 men had been enrolled and 42 camps set up. The pay was low; $30 a month of which $8 was given to the enrollees and the rest sent home to their families. The workers were between 18 and 25 years old, and from the bulging relief rolls.

The work and benefits of this program were vast and can be seen at the CCC Museum, located in the 429-acre North Higgins State Park near Roscommon. The legacy of the crews included the construction of 22 landing strips, 221 buildings, stocking roves with 156 million fish and planting 485 million trees. They also spent 140,000 days fighting forest fires. A remarkable achievement during the six-year period.

CCC Museum, Roscommon, County.

From the second you enter the museum, you'll have a sense of the hardships that the workers endured to make Michigan a better place. One of the first structures visitors will see is the 50-foot tall three-legged fire tower where enrollees spend eight to 10-hour shifts above the ground with no protection from the bugs and rain. Maybe the most impressive building is the replica CCC barracks. Here you view an enrollee's bunk room and what little belongings he possessed. Well-worn boots, and the clothes that were issued hang in display case next to head nets that were worn to escape the pesky black flies and other forest bugs.

Particulars: From I-75 depart at exit 244 and head west for 4.5 miles to the park entrance. The museum is posted on the north side of CR-200. The museum is open daily from mid-June through Labor Day from 11 a.m. to 4 p.m. A $4 daily vehicle permit or an $20 state park pass is needed to enter the park.

SAGINAW COUNTY

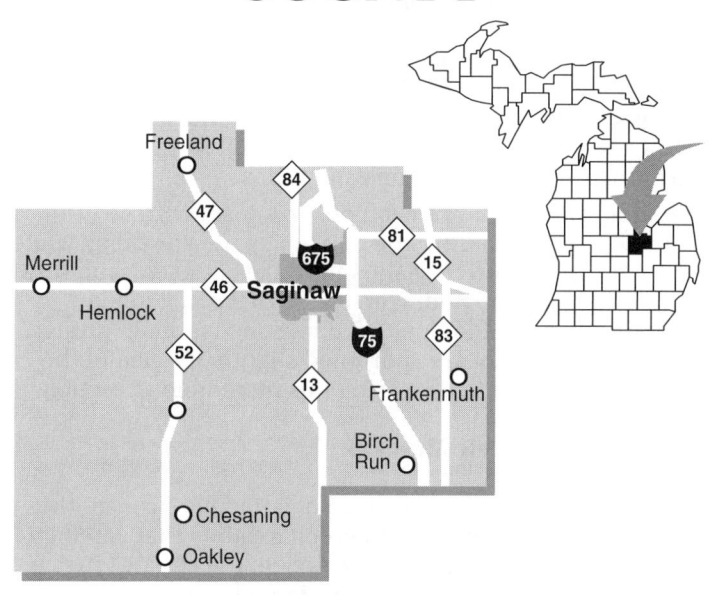

VISITOR INFORMATION

**Saginaw County
Convention & Visitors Bureau**
515 N. Washington Avenue, Third Floor
Saginaw, MI 48607
989-752-7164 or 800-444-9979

**Frankemuth
Convention & Visitors Bureau**
635 S. Main Street
Frankenmuth, MI 48734
989-652-6106 or 800-FUN-TOWN

www.visitsaginawcounty.com

Saginaw County

▼ Frankenmuth

Bronner's CHRISTmas Wonderland
(989) 652-9931

It's the "World's largest Christmas store," with over 50,000 trims and gifts, and arguably the post popular attraction in Michigan. Complete with a free slideshow, the huge complex covers several football-sized arenas, which features a food court, Christmas Lane and miles of aisles.

Particulars: Bronner's is off of M-83, just south of downtown Frankenmuth. You can't miss the sprawling white store, it's surrounded by giant snowflakes, season sculptures and twinkling lights. Hours are 9 a.m. to 9 p.m. Monday through Saturday and noon to 7 p.m. Sundays June through Christmas Eve. They are shortened slightly the rest of the year. No admission for browsing this incredible attraction.

Frankenmuth Historic Museum
(989) 652-9701

Accredited by the American Association of Museum, the Frankenmuth Museum has top-notch exhibits that carefully, but in an entertaining manner, chronicle the story of the Bavarian-like community. Services include a guided tour, educational programs archives, genealogical research and community cultural activities.

Particulars: The museum is located downtown Frankenmuth at 613 South Main St. It is open April to December from 10:30 a.m. to 5 p.m. Monday through Saturday and 12:30-5 p.m. on Sunday. From January through March the hours are slightly reduced. Admission is $1 for adults.

Frankenmuth Brewery
(989) 652-6183

Beer has been brewed on the corner of Tuscola and Main Street in Frankenmuth since 1862 when Cass River Brewing Company began operations. It eventually became Geyer Brothers Brewing Company but began to falter in 1986 when it caught the eye of Fred Schumacher, a beer importer passing through town on a sales mission. A year later the importer became a brewer when he headed a group of investors who purchased the facility.

A fire destroyed the original building in August of 1987, but the brewery was quickly rebuilt and included wonderful imported copper brew kettles from West Germany along with a top German brew master. By March, 1988 Frankenmuth Brewery has produced its first bottle of beer and open a Hospitality House and began plant tours. Although the company has the brewing capacity of 50,000 barrels annually, it's labeled a microbrewery because it produces less than 15,000 barrels a year.

The tour begins with visitors sampling the brewery's different brands and then watching a short video on how beer is made. From the hospitality house, the group walks into the brewery where the guide explains each step of the process and workers actually stop and chat with you.

Particulars: The brewery is located in downtown Frankenmuth at 425 S. Main. Tours are offered by request. Hey, the beer alone is worth it.

Frankenmuth's Covered Bridge
Frankenmuth Visitors Bureau
(989) 652-6106

One of only covered bridges still open to vehicle traffic in the state, Frankenmuth's Covered Bridge spans 239-feet connecting major attractions with parking, lodging and restaurants. The bridge is a replica of an authentic 19th century covered bridge, known as Zehnder's Holz-Brucke, completed a dream by Eddie Tiny Zehnder, owners of the wonderful Zehnder's Restaurant.

Covered bridges were built on dry land and then placed into position over the rivers during the 19th century and so was the 230-ton Frankenmuth structure. Milton Graton, builder of the bridge engineered a complex system of block, capstan, and pulleys that enable just two oxen to pull what would normally take 180 oxen to displace. The bridge includes almost 164,000 board feet of lumber.

Particulars: The bridge is just off Main Street near Zehnder's Restaurant. Free.

Memory Lane Arcade
(989) 652-8881

Bring a pocket-full of coins and step back in time to play unusual and historic arcade games that span the past 90 years. Discover the collection of music and game machines that are amazing ingenious and represent the highest order of craftsmanship. Kids love the place, and there are some excellent chances to talk with them about history and technology, especially as it relates to modern electronic video games.

Particulars: The arcade is located downtown at 626 South Main St. Hours are 12 noon to 9 p.m. daily.

Michigan's Own Military and Space Museum
(517) 652-8005

Stepping from the bright outdoor sunlight into the dimly lit museum immediately sets the mood; a near reverent feeling nurtured by the careful displays that interpret the military service of Michigan residents. The museum features information on the six foreign wars and also honors the peacetime bravery of Michigan astronauts.

Over 300 exhibits are diligently researched and carefully arranged to convey the emotion of those Michigan-bred who served and the families that donated their uniforms and other artifacts.

Particulars: Located in Frankenmuth at 1250 S. Weiss St. Hours are 10 a.m. to 5 p.m. Monday through Saturday and 11 a.m. to 5 p.m. Sunday. Admission is $3 for adults $2 for seniors and $1 children.

Nickless-Hubinger Flour Mill
(989) 652-6850

FREE

"Welcome to the historic Frankenmuth Flour Mill & General Store," says a free brochure that will guide you on a tour of the three and one-half story flour mill. Each level of the mill has rebuilt and refurbished chutes, sifters, grinders, roller miles, and a 13-foot water wheel. You'll learn how wheat is handled, processed, and a carefully purified by capturing the waterpower from the mill's dam that was built in 1847. There is also a gift shop offering flour mill products and gifts (authors note: the Mill's pancake mix is terrific!)

Particulars: The mill is just off Main Street in downtown Frankenmuth at 703 Mill St. at the river. Hours are 10 a.m. to 9 p.m. daily.

Schnitzelbank Woodcarvings
(989) 652-8331

The quaint woodcarving shop has a sweet smell of freshly shaved wood from the busy carvers waving razor-sharp tools and squinting at the object with an expert's eye. The largest selection of Ferrandiz-Anri woodcarvings and music boxes in Michigan gives this crafts shop its distinction.

Particulars: Located in downtown Frankenmuth at 545 S. Main St. Hours are 9:30 a.m. to 9:30 p.m. daily. Free.

Zeesenagel Italian Alpine Village
780 Mill
(989) 652-2591

The lovely miniature village uses over 400 hand-made figures in an elaborate Italian mountain village and is located in the back portion of the Zeesenagel Italian Alpine Village Gift Shop.

When artists David Zeese and Don Nagel visited Italy during a Christmas-time trip, they were overwhelmed and inspired by what they saw, especially the antique nativity settings. With their usual artistic enthusiasm, the men committed themselves to create their own original village of beautiful figures and background scenery.

Particulars: Located south of Zehnder's and the Bavarian Inn restaurants near the flour mill. Only guided tours are offered daily from 10 a.m. to 6 p.m. May through December and weekends the rest of the year. Admission is $2 for adults and $1 for children.

Bee Bee's Fun Place

Located in River Place shopping development, the arcade is a great side trip for youngsters and video game players. Dozen of buzzing and whirling token-operated machine are available.

Particulars: 925 South Main (in River Place), call (989) 652-3070.

▼ Saginaw

Castle Museum of Saginaw County History
(989) 752-2861

"Once upon a time," according to the brochure, "in the fair city of Saginaw was built the most extraordinary Castle," which is today the home and repository of Saginaw County history. The "Chateau" designed building looks like a castle and was built in the French tradition in 1897. The museum is located next door to the recently renovated Hoyt Library, a late 1800's historical building which is open daily.

Particulars: The museum is in downtown Saginaw at the corner of Jefferson and Federal Avenue. Hours are 10 a.m. - 4:30 p.m. Tuesday to Saturday, Sunday noon to 4:30 p.m. Closed on Mondays. Admission is $1 for adults and 50-cents for children.

Saginaw Art Museum
(989) 754- 2491

FREE

The Saginaw Art Museum has been the corner stone of the region's cultural community for more than 40 years. Situated in a 1904 lumbermen's mansion, the Georgian-revival building is surrounded by formal gardens. The museum has 25 shows annually and a permanent collection that features the history of art from 4,000-year-old Ancient Near Eastern ceramics to contemporary American paintings, prints, drawings and designs. The museum had $7 million expansion in 2003, including a 7,000 square foot glass clad wing added on the south side of the historic building.

Particulars: From I-675, depart at Michigan Avenue exit and head south to 1126 N. Michigan. Hours are 10 a.m. to 5 p.m. Tuesday through Saturday and Sunday 1-5 p.m. Free.

Saginaw Antique Warehouse

One of Michigan's largest and finest collection of vendors. The new building is only a mile or so from I-675 and has more than 20,000 square feet and 70 dealers. Lunch and specialty shops.

Particulars: 1122 Tittabawassee Road. Call (989) 755-4343. Only minutes from Gander Mountain sport shop, Fashion Square Mall, Sam's Warehouse and many other stores.

Celebration Square Children's Zoo
(989) 771- 4966

First opened in the early part of the century as the Phoenix Zoo, the renamed Celebration Square Children's Zoo has since become a popular attraction, hosting nearly 100,000 visitors annually. The compact zoo features a miniature steam locomotive that carries up to 60 passengers on a half-mile journey around the 13-acre tract, chugging and clanking by wandering fowl and excited children.

A small pond, large gift shop, concession stand and pony rides are also at the zoo. Recent improvements include a one-quarter-million dollar renovation includes a new Timber County exhibit, featuring timber wolves, hawks, and other native specimens. A new contact area also offers small children the opportunity to pet and learn about our natural world. The festive wood carousel and new gift shop is making the Saginaw-based zoo a regional destination.

Particulars: From I-75, depart at exit 149 and head west on M-46. The zoo is at the corner of M-46 and Washington Blvd. Admission for adults is $4.75; students and seniors are $3.75, and the train ride is $1.50.

Japanese Cultural Center and Tea House
(989) 759-1648

Take a trip to the Orient - in Saginaw. The quiet serenity of a Japanese garden and authentic tea house is providing an enlightening cultural experience for thousands of visitors annually. Part of nearly 30 years of friendship between the city of Saginaw and Tokushima, Japan, the Cultural Center and Tea House offers broad educational programs about the Japanese cultural that is often misunderstood.

After years of cooperative fundraising, the center was completed in 1986 using the design of skilled Japanese architects and set on soils partly owned by Saginaw and land deeded to Tokushima, Visitors will be most taken with the exquisite design and construction of the tea house... built without using nails or screws.

The garden and Tea House are open year-round with many special events and monthly formal tea ceremonies planned. The rapidly developing garden is pleasant area to visit while in Saginaw's Celebration Square. The zoo and historic water treatment plant is across the street.

Particulars: From I-75, depart at exit 149 and head west on M-46 and then north on Washington Avenue. Signs will direct you to the zoo at 527 Ezra Rust Drive. The garden is open 9 a.m. to 4 p.m. Tuesday through Sunday during the summer and the tea house from noon to 4 p.m. Tuesday through Sunday. The house is also open in the winter on more limited basis while the tea ceremony is held the second Sunday of each month at 2 p.m. There is a small admission fee.

Marshall Fredericks Sculpture Gallery
Saginaw Valley State University   **FREE**
(989) 964-7125

"I love people, for I have learned through many experiences, both happy and sad, how beautiful and wonderful they can be; therefore, I want more than anything in the world to do Sculpture which will have real meaning for other people, many people, and might in some ways encourage, inspire, or give them happiness," —Marshall Fredericks.

The gallery, which is a real hidden gem in mid-Michigan, houses an extraordinary collection of over two hundred works which span the career of famed artist Marshall M.

Fredericks. He is known throughout the world for his monumental figurative sculpture, inspiring public memorials,

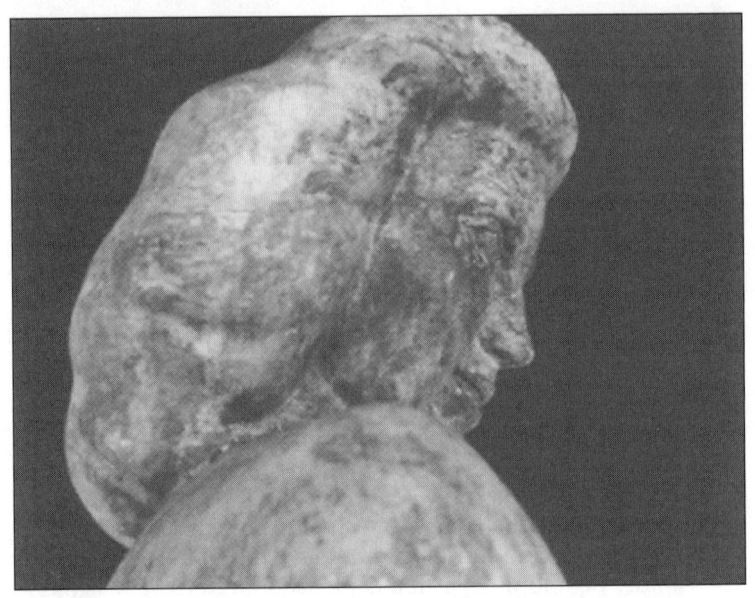

Marshall Frederick's Gallery, Saginaw Valley State University.

exuberant fountains, insightful portraits, and whimsical sculptures of animals. In the gallery are original models for many of his greatest sculptures: Christ on the Cross (Indian River, MICHIGAN); The Fountain of Eternal Life (Cleveland, OH); The Expanding Universe Fountain (Washington, D.C.); The Freedom of the Human Spirit (New York); The leaping Gazelle and the Spirit of Detroit, and many others.

The sculpture garden adjacent to the gallery includes a growing collection of more than a dozen bronze casts of Fredericks' sculptures, most with the green patina favored by the artist throughout his career.

Particulars: Depart I-75 at Bay Road (M-84) exit and head south to Saginaw Valley State University. Hours are noon to 5 p.m. Tuesday through Sunday. Free.

▼ St. Charles

St. Charles Waterfowl Observatory
(989) 865-8287

FREE

Building an understanding of wetlands and wildlife is the working motto of the volunteer operated observatory located in St. Charles. Located near the banks of the Bad River, the observatory is actually part of a small Wildlife Habitat Demonstration Area purchased by the DNR using Pitt-

Robertson Wildlife Restoration Funds. The small observatory features a pond, flight-areas, nesting boxes, benches and interpretive signs for visitors. A wide variety of waterfowl are exhibited.

Particulars: The observatory is located adjacent to the DNR field office in St. Charles, 12 miles southwest on M-52. Free.

SANILAC COUNTY

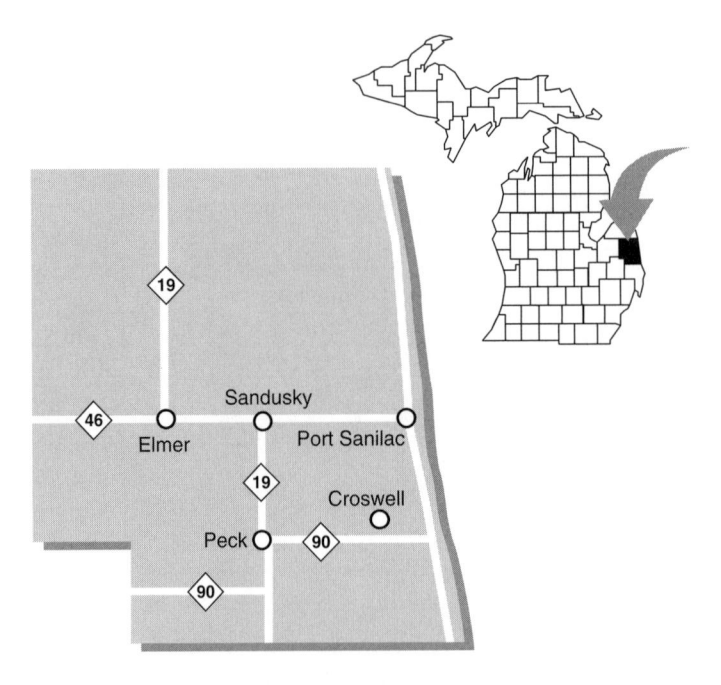

VISITOR INFORMATION

Greater Sandusky Area Chamber of Commerce
26 W. Speaker Street
Sandusky, MI 48471
810-648-3330

Sanilac County

▼ Port Sanilac

Loop-Harrison House Historical Museum
(810) 622-9946

The port town's most impressive man-made landmark is the Post Sanilac Lighthouse with its red brickhouse and whitewashed tower overlooking the harbor and watery horizon o Lake Huron. Like many shoreline communities on Michigan east side, the wealth and rich history of the region can be seen in its old homes that border the quiet street. One is the Loop-Harrison Mansion the home of the Sanilac Historical Museum, a Pioneer Log Cabin, Barn Theater and a tiny Dairy Museum located next to the huge Victorian house.

The home was built in 1873 by Joseph Loop, who arrived in Sanilac County in 1854, and began a medical practice that served a 40-mile radius for three decades. The active historical society has kept the home intact and visitors can leisurely wander among tow floors of original furnishings left just the way they were in the 1870s.

Particulars: The Loop-Harrison House is just south of town on M-25 and open from mid-June through Labor Day. Hours are 11 a.m. to 4:30 p.m. Tuesday through Friday and noon to 4:30 p.m. Saturday and Sunday. Admission is $2 for adults and $1 for children.

▼ Croswell

Mother-In-Law-Bridge
(810) 359-2262

FREE

Dear Abbey loves this tiny bridge in Croswell. It's unlikely she swings on it like area teen, but the message the bridge carriesBABe Kind to your Mother-in-Law B is sound advice.

Michigan has lots of bridges, the five-mile long mighty Mackinaw, the Manistique Siphon Bridge and great covered bridges are scattered around the state. In Croswell a small suspension bridge links one park to another, history to the present and offers a bit of advice to newlyweds. The "Be Good to Your Mother-in-Law" Bridge was first constructed in 1905 and was rebuilt three times since then with David Weis, a local businessman, assisting in the effort.

"But he was best known for offering sage advice to newlyweds," said Kate Meneghin, former Croswell mayor and area historian. AHe even hung a sign at one end of the bridge that reads, "Be Good to Your Mother-in-Law,' and at the other end there used to be a sign that said, "Love Ye One Another."

It's such good advice that the bridge has become something of a ritual with both newlyweds and long-time married couples who are photographed under the black and white sign than walk hand-in-hand across the swaying structure.

They hold hands partly out of devotion to each other and partly to keep their balance. The 139-foot long suspension footbridge is held-up by four thick cables that make you bounce with each step across. The wooden slates sway, jiggle and dip toward the Black River, coming within eight feet of its murky surface.

Particulars: Croswell is just off M-90, five miles west of M-23. The bridge is in a park near the library in the downtown area. Free.

▼ Deckerville

Deckerville Historical Museum
(810) 376-6695

Located on a farm, the museum is more of a historical complex featuring a log cabin, railroad depot, sawmill and pioneer museum that also features Indian displays and exhibits on Great Lakes shipping and lighthouses. Perhaps its most noted collection, however, is its John Deere tractors. The museum has more than 20 on display all in working condition and some dating back to the 1930s.

The museum stages flea markets and antique shows every Saturday as well as other special events and activities. Groups can also arrange horse wagon and sleigh rides as part of their tours.

Particulars: Located a mile north of Deckerville at 4028 Ruth Rd on the farm of Joyce and Harold Reid. Open May through September by appointment. Admission is $2 for adults and $1 for children.

▼ New Greenleaf

Petroglyphs State Historical Park
Michigan Historical Museum
(810) 373-1797

FREE

Just south of Germania, occupying a 238-acres, is one of the most unique cheap and free destinations in the Lower Peninsula. Located in a wooded portion of the Thumb, the parks has a huge slab of stone with petroglyphs, Indian carvings that archaeologists believe to be between 300 and a 1,000 years old and the only examples of the art in the state. The Michigan History Division and the DNR have worked together to erect pavilion and beginning in 1993 have staffed the area during the summer.

The petroglyphs are a short walk from the parking area but try to make effort to hike the 1.5-mile trail that loops through the site. The interpretive trail passes several interesting stops including stone mortars that Indians used to grind corn and the remains of old 18th century cabins.

Particulars: The park is located 13 miles south of Bad Axe. From M-53 head east onto Bay City-Forestville Road to a posted corner on Germainia Road. The entrance is half mile south on Germainia. The site is open Wednesday through Sunday from 11:30 a.m. to 4:30 p.m. mid-May through Labor Day. Free.

SCHOOLCRAFT COUNTY

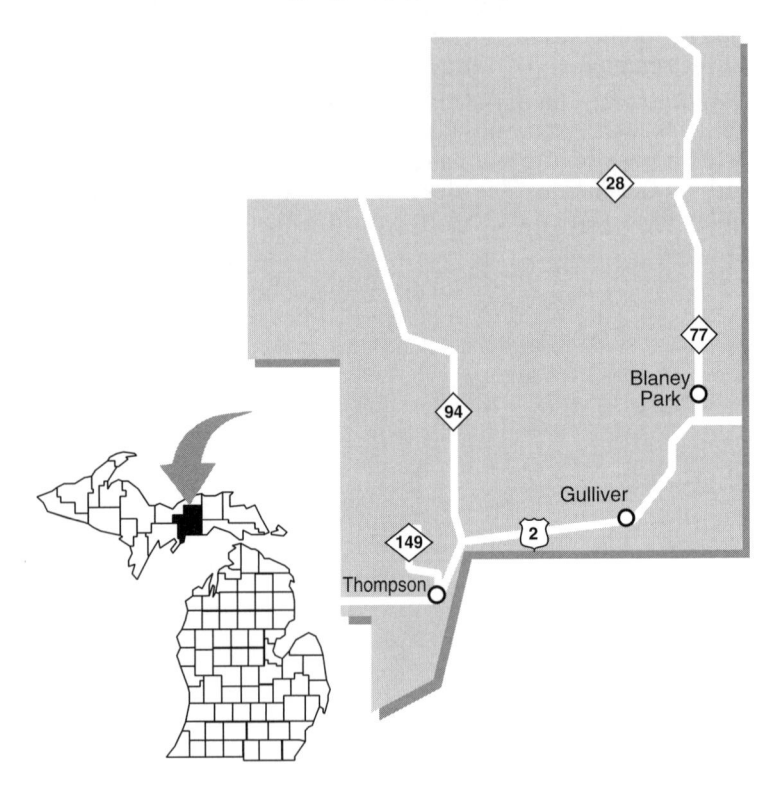

VISITOR INFORMATION

**Upper Peninsula
Travel & Recreation Association**
618 Stephenson Ave.
P. O. Box 400
Iron Mountain, MI 49801
906-774-5480 or 800-562-7134

www.uptravel.com

Schoolcraft County

▼ Manistique

Kitch-Iti-Kipi
Palm Brooks State Park
(906) 341-2355

At the beginning of the century it was a deep black hoe hidden by a mass of fallen trees, obscured to all but John Bellaire. Today, that black hole is Kitch-Iti-Kipi, a Michigan's most lovely spring offering a leisurely raft trip and outstanding scenery located in the middle of the Upper Peninsula.

Kitch-Iti-Kipi, the Indian name for "Big Spring," was cleaned up by Bellaire, a Manistique merchant who also convinced the state to purchase and preserve the land in 1926. The state paid only $10 for it but today nearly 65,000 people ride the raft over the bubbling sands and emerald waters of the spring. The natural spring pours out 10,000 gallons of water per minute from narrow openings in the underlying limestone that were created by a glacial drift. The result is crystal-clear pond 200 feet long and 40 feet deep.

Visitors board a wooden raft with observation holes in the middle and pull themselves across to get a good view of the underwater world below. You'll see century-old trees below and bubbles and swirls of sand making the bottom almost alive. If you are lucky you might see a brown trout slip silently by on its foraging run.

Particulars: The park entrance is eight miles north on M-149 from US-2. The park is open daily year-round but in the winter the entrance drive is not plowed and you have to walk to the springs. A $4 daily vehicle permit or a $20 state park pass is required to enter.

Siphon Bridge
Schoolcraft County Chamber of Commerce
(906) 341-5010

FREE

Built in 1919, this 300-foot bridge over the Manistique River is actually below the river because the water is atmospherically forced below it. The bridge became famous when it was featured in "Ripley's Believe It Or Not" newspaper column. Nearby is the Manistique Pioneer Park which includes the city's Water Tower that is listed in the National Register of Historical Places.

Siphon Bridge at Palms Brook State Park, Schoolcraft County.

Particulars: The bridge is downtown. From US-2 follow M-94 north. Free.

▼ Germfask

Marshland Wildlife Drive
Seney National Wildlife Refuge
(906) 586-9851

FREE

Fires were once intentionally set to clear the timber that the lumbermen missed in the late 1800s at the Seney National Wildlife Refuge, the largest (96,000-acres) national wildlife refuge east of the Mississippi River. Totally healed, the wilderness area surrounds the Great Manistique Swamp and is heavily used nesting and resting place for migratory waterfowl.

The visitor's center overlooks one of the many ponds and has many traditional natural history displays, films and programs in the auditorium.

But the most interesting element of the refuge is the seven-mile-long Marshland Wildlife Drive that you can motor along with a guide that points out items of interest at 20 marked stops. The motor tour is like entering a zoo without fences where you are virtually guaranteed to see wildlife that may include geese, herons, whitetail deer, muskrats, turtles, beavers, songbirds and others. The Marshland Drive actually winds across the dikes built by CCC workers.

You can increase your chances of encountering wildlife in this fenceless zoo by bringing a pair of high-powered binoculars and keeping an eye out for slight movements among the ponds and forest treetops. Timing is also important. Spring, late summer and fall are the best seasons for the tour and most species are active in the morning and evening hours.

Particulars: The entrance of Seney National Wildlife Refuge is off of M-77, five miles south of the town of Seney or two miles north of Germfask. The visitor's center is open daily from mid-May through September from 9 a.m. to 5 p.m. The Marshland Drive is open from dawn to dusk. Free.

SHIAWASSEE COUNTY

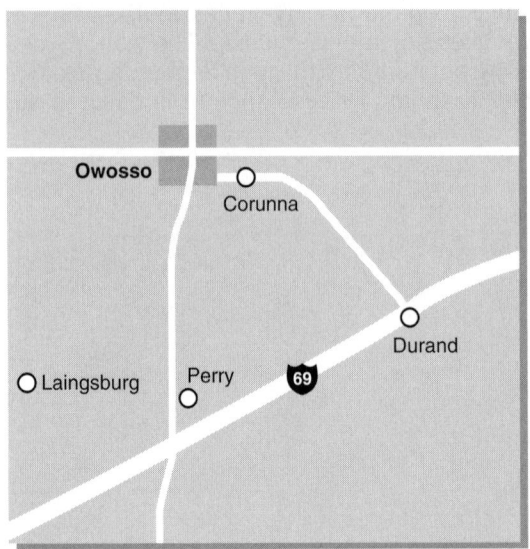

VISITOR INFORMATION

Shiawassee Regional Chamber of Commerce
215 N. Water Street
Owosso, MI 48867
989-723-5149

www.shiawasseechamber.org

Shiawassee County

▼ Owosso

Curwood Castle
(989) 723-8844, ext. 554

Perched on the banks of the Shiawassee River in Owosso, Curwood Castle is indeed a stone castle that was built by Jams Oliver Curwood, one of Michigan's most noted authors. The fact that Curwood never wrote a book in his castle doesn't matter to visitors. Literary buffs flock to the Castle, mush like Hemingway devotees are attracted to the Horton Bay General Store, where young Ernest used to hang out.

Born in Owosso in 1878, in the backroom is his fathers cobbler shop, Curwood published his first short story in the local newspapers when he was a mere 16 years old after his father converted a sewing machine stand into a desk for him, on display in his castle.

In 1907, the Canadian government hired him to travel and write about the unsettled regions of Canada. During this period he wrote an amazing 33 novels about the fact-paced and exciting Northwest Territory, or "god's country" as the popular author so often called it.

But it was in British Columbia where Curwood was changed forever. He was tracking a grizzly hear he shot when the wounded bear suddenly appeared and trapped him on a

Curwood Castle, Shiawassee County.

narrow mountain ledge. Breathlessly he later wrote, Asudden death seemed the hunter's inevitable fate. Then the huge bruin turned away, leaving the hunter unharmed. But not unchanged "the author packed away his guns and never hunted for sport again." The experience was later related in his best-selling novel, "The Grizzly King," published in 1916 and more recently served as the basis for the popular move, "The Bear."

The large castle, with its looming turret and 16-inch thick walls is virtually soundproof and constructed of fieldstones Curwood handpicked in neighboring farm fields. Most of the castle's original furnishings are in the great room where the author often hosted his famous Hollywood friends an on occasion actors even tried out for roles in movies based on his books.

Particulars: From I-69, depart north on M-52 to reach Owosso in 12 miles. Head east on M-21 and in one block, just before crossing the Shiawassee River, turn north on Curwood Castle Drive. The castle is open from 1-5 p.m. daily except on Monday.

Admission is by donation.

▼ Durand

Union Railroad Station
(989) 288-3561

FREE

If you're hungry when you're in Durand, stop at the Golden Spike Restaurant. If you need some golf balls or a fishing pole, there's the Sports Depot, and for a new pair of pants, cross the street to Jeans Junction, just down from Ironhorse Pub. Does this town love trains or what?

It does and for a good reason. At the turn of the century Durand was what Detroit's Metro Airport is today - the transportation hub of the Midwest. The first railroad, the Detroit-Milwaukee Line, arrived at the small town at 1865, partly because of Durand's central location, but mostly because of money. In those days, towns paid the railroad to cross its main street and one railroad had a way of attracting another. And another and another until seven different lines passed through Durand in 1903 and prompted the construction of its Union Station, a massive 239-foot long building that cost $60,000.

Unfortunately the depot burned down two years later but was quickly rebuilt by Grand Truck Railroad as the age of railroading and the town of Durand entered their golden era. At this time nearly half of the towns 2,500 people worked for

Grand Truck servicing 142 trains daily. Today, two Amtrak passenger trains pass through, but what the town and its station really attract are railroad buffs.

The Union Station is usually the first stop for them. Often called "the most photographed depot in the country" the station was recently designated the Michigan Railroad History Museum and Information Center and in the years to come will feature new and expanded exhibits. But even today you can view a gallery full of railroading artifacts, handcarts, engine lights, toll top desks and lots of other furnishing of a 1900-era train station.

From the museum you can wander along Main and Saginaw Streets, past Depot View Park with its bronze statue of an engineer oiling a drive wheel of an engine to the town's other railroad museum. The park features Engine No. 5632, a 260,000-pound locomotive built in 1929, Gate Tower M-25 that was used in town until automatic crossing gates replaced it in 1979 and the museum itself, a 1919 Pullman baggage car, crammed with more railroad history.

Particulars: Durand is 30 miles east of Lansing and 16 miles west of Flint and can be reached from I-69 by departing south at exit 116. The depot is in the heart of town (just follow the tracks) at 205 Clinton St. The Union Station Gallery is open Tuesday through Sunday from 1-5 p.m. Free.

ST. CLAIR COUNTY

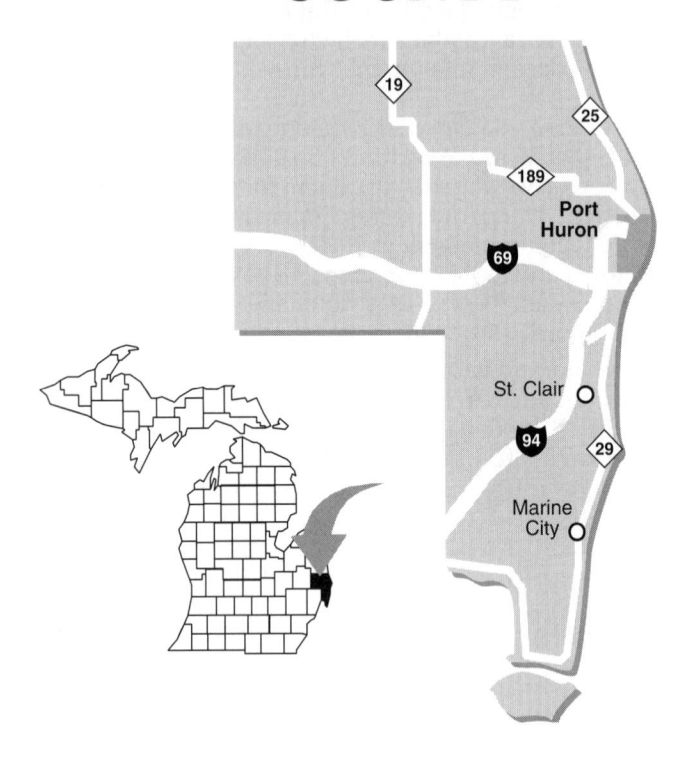

VISITOR INFORMATION

Blue Water Area Tourism Bureau
701 McMorran
Port Huron, MI 48060
517-349-8881

MDOT Welcome Center
2260 Water St.
Port Huron, MI 48060

www.bluewater.org

St. Clair County

▼ Port Huron

Blue Water Trolley
(810) 987-7373

Clanking bells and a red trolley recapture the past on public transportation in the Blue Water area passing local points of interest on a 40-minute ride for just a dime. The regular tour takes you through the heart of Port Huron and along the river-front,Edison Parkway, for a panoramic glimpse of the Blue Water Bridge. Thomas Edison Statue and Historic Depot.

Particulars: Among the stops you pick up the trolley is at the corner of Quay and Huron Street in downtown Port Huron. The trolley runs from Memorial Day to Labor Day from 10 a.m. to 5 p.m. A ride is 10 cents.

Huron Lightship
(810) 982-0891 ext. 14

Lightships are like floating lighthouses anchored in areas where it was too deep or impractical to construct a traditional lighthouse. Lightships displayed a light at the top of a mast and when fog developed also sounded a horn.

With the advent of better lighted buoys and navigational aids, lightships have since been discontinued. The "Huron" was decommissioned in 1971 and a year later the city of Port Huron acquired the vessel and enshrined it at Pine Grove Park. In 1989, the Huron was designated a National Historic Landmark, the only lightship on the Great Lakes to be honored this way.

A visit to the ship includes a handy self-guided brochure that will describe the main deck, engine room. Weather deck, crew's quarters, galley, and more.

Particulars: Pine Grove Park is in the downtown area on Pine Grove Street along the water. The ship is open 7 days a week Memorial Day through Labor Day from 1-4:30 p.m. The rest of the year it is open on Sundays from 1-4:30 p.m. Admission is $3 for adults and $2 for children and seniors.

Ice Museum
(810) 984-3369

FREE

At first, the idea of an Ice Museum was pretty comical B did they house the hard water in a refrigerator? Do we wear heavy coats? Or is the place extra popular in August?

Well, I've found out that it's not that kind of a museum. Actually, the museum chronicles ice harvesting from Lake Huron, the equipment used, and a film showing ice farmers hauling huge ice cubes from the lake waters to the cold houses.

Particulars: The museum is at 1755 Yeager Street. You must pre-register by calling before arriving at the museum. Free.

History and Art Museum of Port Huron.

Museum of Arts & History
(810) 982-8091

Be a captain by stepping into an actual pilothouse of a Great Lakes freighter. In the polished brass pilot house you can turn the big wheel, ring the bell and pretend that you are in charge by yelling commands into speaker horn while all around is a huge mural that gives you the impression you are departing the north end of the St. Clair River for Lake Huron.

After your jaunt on the ship you can also see some of Tom Edison's stuff from his childhood home in Port Huron along with displays of bones of prehistoric mammoths that roamed Michigan 10,000 years ago and a room full of model ships among other things.

Particulars: The museum is two blocks west of M-29 in downtown Port Huron at 1115 Sixth St. Hours are 1-4 p.m. Wednesday through Sunday. Free.

Times Herald Newspaper Tour
(810) 985-7171

FREE

Sneak a peak at the working of a modern newspaper as

reporters, editors, and production staff work under daily deadlines to produce the news you can use. The tour takes about an hour and there is not cost.

Particulars: The newspaper office is right downtown at 911 Military St. You must call in advance to set up a tour. Free.

▼ Ruby

Ruby Farms
(810) 324-2662

The Ruby Farms offers pure country relaxation in an old-fashioned atmosphere complete with farm buildings, cider mill, pony rides, wax museum, carousel, petting zoo, and restaurant. Fall is the best time to visit when the wagon rides will take you over the countryside to view the blazing autumn colors, while you sip a cup of fresh hot cider from the mill. Stop back later in the year to custom cut your own Christmas tree.

Particulars: Located nine miles west of Port Huron on Imlay City Road. The farm is open daily September through December.

Palmer Park
(810) 329-2962

FREE

Ship watching is the Blue Water Area's number one visitor attraction...and it's free! Residents and visitors alike find ocean-going ship traffic fascinating as huge freighters steam through the St. Clair River so close to Palmer Park you can almost talk to the crew members.

The park, a beautiful spot to whittle away a sunny afternoon, is often called the world's longest fresh water boardwalk. The 1,500-foot long riverwalk passes tables, benches and play areas, all facing the St. Clair River and Canada on the other side. Watching freighters is the favorite activity but many chose summer days for fishing for walleyes from the shore.

Particulars: St. Clair is 15 miles south of Port Huron M-19. Palmer Park is right downtown. Free.

▼ Marine City

Pride and Heritage Museum
(810) 765-3043

The Newport Academy was established in Marine City in 1845 and two years later a schoolhouse was built. Eventually the building was used for a village hall, jail, and a church (not at the same times as the jail). Today the two-story school is a Michigan Historical Site and home to the Pride and Heritage Museum.

Inside you find a recreated blacksmith shop, exhibits on World War I artifacts and local displays as well as dozens of model ships that help trace the era when Marine City was the site of five shipyards that built more than 250 vessels.

Particulars: The museum is just off M-29, seven miles south of St. Clair, at 405 Main Street. Hours are 1-4 p.m. Saturday Sunday March through December. Admission is by donation.

ST. JOSEPH COUNTY

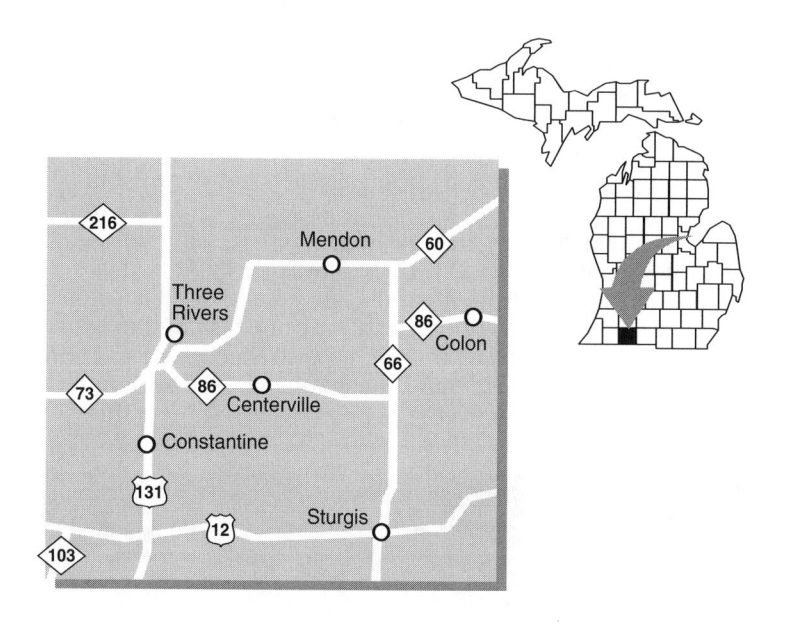

VISITOR INFORMATION

Three Rivers Area Chamber of Commerce
57 N. Main Street
Three Rivers, MI 49093
269-278-8193

www.trchamber.com

▼ Colon

**Abbott's Magic Company
(269) 432-3235**

FREE

If you tie a finely clipped toy poodle onto your car's hood, and drive exactly 53 mph, there will be a vague whistling of "Born Free." That's not magic, that's science. At the Abbott's Magic company they don't deal in reality, they sell magic.

Colon has only 1200 people but it's the "Magic Capital of the World." It's not an illusion. Back in the 1920s, famed trickster Harry Blackstone performed in Kalamazoo when his wife took a trip through Colon. She was delighted and convinced Harry, Sr. to buy a summer home near the town on Sturgeon Lake. At this time there wasn't much magical in the sleepy town, but Harry liked it.

It wasn't long before other magicians were passing through Colon (no pun intended). One of them was Percy Abbott, a slight-of-hand expert from Australia and a buddy of Blackstone. Abbott fell in love with a local girl during one visit and moved to Michigan and formed a partnership with Blackstone to build magical tricks. The partnership lasted only Free. Few months, and the two magicians never spoke again, even though they

Magic at Abbot's in Colon, St. Joseph County.

both lived long in Colon. Abbott soon found another partner with money and in 1933 launched the company that sponsored open houses and the popular festival known as Magical Get-Together.

The annual festival is held in late August each year when the town's population triples and slick professional and want-a-be amateur magicians in greater numbers that spectators arrive for four days of acts and shows.

The Abbott factory is open year-round and housed in a former carriage factory. Abbott is known as the "world's largest maker of magic tricks," and even though 80 percent of its sales is catalogue orders, it's showroom is still impressive. The walls and ceiling are covered with colorful posters and photographs of magicians. Near the front there is a small stage and on each side are rows of books with such titles as "How to Pick Pockets" and "Self Working Card Tricks."

All around are glass cases and shelves filled with only a portion of the 2,000 tricks and gadgets Abbott's produce. Although there aren't regular shows or tours of the company, eager resident magicians will take time out for a quick trick, especially if you have kids in tow.

Particulars: Colon is 16 miles west of Coldwater on M-86 and Abbott's is a block off M-86 at 124 St. Joseph St. Hours are 8 a.m. until 5 p.m. Monday through Friday and until 4 p.m. on Saturday. Free.

Colon Community Museum

More magical memorabilia can be seen at the Colon historical Museum, which is housed in a former church. Although many artifacts deal with the town's first pioneer families, one area is devoted to the personal items and photographs of its two most famous performers, Blackstone and Abbott. Blackstone's grave is also in Colon at the Lakeview Cemetery.

Particulars: The church is located north of M-86 at 219 North Blackstone Rd. Hours
are Tuesday, Thursday and Sunday from 2-4:30 p.m. Free.

▼ Three Rivers

Scidmore Park Zoo
(800) 447-2821

Only one block west of downtown Three Rivers is a small, somewhat ragged, animal park that exhibits about 20 species of animals. The park has a collection of mostly barnyard animals that are cared for by the city and a group of volunteers.

About ten years ago the facility housed wolves and a bear, but according to local legend, an intoxicated resident one day hopped the fence and decided to wrestle a bear. Well, the human lost the battle, and the facility lost the war. The bear and wolves were correctly shipped out, and the downsizing of the zoo began. Today, the small collection includes turkeys, ducks, goats, white-tailed deer, fallow deer, raptors, peacocks, donkey, and honking geese.

Nearby are picnicking and park facilities including game courts, a group camping area, tennis courts, and plenty of playground equipment.

Particulars: One black west of downtown Three Rivers at 333 West Michigan Ave.

across from the fire station. Open daily from 7 a.m. to 7 p.m. Free.

FREE

CARNEGIE CENTER for the ARTS

The Carnegie Center's building was built in 1904 and is on the National Historic Register. It's one of the few remaining original "Carnegie Libraries" built by Andrew Carnegie in the early 20th century. The Center is a non-profit org. supported by annual memberships and grants. The CCA features three exhibit galleries for fine arts, annual concert series, educational art programs on site and at schools and an adult lecture series. No admission for gallery exhibits. Gallery hours are Tuesday-Saturday 10-4, Sunday 1-5 p.m.

Particulars: 107 N. Main Street, Three Rivers, call (269) 273-8882.

▼ Centreville

FREE

Langley Covered Bridge
River Country Tourism Council
(269) 467-4452

Langley Covered Bridge is the largest one still standing in Michigan.

It's not only the longest at 282 feet but also the heaviest at three tons. Built in 1887, the bridge had to be raised eight feet to avoid the surging waters of the St. Joseph River when the Sturgis Dam was completed in 1910.

Nearby is Covered Bridge Park, a 15-acre park that features tables, grills, a short nature trail and a good view of the historical bridge. Particulars: From Centreville

head north on Covered Bridge Road to reach the historical structure in four miles. Free.

TUSCOLA COUNTY

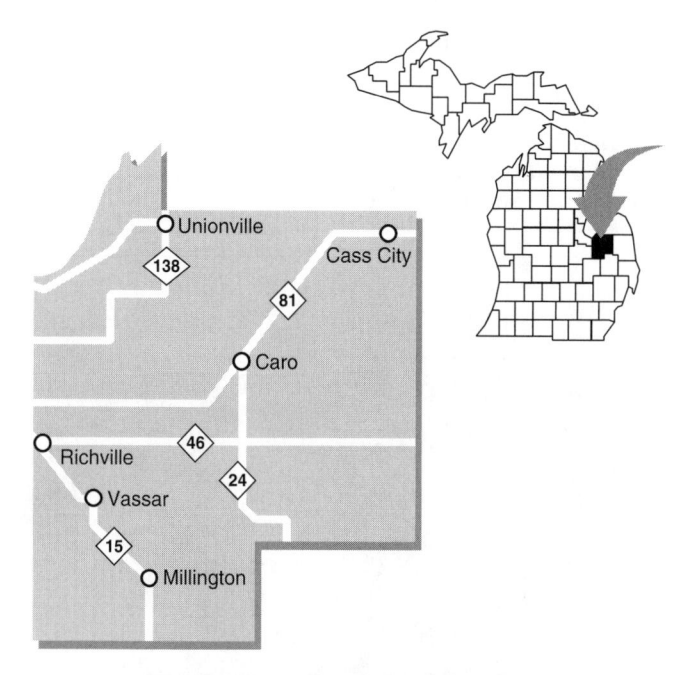

VISITOR INFORMATION

Vassar Chamber of Commerce
116 N. Main Street
Vassar, MI 48768
989-823-2601

Tuscola County

▼ Mayville

Mayville Historical Museum
(989) 843-7185

FREE

Local history is preserved in the newly restored Mayville Depot that's open during the summer months. Arrive the second weekend of the month and you can also enjoy a good old flea market with items almost as historical as what you'll find inside the depot.

Particulars: The depot is half-mile east of Mayville on M-24. It's open May through September from 11 a.m. to 3 p.m. on Friday and Saturday. Free.

Paddling the Cass River is a fun adventure in Tuscola County.

Glovebox Guidebooks of America **351**

VAN BUREN COUNTY

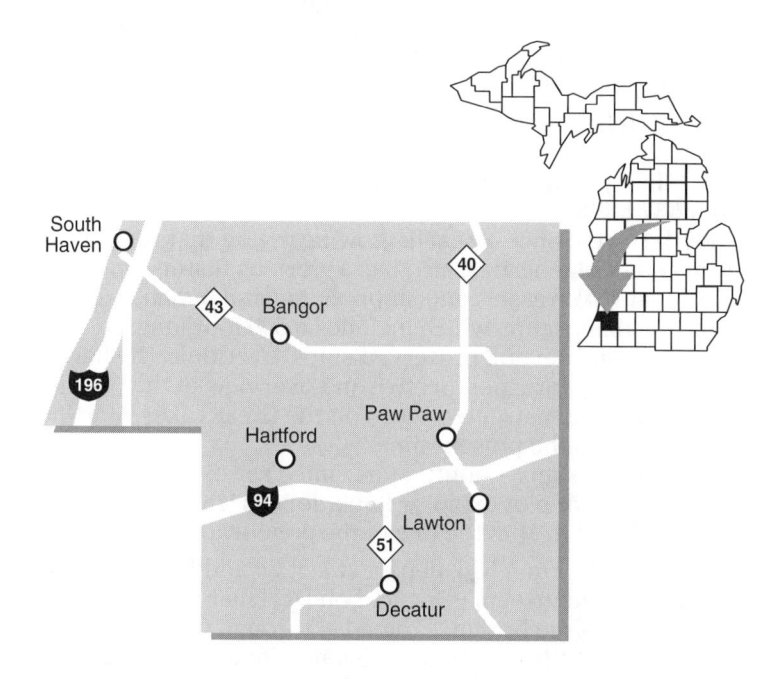

VISITOR INFORMATION

**South Haven
Convention & Visitors Bureau**
546 Phoenix Street
South Haven, MI 49090
269-637-5252

www.southhaven.org

Van Buren County

▼ South Haven

Waterfront Skate Park — *FREE*

Grab your skateboard or in-line skates and practice your moves on multiple ramps. Located right next to the South Beach and the Black River, this park is a great place for kids to spend the day and burn off some of that extra energy!

Particulars: Everyday, 9 a.m.-11 p.m., Water Street across from South Beach, South Haven, MI 49090

**Lake Michigan Maritime Museum
(269) 637-8078**

South Haven, once a peach- growing region that turned to tourism and blueberries, also has a glorious history spiced with Great Lake vessels and shipbuilding and Indian lore.

The small museum, which includes a 600-foot long boardwalk and several preserved ships, overlooks the harbor and offers a historic perspective and overview of the people who used and constructed boats on the Great Lakes, starting with Indians to the present time.

Interpretive signs, photographs, and a series of maps of the Great Lakes that plot explorer Louis Joliet's travels in the late 1600s are used to spin the tale of the great waterways.

Particulars: From I-96, depart at exit 20 and head west for 1.5 miles. The museum is located on Dyckman Avenue on the Black River by the bridge. From May through October the museum is open from 10 a.m. to 5 p.m. Monday, Wednesday through Saturday, and 12 noon to 5 p.m. on Sunday. Admission is $2.50 for adults.

South Haven Center for the Arts.

We feature exhibits, events, and education. Our ever-changing exhibits are by local, regional and national artists. Events include concerts, the Art Fair in the summer, the Miniature Art Auction in the fall, and the Mistletoe Market in the winter. We also offer education for all ages, including intensive 1-3 day workshops, summer children's camps, and six-week classes

Particulars: Tuesday-Thursday, 10 a.m.-5 p.m.; Friday, 10 a.m.-4 p.m.; Saturday-Sunday, 1 p.m.-4 p.m. 600 Phoenix Street, South Haven, MI 49090, call (269) 637-1041

Liberty Hyde Bailey Museum *FREE*
(269) 637-3251
The 19th century homestead preserves the birthplace and honors the world-renown horticulturist and botanist. Bailey was native of South Haven and founded the nation's first horticultural and landscaping department while teaching at Michigan State University.

The museum presents the life of a 1850s family as well as preserving family memorabilia, period furnishings and Indian artifacts.

Particulars: The museum is located in South Haven at 903 S. Bailey. Hours are 2-4 p.m. Tuesday and Friday. Free.

▼ Hartford   *FREE*

Van Buren County Historical Museum
(269) 621-2188
The museum, located next to the county fairgrounds, is a three-story, 44-room building that was built in 1884 as the county poor house. Today it's a state historical site and houses the rich history of this area.

Inside you'll find pioneer tools, housewares, toys, musical instruments and clothing. One room is set as an old fashion kitchen, another as a school and others as an old country store, pre-1900 dentist office and turn-of-the-century parlor. Outside is a working blacksmith shop and, my favorite, old-time whiskey still that, unfortunately, is not in working shape.

Particulars: The museum is on Red Arrow Highway between Hartford and Lawrence. It is open May through October from 10 a.m. to 4 p.m. Wednesday through Saturday, and 1-5 p.m. on Sunday. Free.

▼ Paw Paw   *FREE*

Warner Vineyards
(269) 657-3165
Of all the wineries in the "Wine Capital" of Michigan, this is my favorite place to stop, tour and taste. Its Wine Haus was originally the water-works station for Paw Paw and was built in 1898, straddling a small rushing stream.

Warner purchased the building in 1967 and renovated it using lumber from old wine casks. Nice touch.

Today you can stop at the scenic spot, join a walking tour, step up to the counter in the tasting room, purchase a bottle or two and, if the weather is agreeable, enjoy it outside on a deck overlooking the stream.

Particulars: From I-94, depart at exit 60 and head north into Paw Paw where you'll find the winery in the heart of town at 706 S. Kalamazoo St. Hours of tours are 10 a.m. to 5 p.m. Monday through Saturday and noon to 5 p.m. on Sunday. Summer and fall are the best times to take them. Free.

WASHTENAW COUNTY

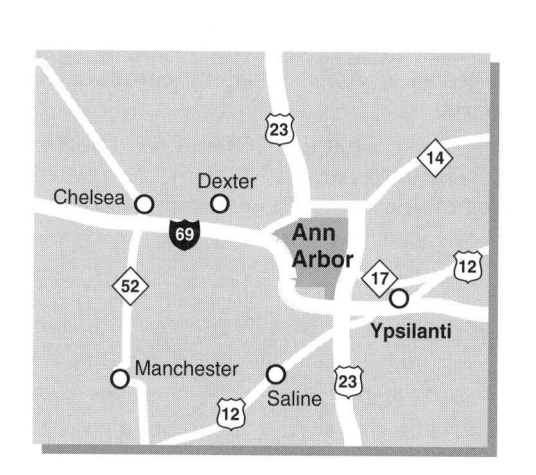

VISITOR INFORMATION

**Ann Arbor
Convention & Visitors
Bureau**
120 W. Huron
Ann Arbor, MI 48104
734-995-7281

www.annarbor.org

**Ypsilanti
Convention & Visitorss
Bureau**
106 W. Michigan Avenue
Ypsilanti, MI 48197
734-547-6855

www.ypsilanti.org

Washtenaw County

▼ Chelsea

Chelsea Milling Co.
(734) 475-1361

FREE

Chelsea Millings is the world headquarters of nationally known Jiffy mix, of which I have eaten hundreds of their blueberry muffins (I add my own fresh blueberries that's a no cost cooking tip from a guidebook writer). The little boxes of baking products are especially wonderful for us bakers that can't handle complex recipes. Just add an egg, a little water, stir, and wait until the smoke detector goes off.

The Jiffy people offer a brief slide show about the historic mill and a snack, you'll tour the factory in operation and take home a free souvenir box of Jiffy Mix. What a great place for the cheap and free tourist.

Particulars: From I-94, depart at exit 159 and head north on M-52 into Chelsea. The mill is at 201 North St. The tour is offered Monday through Friday but you must call ahead for exact times. Free.

▼ Ann Arbor

Cobblestone Farm
(734) 994-2928

There are many experts on this sort of thing, people who study architecture and old buildings, and many of them agree that this is the site of the finest restored cobblestone house in the state. Heck, I agree, too. The small garden, old barn that houses common livestock, log cabin, and adjacent Buhl Park with a pool and tennis court, makes this an excellent destination for the budget-minded travelers.

Polished and restored with loving care, the interpretive tour is designed to instill this reverence for farm lifestyles and Classic Revival styles. The farm was recorded in the Historic American Buildings Survey in 1936, and placed on the National and State Registers of Historic Places in 1972.

Particulars: From US-23, depart at the Washtenaw Road exit and head west. Turn south on Platt Road and then west on Packard Road. The museum is at 2781 Packard Rd. and open May through from 1-4 p.m. Friday and Sunday. Admission is $2 for adults and $1.50 for children and seniors.

Hands-on Museum, Washtenaw County.

Hands-on Museum
(734) 995-KIDS

Located in a century-old firehouse, this popular Hand-on Museum offers more than 80 exhibits on floors. The displays range from bubble capsule, where kids actually stand inside a giant bubble, and a sand pendular to computers that help explain complex theories to exhibits as simple as touch boxes. The theme is taking science to the people and staff recommends it for children eight years and older.

Particulars: The museum is at the corner of Huron and Fifth Avenue and can be reached by following Business US-23 from M-14. Hours are 10 a.m. to 5 p.m. Monday through Saturday, and 12 noon to 5 p.m. Sunday. Admission is $7 for adults and $5 for children.

Kelsey Museum of Archaeology
(734) 764-9304

FREE

How's your tummy? How did they make mummies? Why do they call them mummies, anyway? Learn the answer to these and lots more questions when you visit one of Michigan's museum of archaeology.

During the Victorian era, the common practice was to unwrap mummies (they actually had unwrapping parties) which, of course, destroyed the artifact. Today, non-evasive research is the norm because in the 1960s, U Of M pioneered the method of x-raying mummies and for the first time in history they were able to look closely at preserved bodies without unwrapping them.

The museum does have a couple of unwrapped mummies, two cats and a dog to be exact, but most of the displays deal with the x-rays taken by university researchers. You can step into a mummy tomb, push a button and there is Rames II, whose x-ray revealed he was 5-foot-8-inches, had long hair, and was 70 years old when he died. Other x-rays reveal interesting facts about other pharaohs. Siptah died of polio when he was 20 years and Segenre Taa II didn't die from a gaping axe wound in the forehead as once thought, but from an arrow in the back. Nice guys, these pharaohs.

The museum is also known for many antiquities, including its collection of Roman-Greco glass, the largest collection of intact vases, flasks and bowls of North America.

Particulars: From I-94, depart at exit 177 and head north on State Street for two miles. The museum is at 434 S. State St. in Newberry Hall on the U of M campus, almost directly across rom the U of M Museum of Art. Hours are 9 a.m. to 4 p.m. Tuesday through Friday and 1-4 p.m. Saturday and Sunday during the school year. In the summer the hours are less. Free.

Matthaei Botanical Garden
(734) 998-7061

One of the best places to visit during Michigan's long winters is the toasty warm and tropical Matthaei Botanical Gardens, near Ann Arbor. U of M's conservatory always has glorious blooms and beaming tropical plants on display year-round. In fact, 50,000 visitors annually head inside the conservatory.

The garden dates back to when the university was founded and originally located on the main campus. But that was impractical and they moved, lock, stalk, and leaves, several times. An interest in broader agricultural research plots prompted the final move in 1962. The huge greenhouse now houses more than 3,000 plants from around the world, ranging from Asian jungles to tundra plants.

Your visit begins with a walk through the tropical house with its broad stagehorn fern, aromatic orchids and elegant Bird of Paradise, whose purple and orange flower is actually a giant herb of the banana family. From the steamy tropic area you step into the warm temperate house with its eucalyptus tree, common fig, towering bamboo and gorgeous orchids above the small pool.

Nearby is a large assortment of insect-eating plants like the Venus fly trap with its hinged lid that traps curious bugs, the butterworth with its sticky leir and the picture plant that has a long throat covered with tiny downward pointing barbs. Finally there is the desert house, home of barrel cactuses, yucca, familiar aloe plants and an interesting group of stone plants that camouflaged themselves among the rocks of the Namib Desert in South Africa.

Particulars: From US-23, depart at exit 41 and head east on Plymouth Road. Turn south on Dixboro Road to reach the entrance in half a mile. Hours are 10 a.m. to 4:30 p.m. daily. Admission is $3.

U-M Football Stadium
(734) 747-BLUE

FREE

The U of M Stadium, built in 1927, is the biggest collegiate stadium in the country, capable of seating nearly 102,000 screaming fans. Here and at nearby Yost Field House, you can occasionally see teams practicing or participating in promotional events. Particulars: From I-94, depart at exit 177 and head north on State Street and then west on Stadium Boulevard. Visitors may view it by entering the gates on Stadium Boulevard but it's best to call before you visit. Free.

Sterns Musical Collection
(734) 763-4389

FREE

Since Frederick Sterns, a 19th century rich guy, donated a collection of musical instruments, including several Tonettes, there have been more than 2,000 others acquired. Some pieces are ornate and many others have great historic value. The U-M School of Music manages and houses the important collection that can be seen on a guided tour.

Particulars: The collection is housed at the School of Music on the North campus, reached from US-23 by departing west on Plymouth Road. Hours are 10 a.m. to 5 p.m. Monday through Friday. Free.

U-M Museum of Art
(734) 764-0395

FREE

A top ten art museum for a Big Ten school. The impressive museum has over 20,000 pieces of art in its collection featuring the works of Monet, Rodin, Whistler and many works of Oriental art.

Twentieth century sculpture of both American and British artists and 19th-century landscapes are also features in galleries that echo your whispers and focus your attention on each work.

Particulars: From I-94, depart at exit 177 and head north on State Street. The museum is at 525 S. State on the U of M main campus and is open 10 a.m. to 5 p.m. Tuesday through Saturday, 10 a.m. to 9 p.m. on Thursday, and 12 noon to 5 p.m. Sunday. Free.

Exhibit Museum
(734) 763-6085

FREE

If it's too nasty to go outdoors to study or natural world, go indoors where you can keep your boots dry and your ears warm. That paradox is possible in the University of Michigan's Exhibit Museum. There you'll find three floors of displays and exhibits, including the Hall of Evolution on the second floor where you can see a completely assembled skeleton of a mastodon, the elephant-like mammal that existed 10,000 years ago and was eventually found on a farm near Owosso. Next to it is standing skeleton of a sabertooth tiger with its huge front teeth as well as an Allosaurus, the forerunner of the Tyrannosaurus.

The third floor is the Michigan Wildlife Gallery that is filled with every plant and animal thriving in our state and a few no longer around like the wolverine. The dioramas here will make you feel like you're outdoors. There is a swamp forest with a family of opossums and wildflowers all around, a freshwater

University of Michigan Exhibit Museum.

pond with a snapping turtle, frogs and a huge pike lurking underneath a lily pad and a oak-hickory forest in brilliant fall colors.

The fourth floor houses the planetarium and galleries devoted to native North Americans, astronomy, geology and mineralogy.

Particulars: From I-94 depart at exit 172 and head east, which in 2.5 miles becomes Huron Street in downtown Ann Arbor. Turn south on State Street for two blocks and then east on N. University Avenue. Exhibit Museum is located on the corner where N. University curves to the South and becomes Geddes on U of Ms central campus. The museum is open year round Monday through Saturday from 9 a.m. to 5 p.m. and Sunday 12 noon to 5 p.m. Free.

▼ Ypsilanti

Yankee Air Museum
(734) 483-4030

The annual open house and weekend fly-ins are probably the best times to visit the air museum then planes are reviving on the ramp and take-offs and landings and jets are thick in the air. If you can't go when the plans are out and about, a visit to the mostly upstairs museum is a budget tour worth an hour-long visit.

Crowded with ages aircraft, the hangar and grounds of the Willow Run Airport are a bit rundown, but the dedicated and hardwork of the volunteers has maintained and aura of excitement and many of the old war birds are still flyable. One that is still flying is the 1945 C-47, the cargo version of the DC-3, another is the 1943 B-25 gunship that patrolled the skies of Europe during World War II.

Particulars: Depart 1-94 at exit 190 and head north on Belleville Road and then west on Tyler Road to reach the Willow Run Airport off Beck Road. Hours are 9 a.m. to 4 p.m. Tuesday through Saturday and noon to 4 p.m. on Sunday. Admission for adults is $7.

Ypsilanti Historical Museum
(734) 482-4990

FREE

This 1860 home of a prosperous businessman had been restored and refurbished to convey a Victorian-era living style.

Particulars: From I-94 depart at exit 183 and head north into Ypsilanti where the museum is at 22 N. Huron St. Hours are 2-4 p.m. Thursday, Saturday and Sunday.

Free.

WAYNE COUNTY

VISITOR INFORMATION

**Metro Detroit
Convention & Visitors Bureau**
211 W. Fort St., Suite 1000
Detroit, MI 48226
800-DETROIT
www.visitdetroit.com

Wayne County

▼ Detroit

Belle Isle Aquarium
(313) 852-4141

Built in 1904, the green-tiled, domed building is the oldest aquarium is America Inside the 4,200-square-foot facility are 60 exhibits with a total capacity 32,000 gallons of water offering moist housing for over 1,300 aquatic specimens. The two largest aquaria are 2,800 and 4,000 gallon tanks, most of the other tanks are between 200 to 600 gallons in capacity.

Cold freshwater species like trout, muskies and salmon are accommodated by more than 10,000 gallons of refrigerated waters. Several freestanding interpretive displays detail aquatic life cycles, information on fish scales, growth phases, and lots of other natural history facts. The most popular activity at the aquarium are the eel feeding shows, which is really and educational program on how eel's discharge electricity. Plan about an hour for your visits.

Particulars: Located less than 2.5 miles from downtown Detroit, Belle isle is accessed by the Douglas MacArthur Bridge at the corner of East Jefferson and East Grand Boulevard. Hours are 10 a.m. to 5 p.m. daily. Admission is $4 for adults and $2 for seniors and students.

Dossin Great Lakes Museum
(313) 833-9721

One exhibit at the Dossin Great Lakes Museum allows you to slip an old cork block life jacket for a feel of the sometimes heavy, sometimes dangerous equipment used a few decades ago on the ships that sailed the lakes. Another is the Morse Code exhibit where you spend two minutes tapping out "my ship is sinking" message.

At the Great Lakes Museum, visitors genuinely gain empathy with sailors and crews that sailed the Great Lakes on old-fashioned ships long before radar, satellite navigation and radios. Much of the museum is dedicated to interpreting the fury of the lakes and the hazards of sailing.

Other permanent displays in the museum include dozens of model ships, a captain's room from a freighter and a pilot's house situated on the banks of the Detroit River where you feel like you're actually steering the ship as it stems past Windsor, Ontario.

Particulars: The museum is located near the Belle Isle

Aquarium and is open from 11 a.m. to 5 p.m. Saturday through Sunday. Admission is $3.50 for adults and $2.50 for seniors and students.

Whitcomb Conservatory
(313) 852-4064

The best time to visit a conservatory is in the dead of winter when our outdoor plants re dormant and gray like the skies. Inside the Whitcomb Conservatory, under the 85-foot dome that opened in 1904, it's almost summer-like with hundreds of lush plants breathing out oxygen, some displaying blossoms and all helping to raise your spirits. Marshall Frederick's famous sculpture the "Bronze Gazelle," is outdoors in the fountain and formal garden area.

Particulars: The conservatory is on Belle Isle on Loiterway Drive. Hours are 10 a.m. to 5 p.m. daily. Admission is $2 for adults and $1.00 for seniors and students.

Detroit Historical Museum
(313) 833-1805

The Detroit Historical Museum is history but it's fun too. The museum opened in 1951 and one of the most popular exhibits has been the Detroit Antique Toy Museum, a 2,900 square foot hall that contains hundreds of wonderful collectible toys.

Your kids will love viewing the toys of you and your grandparents past. You'll see 19th century board games, a wooden Felix the Cat doll, and old Slinky and a great model train exhibit.

From here go upstairs to the Booth-Wilkinson costume Gallery to view the mannequins dressed in uniforms, business suits of the past, sport uniforms and even a Playboy bunny suit. Other displays include "Streets of Detroit" that allows you to walk through the history of the city's changing main street.

Particulars: From I-75 depart at exit 53 and go west on Warren and then north on Woodward. The museum is kitty-corner from the DIA. Hours are 9 a.m. to 5 p.m. Tuesday through Friday and 10 a.m. to 5 p.m. on Saturday –Sunday. Admission is $5 for adults and $3 for students and seniors.

Detroit People Mover
(313) 962-RAIL

After what seemed like years of controversy, the 2.9-mile loop of computerized transit cars and 13 stations known collectively as the people mover started serving the public in July of 1987. Remarkably clean and speedy, Detroit Transportation officials estimate that about one-third of the passengers are downtown workers, while most of the rest are visitors and convention goers.

Elevators and escalators take you from street level to the stations in the sky where you wait only two to three minutes from the next transit car. Frankly, waiting from the next sleek car was almost as much fun as the ride with $2 million dollars in works of art adorning the walls and common areas of the People Mover stations. The art ranges from mosaic tile cathedral windows at Cadillac Square and a lifelike statue of a man reading newspapers at Grand Circus Park to a 105-by-10-foot mosaic of seven antique autos in Cobo Hall.

The ride is 14-minutes long above the streets of Detroit for a wonderful view of streetscapes and roadways, buildings and pedestrians. The fair alone is worth the segment between Joe Louis Arena and the Financial District when the transit cars follow the Detroit River for a panorama of the Renaissance Center and the Windsor skyline across the water.

Particulars: Stations are located at Joe Louis Arena, Cobo Center, Financial District off Larner Street, Millender Center, Renaissance Center, Bricktown on Beaubein Street, Greektown at Trapper's Alley, Cadillac Center, Broadway, Grand Circus Park, Times Square, Michigan and at Fort and Cass. Hours are 7 a.m. to 11 p.m. Monday through Thursday, 7 a.m. to midnight Friday, 9 a.m. to midnight Saturday and noon to 8 p.m. Sunday. Tokens are 50-cents each.

Detroit Trolley
(313) 933-1300

Rumbling and swaying with a bump and clank, the Detroit Trolley cars are no modern bus...or, maybe, better yet, a modern bus is no trolley. The polished oak panels, brass trim, and red cushion seats make the trolleys a "best buy" for the budget-minded travelers visiting downtown Detroit.

Particulars: The cars operate on Washington Boulevard and Jefferson Avenue from Grand Circus Park to the Renaissance Center. Hours are 7 a.m. to 6 p.m. Monday through Friday and 10 a.m. to 6 p.m. Saturday and Sunday. The fare is 50 cents per person.

Detroit Water & Sewer Department Tours   **FREE**
(313) 297-9187

Tours of this wastewater treatment, one of the largest of its kind in the nation, include an overview of the plant functions and a film presentation. More than 700 million gallons of water are treated daily.

Particulars: The plant is located at 9300 W. Jefferson. The one-hour tours are for children 10 years and older and you most register two weeks in advance. Free.

Eastern Market
(586) 393-8800

FREE

At Detroit's Eastern Farmer's Market, one of the largest in the country, you can see, touch, taste and even haggle over the freshest produce in the country. Especially haggle. The vendors love it in on Saturday afternoons as they rather barter then take home their produce.

Spreading across 11 acres, the Eastern Market features five large sheds, two of them winterized, offering wholesale sales only Monday-Friday. On Saturday, the public invades the market and can buy any volume of produce, herbs, meats, and so on.

During the summer the market draws up to 14,000 shoppers on a Saturday but even in the winter its bustling with people closely inspecting the produce of more than 200 vendors. They come for the atmosphere of an open market and the variety of food that can be purchased. There are always head of iceberg lettuce, but how may supermarkets also carry crates of curly endive, beet green or kale? From capons to feathered chickens and cider, shoppers flock to the booths.

Around the perimeter of the market are side streets of specialty shops restaurants, butchers, bakers, and packinghouses. Specialty shops and importers offer exotic mustards and wines, 200 kinds of cheeses, custom cut meats, ethic bakeries and spices. Plan to munch as you shop, everyone else seems to eat what they buy before it gets home.

Particulars: From I-75 exit at the Mack Avenue and head east two blocks to the corner of Russell Avenue. The retail market on Monday through Saturday is from 7 a.m. to 5 p.m. Free.

Money Museum
Bank One
(248) 680-2600

FREE

Frankly, I love collecting money. But not necessarily the kinds at the Money Museum which Nate Shapiro began many ears ago and occupies a space in the large lobby at
the bank on Woodward Avenue near Congress. Although to

collectors some of the weird kinds of money ranging from coins made from coal and porcelain to fabric and odd metals are highly valuable and interesting, most couldn't buy you a cup of coffee.

Nevertheless, the story of money and all of the oddball currencies are interesting and often very beautiful.

Particulars: The museum is at 611 Woodward Ave. and open Monday through Friday from 9 a.m. to 5 p.m. Free.

Graystone Jazz Museum
(313) 963-3813

In 1974, James Jenkins booked Duke Ellington for a concert at the Light Guard Armory but the great jazz musician never made it. Three months later Ellington died and suddenly Jenkins felt that something was mission in the city of Motown where pop music reined supreme. So the retired city bus driver started collection jazz memorabilia, rented out a room in the New Center area of Detroit and that year officially

Graystone Jazz Museum.

opened the Graystone International Jazz Museum.

Its moved twice since then, most recently to Broadway Avenue in 1991, and has expanded to five rooms of displays but it's still the only public jazz museum in the United States. Motown move over.

Long before there was Stevie Wonder or the Temptations, black musicians were picking up their horns to play on the steamers that in the mid-1800s were making regular runs to the Lake Erie resorts on Put-In-Bay. By the early 1900s, Paradise Valley, an unsegregated entertainment area centered near St. Antoine and Adams street in the heart of Detroit's black community, had emerged as a major force in the development of jazz talent through regular house bands and after-hour jam sessions.

Then in 1922, the University of Michigan built the Graystone Ballroom along Woodward Avenue, and Detroit entered its golden era for jazz. For years the Graystone was the city's leading dancehall. In 1928, it ended its strictly segregated policy by admitting blacks on Monday Nights in an the event that became a long running jazz tradition known as Blue Mondays. Eventually Ellington, Tommy Dorsey, Glen Miller, Jimmie Lunceford and many others played to capacity crowds before the ballroom was torn down in 1980 by its last owner...Motown.

The furnishing that survived the demolition of the Graystone is now used to replicated a section of the ballroom in the museum. In the other small rooms on the first floor are posters, musical instruments, album covers and other memorabilia that have been chronologically arranged as a history of jazz, highlighting such greats as Miles Davis, John Coltrane, Nancy Wilson and many others. There is also a gift shop that sells hard to find albums and in every room you can hear the rich, soulful heritage of jazz.

Particulars: The museum is on the corner of Broadway and John R. Street, across from the Broadway Station of the Detroit People Mover. Easiest way to reach it from I-74 is to depart at Lafayette Avenue, park in Greektown and catch the People Mover. Hours are 10 a.m. to 5 p.m. Tuesday through Friday and 11 a.m. to 4 p.m. on Saturday. Admission for adults is $2.

▼ Northville

Mill Race Village
(810) 348-1845

The upstairs rooms of the Cady Inn are once again open to

travelers. The inn is part of the Mill Race Historical Village, where visitors go, not for a night rest, but an afternoon with an insight on the way things used to be. The inn, which once hosted travelers, is spartan, in fact the guests bed is a mere 15 inches wide and the metal toilet pot would be a real experience on a cold winter's night.

Mill Race Village and Northville itself is the result of John Miller arriving in 1827 and building a humble gristmill on what is not the parking lot of the village museum. The mill stood there until Henry Ford bought the land in 1919, and built a factory. Today, with the help of Ford Motor Company, there are eight historic buildings overlooking scenic Mill Race Creek with gaslight lamps and white picket fences for a park-like setting.

There's Wash Oak School with slate boards at every desk, the Hunter House, a classic Greek Revival home built in 1851, a Victorian home of a 19th century judge, the Hirsch Blacksmith Shop, New School Church, even the Interurban Station, where Northville riders waited for the Farmington Line's high speed electric transit trains until the 1930s.

Particulars: From I-275 depart at exit 167 and head west on Eight Mile. Within two miles turn south onto Griswold Road and the Mill Race village is passed just before entering Northville. You can stroll the village year-round but the buildings are opened and staffed from 2-5 p.m. Sunday May through October.

Maybury State Park
(810) 349-0817

Developed using Recreation Bond Funds the Living Farm at the 1,000-acre Maybury State Park is surrounded by meadows, forests, hiking trails, and bike trails, along with a horseback riding concession.

The 25-acre living farm has a windmill water pump that clicks in the garden while visitors while visitors often hear a turkey gobble in the distance. Ten outbuildings, a small red barn houses goats and fowl, while a larger barn has pigs, sheep, lambs, and "Sam" and "Sarge," draft horses standing ready to be hitched.

The pastoral farmland rolls into the distance divided into many square pastures where Percheron horses graze in the afternoon sun.

Clean and well maintained a small group of donkeys occasionally bray, shaking of flies, and nuzzling small children.

One of the better living farms in the state, the Maybury

farm is less "slick" then some farms built for the purpose.

Particulars: The main entrance to the park is on Eight Mile Road, five miles west of its exit off I-275. Hours for the farm are 9 a.m. to 6 p.m. daily June through September and 10 a.m. to 5 p.m. the rest of the year. A $4 vehicle entry permit or a $20 state park pass is required to enter.

▼ Dearborn

Commandant's Quarters
Dearborn Historical Museum
(313) 565-3000

FREE

Built in 1833 as Commandant's Quarters, U.S. Arsenal, the building has since been restored and is on the National Register of Historical Places. Adjacent to it is the McFadden-Ross House, which originally was built in 1839 as the powder magazine of the U.S. Arsenal. It features thick brick walls while inside there are exhibits on farming, transportation and local history.

Particulars: The buildings are located in Dearborn at 21950 Michigan Ave. It is open from 9 a.m. to 5 p.m. May through October and 1-5 p.m. Monday through Saturday in November through April. Free.

▼ Livonia

Greenmead Historical Village
(248) 477-7375

The village includes the 1842 Hill House Museum, village houses, general store, church and surrounding gardens. There are a total of 25 buildings with eight of them furbished and opened along a 19th century intersection. There is even an authentic outhouse from the 1800s on display here.

Particulars: Located at 38125 Eight Mile Road and can be reached from exit 167 of I-275 by heading east. Hours are 1-4 p.m. Sunday from may through October. Admission is $2 for adults and $1 for seniors. Children are free.

▼ Grosse Ile

Grosse Ile Historical Museum
(734) 675-1250

Before the French landed in Detroit, they first stopped in Grosse Ile. This island in the middle of the Detroit River is loaded with history and thus those green Michigan Historical Site signs. You can also learn of its past with a visit at the 1904 Michigan Central Railroad Depot, which has been restored as the Island's Museum.

Overlooking the Detroit River, the depot contains historical artifacts and exhibits. Behind it is the 1871 U.S. Custom House, which has antique furnishings.

Particulars: From Jefferson Road in Trenton, cross the Free Bridge and continue east along Parkway Avenue on the other side. The depot is at the corner of Parkway and East Road and is open 1-4 p.m. Sunday April through December. Admission is by donation.

▼ Plymouth

Plymouth Historical Museum
(734) 455-8940

Located in a building in downtown Plymouth, this two level museum is packed with interesting local historical displays. One exhibit includes the only remaining Alter car that was put together in Plymouth from 1916-1917 and sold for $850. Another display is devoted to Daisey BB guns, which was founded in this town in 1890 and manufactured its weapons until 1957 when it moved to Arkansas.

Particulars: The Museum is on the corner of Church and Main Street and is open Wednesday, Thursday and Saturday from 1-4 p.m. and Sunday 2-5 p.m. Admission is $2 for adults. There is also a family pass.

Wyandotte Museum
(734) 324-7297

Housed in a restored Queen Anne Mansion that was built in 1896, the Wyandotte Museum has three floors of exhibits and displays of local history and a changing art gallery.

Particulars: The museum is located at 2610 Biddle Ave. (Jefferson Avenue) just north of downtown Wyandotte. Hours are noon to 4 p.m. Monday through Friday. Admission is $1 for adults.

WEXFORD COUNTY

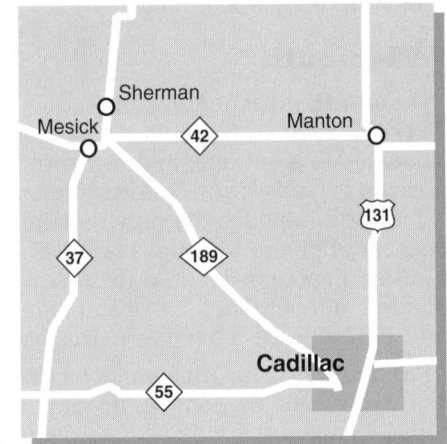

VISITOR INFORMATION

**Cadillad Area
Convention & Visitors Bureau**
222 Lake St.
Cadillac, MI 49601
231-775-0657

www.cadillac.org

Wexford County

▼ Cadillac

Carl T. Johnson Hunting and Fishing Center
Mitchell State Park
(231) 775-7911

Fishing and hunting have always been important to us and this state park interpretive center does an excellent job conveying Michigan's love for those sports. Exhibits trace the history of both activities from when they meant survival to the recreational pastimes they are today. There are also displays on the future of Michigan wildlife and its habitat and the efforts of anglers and hunters to save it.

From the center a path then heads north into the Heritage Fisheries and Wildlife Nature Study Area. The two-mile loop passes marshes and ponds where you might spot a variety of bird life including blue herons, mallards and woodducks.

Particulars: The center is in Mitchell State Park at the corner of M-115 and North Boulevard, just after you cross the channel between Lake Mitchell and Lake Cadillac. Hours are 10 a.m. to 4 p.m. Friday and Sunday, and 10a.m. to 5 p.m. on Sunday most of the year and 10 a.m. to 6 p.m. Tuesday through Sunday during the busy camping season. Admission is $1 for adults and 50 cents for kids.

The Sweet Shop   *FREE*
(231) 775-2201

Candy making demonstrations, and home of the Cadillac snowbirds. The tours are free, but the calories are not.

Particulars: The shop is located in downtown Cadillac at 122 Mitchell St. Hours are 9 a.m. to 5 p.m. Monday through Saturday. Free.

Four Winns Boat Factory Tour   *FREE*
(231) 775-1351

Tour the factory where the popular Four Winns boats are designed and engineered, built and tested on Lake Cadillac.

Particulars: The factory is off Cadillac at 925 Frisbie St. The tours are offered between 10 a.m. and 2 p.m. Monday through Friday. You must register in advance for the factory tour. Free.

Lake Mitchell, Wexford County.

Shay Locomotive
Cadillac Chamber of Commerce
(231) 775-9776

Ephriam Shay invented a locomotive that could navigate sharper curves and climber steeper grades and its development in Cadillac in the late 1870s gave the logging industry a boost in Michigan. Today there is an early model on display in the heart of the city that made it famous.

Particulars: The Shay Locomotive is on display in the City Park just off the Lake Cadillac in the downtown area. Free.

Wexford County Museum
Cadillac Chamber of Commerce
(231) 775-9776

FREE

The territory that was to become Wexford County was organized by the State Legislature in April 1840 under the Indian name of Kautawabet, meaning "broken tooth." Three years later the name Wexford was designated with the first settler arriving in Hanover Township in 1863.

Housed in the former Cadillac Carnegie Library that was built in 1906, the museum chronicles the history of people, occupations and businesses of Wexford County. The main Floor is divided into several exhibits areas that include an early home interior, general store, post office, small shops, and a post office. Many exhibits for children are also offered.

Particulars: The museum is located in downtown Cadillac at 127 Beech St. Hours are noon to 4 p.m. Wednesday, Thursday, and Sunday in the summer and noon to 4 p.m. on Saturday the rest of the year. It is closed January through March. Admission is by donation.

▼ Harrietta

Harrietta State Fish Hatchery
(231) 389-2211

FREE

Renovated and dedicated in 1979, the hatchery has both indoor and outdoor tanks and raceways. Two to four million fish can be produced annually depending on the species being reared. The hatchery often produces a number of species a year including rainbow trout, coho salmon and brown trout that are ultimately released into area waterways.

A visitor's station offers a look at the nine indoor rearing tanks while interpretive wall charts and displays are everywhere showing modern rearing techniques and giving anglers courage. You'll see hundreds of thousands of tiny fish teaming to the surface and swimming about in large tanks designed so even small children will be able to see.

A self-guided brochure is available that further explains the science behind the efforts, while wall posters give tips on fish identification as A"mother hen-type" biologists work in the background.

Particulars: The hatchery is located just west of the small hamlet of Harrietta at 6801 W. 30th Rd. Hours are 8 a.m. to 4:30 p.m. Monday through Friday and weekends 8 a.m. to 4 p.m. Free.